Situational Context of Education

A Window Into the World of Bilingual Learners

Situational Context of Education

A Window Into the World of Bilingual Learners

María Estela Brisk
Boston College

Angela Burgos
Boston Public Schools

Sara Hamerla
Framingham Public Schools

LAWRENCE ERLBAUM ASSOCIATES, PUBLISHERS

2004   Mahwah, New Jersey   London

Lawrence Erlbaum Associates, Inc., Publishers
10 Industrial Avenue
Mahwah, NJ 07430

Cover design by Kathryn Houghtaling Lacey

Library of Congress Cataloging-in-Publication Data

Brisk, Maria.
Situational context of education : a window into the world of bilingual learners / Maria Estela Brisk, Angela Burgos, Sara Hamerla.

p. cm.

Includes bibliographical references and index.
ISBN 0-8058-3946-1 (pbk : alk. Paper)
1. Education, Bilingual—Social aspects—United States. 2. Children of immigrants—Education—Social aspects—United States. 3. Personality and situation—United States. I. Burgos, Angela. II. Hamerla, Sara. III. Title.

LC3731.B686 2004
370.117'0973—dc21   2003056101
                                                          CIP

Books published by Lawrence Erlbaum Associates are printed on acid-free paper, and their bindings are chosen for strength and durability.

Printed in the United States of America
10 9 8 7 6 5 4 3 2 1

To Bill

To my parents, Alicia and Miguel

To Oliver Burke

Contents

Preface

Personal characteristics, family support, and quality of instruction shape academic performance. Hardworking students, involved parents, and qualified teachers contribute to a positive educational experience. Life, however, does not deal the same hand to all students. Some are born to families that speak the same language used in schools; others are raised in another language and must cope with the new one when they enter school. Some children are raised in poor homes and neighborhoods and attend poorly funded schools whereas others are well provided for and safe at home and in school. Some children suffer from prejudice; others never experience negative attitudes. Students and teachers have no control over language, socioeconomic status, skin color, particular heritage, and other situational factors that affect learners. The influence of these factors is subtle and indirect. Yet, they contribute to making the educational experience more or less difficult for different students.

This book proposes that the objective study of the situational context of education benefits students, their families, and their teachers. Knowledge of the situational context gives students and teachers a more realistic view to of what they need to do to facilitate students' progress in school. Teachers' use of this understanding should not lead them to feel sorry for students and lower educational expectations. Rather, it should lead them to find productive, useful solutions. Some teachers feel guilty when comparing their situational context with that of their students. Their comfortable middle-class lives seem so easy compared with the lives of their struggling urban students. These feelings are not productive either. It is better for teachers who experience these feelings to acknowledge their reality and recognize that, to a degree, situational factors rather than merit helped them succeed. Most important, they should not judge their students based on their own experience nor take a patronizing attitude toward their students. For example, they should not judge intelligence by their students' level of English ability nor they should feel sorry that children do not know English. The children will learn it and in addition they will know another language.

The approach to the study of the situational context of education presented in this book was designed for a graduate course for preservice and in-service teachers interested in bilingual populations. The approach was originally introduced as an assignment for participants to carry out with their bilingual students. The goal was to have course participants learn about these factors not only from the literature but also from the situational contexts of their own students. At the end of the semester the course participants had learned a great deal about situational factors. This activity gave teachers strategies to get to know their students and their predicaments within the social context of the United States. They also reported that it had a great impact on their students. Thus, both students from first grade through master's level achieved academically while gaining awareness of factors affecting their lives.

This professional development strategy soon turned into an instructional approach implemented with students in bilingual, ESL (English as a Second Language), mainstream, and special education classrooms. Students of different ages and language backgrounds have participated in these projects over the years.

Overview and Use of the Book

This book provides the empirical and theoretical background and practical tools for the study of the situational context of education by teachers and students. Many factors affect the lives of students; this book focuses on those that affect language-minority and immigrant students in the context of the United States. It can be used as a framework for work with other populations in other social contexts, and can also be used in professional development programs or college courses that explore the social context of education. The book contains an introductory chapter, five main chapters, and four appendixes.

Chapter 1, the Introduction, is an overview of the theory and implementation of this approach. It explains the theoretical framework underlying the approach including its evolution and implementation. This section illustrates how situational context (SC) lessons were used across age groups and languages and describes the context of the pilot lessons included in this book. The chapter closes with an explanation of how to use the lessons detailed in chapters 2 through 6.

In chapters 2 through 6 a three-part structure is used. Each chapter focuses on one situational factor: linguistic, economic, social, cultural, or political. Each of the chapters begin with a rich description of the implementation of one of the lessons in a fifth-grade bilingual classroom, followed by theoretical explanation of the factor that is the focus of the chapter. This research overview serves as the basis for lesson objectives. Each chapter includes several lessons for implementation. The lessons are addressed to the teacher, with detailed ideas of how to carry out the lesson and evaluate the students' understanding of the situational context.

Four appendixes provide resources helpful for the implementation of the lessons: an annotated bibliography of children's literature recommended in the lessons; and a step-by-step description of various instructional approaches used in the lessons; scoring rubrics for content objectives; and guidelines for a contrastive study of situational contexts.

Teachers should read the Introduction to develop an understanding of the approach; and review chapters 2 through 6 to choose lessons that will best fit with their curriculum. Ideally, teachers should implement at least one lesson on each situational factor to give students a full breadth of understanding of their social context. These lessons can be interspersed through the school year. Teachers of different grade levels can coordinate with each other to implement different lessons over the course of several grades.

After the lessons are chosen, teachers should read the theoretical section of the chapter to familiarize themselves with the research that provides the rationale for the lessons. The section in each chapter illustrating the implementation of one lesson allows teachers to visualize the dialogue that could occur. The lessons can be implemented in full as they are presented in this book or adapted to the age, grade level, and language ability of the students. Teachers should take advantage of current events or special classroom circumstances appropriate to the lessons.

In planning the implementation of specific lessons, teachers should refer to the appendixes for explanations of the instructional approaches suggested in the lessons, and to look for alternative or additional book selections from the Annotated Bibliography (Appendix A).

Teachers may not have time to implement all lessons. They should also expect variation in the depth of student understanding of the objectives. The piloting of the five lessons in Angela's class demonstrated this variance. Although the students may have been too young to grasp all the relationships in the lessons' objectives and often were unable to fully articulate solutions, they matured intellectually and as learners. All basic concepts for each lesson were fully developed, enriching the students' knowledge of the world around them. Students gained awareness of how language, culture, and ethnicity play a role in the society where they live. The in-depth discussions and reflections challenged them intellectually and taught them how to analyze important issues. In the words of their teacher, "By the time we got to the political lesson, there was no stopping them."

ACKNOWLEDGMENTS

We would like to thank the many teachers who over the years tried this approach and helped us refine it. We are grateful to the many students who participated in critical autobiography projects, inspiring us to carry out the difficult task of designing and writing the book. We appreciate especially the participation of Angela's fifth-grade students. Julie Campanella deserves special thanks for her assistance in identifying, organizing, and summarizing the books included in the Annotated Bibliography. Kim Thienpont also deserves special thanks for her tireless assistance with the final manuscript. We greatly appreciate Naomi Silverman's patient support for the evolution of this complicated project.

—María E. Brisk
—Angela Burgos
—Sara R. Hamerla

About the Authors

María Estela Brisk is a Professor at the Lynch School of Education, Boston College. Her research and teaching interests include bilingual education, bilingual language and literacy acquisition, literacy methodology and preparation of teachers to teach in urban schools. She is the author of the books *Bilingual Education: From Compensatory to Quality Schooling* and, with Margaret Harrington, *Literacy and Bilingualism: A Handbook for ALL Teachers* (Lawrence Erlbaum Associates). For nearly a decade she has been working with teachers who have tested the development of the teaching approach described in this book. For the past 3 years she has taught a course on the social context of education for pre-and in-service mainstream teachers.

Angela Burgos is an elementary school teacher with 24 years experience working with bilingual students. She has taught at the primary, middle, and secondary levels. She is currently teaching in a fifth-grade transitional bilingual education classroom in the Boston Public Schools. She earned her bachelor's degree at Boston College and her Master's degree in bilingual education at Boston University. She has been a presenter at various educational workshops, a cooperating teacher for university student teachers, and has contributed to the professional development of fellow teachers in bilingual education and computer literacy. Her interests are technology and literacy development of bilinguals. Angela was a member of the original group that experimented with situational context lessons. She has used and researched the approach in her classroom for several years.

Sara R. Hamerla has a doctorate in language, literacy, and cultural studies from Boston University. She is a social studies, language arts, and English-as-a-second-language (ESL) teacher. Sara lived for years in South America where she taught middle school students. Currently, she is the Assistant Director of Bilingual Education for Framingham Public Schools. Her research is focused on the revising strategies of young bilingual writers.

1

Introduction

The role of context has been both ignored and stressed in educational research and practice over time. Positivist theories treated knowledge as separate from experience whereas more recent theories underscore the importance of social context (Corson, 2001). This book adheres to the notion that the situational context of education is important: "Learning and development cannot be considered apart from the individual's social environment, the ecocultural niche" (Newman & Celano, 2001, p. 8). The study of situational context helps teachers and students to work together, especially when they come from different backgrounds. Students, particularly language-minority and immigrant students, also profit from a better understanding of the situational factors that affect their lives. Such students' progress in school depends on their acquisition of English academic skills and on their ability to function within the school's cultural norms. These students' individual efforts are assisted or facilitated by situational factors. For example, efforts to learn a language need to be supported by opportunities for use, positive attitudes, and high expectations. Cultural adaptation is assisted when teachers and peers understand cultural differences. Governmental policies toward particular ethnic groups facilitate or lay barriers for the whole family, directly affecting parental support of students. This book explores these and many other situational factors affecting bilingual students' learning experiences.

These factors are numerous, change over time, and vary from one section of the country to another. A deep understanding of the existing research can help understand the situational context of bilingual learners. This understanding can help teachers and students identify new situations unexplored by the research.

SITUATIONAL CONTEXT OF EDUCATION

Students and schools do not perform in a sterilized environment. Research on variables influencing the education of language-minority students indicates that multiple situational and individual factors affect students' school performance.[1] Situational factors, including—linguistic, cultural, economic, political, and social—affect all students. This book focuses on those that particularly influence

---

[1] A review of the research supporting each of these factors is included in chapters 2–6.

bilingual students (Brisk, 1998; Perez, 1998; Spolsky, 1978). These factors influence students' academic and linguistic performance as well as their ability to function in different cultural contexts. Individual students cope in different ways. Some students succeed in spite of unfavorable circumstances due to relentless efforts. Aristide, a Haitian high school student in Miami, succeeded in school in spite of such negative situational factors as poverty, race, and immigrant status. He ignored teasing from students who did not approve of his quest for academic achievement. Aristide looked forward to following in the footsteps of his older brother, a student at Yale (A. Portes & Rumbaut, 2001).

Review of the research supporting each of these factors is included in chapters 2–6.

Situational factors are closely related. Language use (linguistic factor) often depends on societal attitudes to the language (social factor). When youngsters become aware of negative attitudes toward their heritage language, they refuse to use it. Restrictions imposed on children due to gender (social) often have their roots in family values (cultural). Negative attitudes toward ethnic groups (social) arise from unfavorable political relations with their countries of origin (political). Financial status of families (economic) may depend on government policies toward particular immigrant groups (political).

These factors affect students through the institutions with which and people with whom they frequently come into contact, called filters (see Fig.1.1). Situational factors color the advice, attitudes, and pressures that family, peers, and school personnel bring to students. The neighborhood is the social context students experience daily, and the media are the most accessible way to bring the views of the larger society to children.

The manifestation of these factors is fluid, changing over time and varying from place to place. Tollefson (1991) maintained that historical background influences societal factors. Today's attitudes toward an ethnic group may be very different from those evident in the past. Present attitudes toward Japanese immigrants contrast sharply with those held at the time of World War II. Research on the academic achievement of students from different ethnic groups reveals differential performance of whole groups in different countries. For example, Finns tend to do poorly in Sweden but not in the United States, whereas Koreans excel in most countries except in Japan (Cummins, 1981; Ogbu, 1993).

STUDENTS ANALYZE THEIR SITUATIONAL CONTEXT

Students and teachers have no control over situational factors, but they can objectively analyze them. Students can research such factors and reflect on how they affect them as language and literacy learners, as students, and as members of our society. Objective analysis of these factors helps students understand their present circumstances and react in a constructive way. Bilingual and immigrant students often blame themselves, their language, and their culture for what happens to them. "I don't do much wrong in Korea; because I'm a Korean person I keep doing wrong things here," declared a first-grade student. Study of

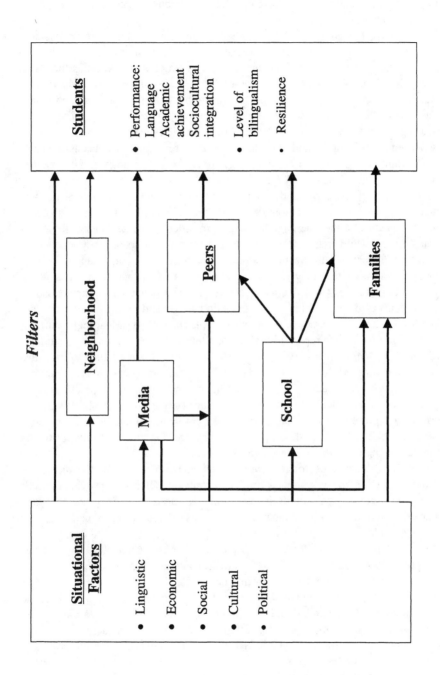

the situational context turns these problematic circumstances into an opportunity for learning.

Carefully planned lessons allow students to objectively analyze external factors influencing their lives as bilinguals. The instructional activities include: reading literature with pertinent themes; discussing and writing responses to this literature; using the library and Internet as resources; conducting interviews, observations, and surveys; and writing reflections to connect the themes of the lesson with their own lives. These activities offer students the opportunity to develop literacy by reading "the word and the world" (this phrase is part of the title of a book by Freire & Macedo, 1987). Freire and Macedo believe that "reading does not consist merely of decoding the written word or language; rather, it is preceded by and intertwined with knowledge of the world" (p. 29).

The tasks are demanding and meaningful. Students explore concepts that are often unknown to them. In a seventh-grade classroom, for example, students had to determine the nature of their heritage languages. In order to decide whether these languages were world, regional, dialects, standardized, and so on, they studied the countries in the world, the languages spoken, and the nature of those languages. Following these activities, they focused on characteristics of their own heritage languages. Exploration of these linguistic factors turned into a major geography lesson.

Students of diverse cultural and linguistic background need to master the language and literacy demands of American schools and society . Meaningful curriculum has proven to be a powerful tool for developing literacy among such students (Bartolome, 1993; Heath, 1983; Moll, 1988; Torres Guzman, 1992). They also need abundant practice. Lessons about situational factors meet these requirements for meaningful and academically demanding lessons and intensive practice of language and literacy. Students tap into their cultural experience and objectively and critically explore their world while they make ample use of language and practice academic skills. Students develop the ability to read, write, and think critically through engaging in in-depth exploration of issues.

Teachers also benefit from this work. Teachers learn best about diversity in the context of their own classrooms . Situational context (SC) lessons provide teachers with a concrete way to explore the lives and conditions that affect their students' learning. As a result of implementing SC lessons, a group of bilingual, ESL, and mainstream teachers learned about the situational factors that played a role in their students' language and literacy development and about their students' abilities (Coppola, 1997). These teachers were surprised at their students' strengths "when the students were engaged in literacy instructional activities that incorporated their background experiences and provided opportunities for the students to demonstrate and build upon their background knowledge" (p. 204). Teachers' learning varied depending on the factors they explored with their students and the depth with which they studied them. Teachers who tested the lessons in classes with bilingual and mainstream students also discovered how little the mainstream students knew about the lives of their bilingual classmates.

This book offers a series of lessons for each of the situational factors. Lessons are based on what the research has uncovered as relevant factors. Teachers are encouraged to try these lessons as well as develop their own as circumstances arise. For example, one teacher from Texas related one such circumstance. Her principal decided to have a ceremony for students who scored high in the TAAS (Texas Assessment of Academic Skills), a state achievement test. After the ceremony her fifth-grade bilingual-program students told her that the principal did not like them because those who scored high but had taken the test in Spanish were not recognized. This was a perfect setting for an SC lesson on the differential value with respect to languages in this society. The principal had not acted out of malice or dislike for them. He was merely unconsciously reflecting the society's higher value for English than Spanish in this country.

Some teachers have raised concerns about implementing SC lessons. They fear probing into personal matters, they question their ability if they do not know their students' languages, and they are concerned with work load, availability of resources, and implementing SC lessons when not all the students have a linguistically and culturally diverse background. These are legitimate concerns, but teachers have provided answers through their experiences with SC lessons. Students love to share their experiences so often ignored by schools. SC lessons move the focus from the individual to the issues; from a student's concern about heritage language loss, the lessons move to the study of opportunities for language development. Collaboration among students and family involvement support teachers unfamiliar with the students' language. For instance, when Joseph brought home a book on Korean culture, the mother felt compelled to get involved to clarify aspects of the culture that were inaccurate in the book. Although the lessons take time to prepare and develop, they can be incorporated into the curriculum and they are productive literacy and social studies activities. The Internet as well as the growing market for multicultural literacy provide excellent materials to implement the lessons. These lessons were successfully implemented in classes with both bilingual and mainstream students. Such lessons provided an opportunity for mainstream students to expand their knowledge of the world and of other students in their class.

TEACHERS ANALYZE THEIR SITUATIONAL CONTEXT

Teachers in the United States are likely to have students of culturally and linguistically diverse backgrounds in their classes. Based on Census 2000 results, about one in five students throughout the nation comes from a home in which a language other than English is spoken . Approximately 30 million people in the United States are foreign born. (C. Suárez-Orozco & M. M. Suárez-Orozco, 2001). In large urban schools, such as New York City, 48% of students represent more than 100 languages. In California, almost 1.5 million children are classified as Limited English Proficient (LEP). But this increasing wave of linguistic diversity is "not only an urban or southwestern phenomenon—schools across the country are encountering growing numbers of children from immigrant families. Even in places like Dodge City, Kansas, more than 30 percent of the children enrolled in public schools are the children of immigrants."(C. Suárez-Orozco & M. M. Suárez-Orozco, 2001 pp. 2–3). By 2020, it is projected that there will be 6 million school-age children between the ages of 5 and 17 whose primary language will not be English. These students are served by unprepared teachers who share little of their experience. A 1999–2000 survey reported that 41.2% of teachers taught students with limited English proficiency but only 12.5% of them had received 8 or more hours of professional development (National Center for Education Statistics, 2002).

Most teaching staff does not come from the background of these students. Over 90% of the teachers are White (Nieto, 2000). Teachers are often unaware that they see, perceive, and judge students through the lens of their own culture and values (Delpit, 1995).

Many teachers working with language-minority students feel they are not prepared to teach those students. (National Center for Education Statistics, 1999). Teachers with a different cultural experience from their students benefit from studying their own SC of education in preparation for working with such students. By understanding their own circumstances, they begin to realize that their experience is just a different kind of experience and not the norm by which to judge their students.

Teachers can engage in studying their SC in two ways. One is by studying their own SC along with their students' as they carry out lessons included in this book. Another is by writing a memoir of their school years and then using the framework of the situational factors (Fig.1.1) to analyze what happened in those years and how the situational factors helped them succeed as students (see Appendix D). Comparing their experience with a student or a person of a different background brings awareness of the effects of situational factors. For example, teachers often complain about the lack of family support for their students. They think back at how their parents were involved in their education. A contrast of differential opportunities due to socioeconomic factors can bring awareness that the situation and not the intention is hindering parents. Most families want the best for their children's education but "parents in lower and middle-class communities [differ] differed widely in the skills and resources they [have] had at their disposal for upgrading children's school performance" (Neuman & Celano, 2001, p. 8).

Study of their situational context is most important for teachers who are native speakers of English and raised in the American culture. These teachers take for granted how linguistic and cultural congruity with the school facilitated their education. Cailin, a pre-service teacher, admitted that she first realized what lack of mastery of the school language meant when she was a student in France. She felt humiliated in class by her inability to express herself intelligently and correctly in French.

EVOLUTION AND IMPLEMENTATION
OF SITUATIONAL CONTEXT LESSONS

The development of SC lessons for students, although guided by the same theoretical principles, has undergone many transformations, including name change over the years. Lessons evolved from one based on literacy activities coconstructed between students and their teachers to a comprehensive set of units based on specific objectives. Originally called "critical autobiography," these lessons are presently more accurately named "situational context lessons."

These lessons emerged as a tool to help pre- and in-service teachers understand the situational factors affecting bilingual students. Inspired by Benesch's work, the approach was initially named "critical autobiography."

Benesch (1993) developed critical autobiographies while working with adult immigrants. She encouraged students to write and analyze their experiences as immigrants. This process helped her students understand that "the problems of living in a new culture are ... the result of social factors rather than of personal shortcomings" (p. 249). Benesch based her work on critical literacy and principles of literacy development. Her students read critically an account by a Chinese journalist of his experiences living in the United States. They then determined what the relevant topics in their own lives were as immigrants. Using a process writing approach, they wrote chapters for their autobiography about the chosen topics.

Practitioners implemented lessons with school-age students of a variety of ages and backgrounds. Teachers helped students identify relevant issues through discussions and critical exploration of literature reflecting immigrant experiences. Students wrote chapter books relating their own experiences (Brisk & Harrington, 2000). Teachers took into account students' age, language skills, and backgrounds. Younger students drew pictures as they talked about the issues. Older students discussed issues, responded to readings, carried out research projects, and interviewed expert adults. These sources of information were used to write essays or reports. Teachers implemented the approach with individual students, small groups, or the whole class. Bilingual teachers allowed the students to choose the language for the various activities. Teachers who did not know the native language of the students used English. All teachers embedded the lessons into their reading, language arts, and social studies curricula.

Brisk and Zandman (1995) reported on the work with Galina, a second-grade immigrant from Russia via Israel. Galina had difficulty relating to students, teachers, and even her mother. Galina refused to speak Russian to her mother, or Hebrew to the bilingual teacher. In critical autobiography lessons, she created three books focusing on each of the countries in which she had lived. Galina dictated the stories to the teacher while she drew illustrations of her accounts. Writing about life in the three countries helped her understand her complex linguistic and cultural development. She improved her relationship with her mother, used Russian, Hebrew, and English freely, and became an overall better student.

Brisk (1999) examined the implementation of critical autobiography projects in four distinct contexts: a Reading Recovery tutorial, a fifth-grade bilingual classroom, a sixth-grade classroom for Spanish-speaking newcomers, and a high school ESL class. In the first context, Joseph had shown no progress in his Reading Recovery program for several months. Ruth, his teacher, adopted critical autobiographies in her weekly meetings with him to improve his English-reading skills. Ruth stimulated conversations around language, culture, politics, economics, and social issues aided by books, maps, coins, and pictures. Joseph drew pictures as the teacher wrote down what he said. Questions and discussion helped expand and clarify points. His mother participated in some sessions to help elucidate confusing ideas. Together they read a typed draft and made additions and modifications suggested by Joseph. Ruth bound the final version into a book with Joseph's drawings. Joseph tested out of Reading Recovery within 8 weeks of implementing Critical Autobiographies.

Angela, a fifth-grade bilingual teacher, embedded critical autobiographies into her literacy and social studies curricula. Students read biographies and autobiographies, historically relevant to the social studies theme of the month. They read and responded to literature that stimulated students' discussion of the situational factors. After careful preparation, students interviewed a parent about her immigration experience and adjustment to the United States. Throughout the lessons, students wrote chapters for their books using a process approach to writing. Students engaged in these activities in their language of greater fluency and preference. The ESL and computer teachers collaborated with the project. In addition to improving their writing and reading abilities, students better understood their immigrant experience.

Carmen, a social studies and language arts teacher, worked with a class of sixth-grade Spanish-speaking newcomers. Students settled on 10 topics for their book. These were listed permanently on the board. Each week Carmen started the exploration of one topic with a variety of activities such as reading and analyzing a poem, interviewing a guest speaker, drawing images of the issues, and others. After intensive discussions, students concluded each topic by writing an essay. Students learned to analyze and support opinions and write extensive text.

Angelique, an ESL high school teacher, worked with a group of beginners from a variety of language and cultural backgrounds. Initial discussions on their lives and hardships brought to light that the students felt ostracized by the English-speaking students in the school. Angelique had her students carry out a research project on attitudes toward immigrants. Students developed a questionnaire to be filled out by their classmates. Answers to questions such as "Have you ever traveled abroad?," "Do you speak a second language?," and "Do you have any foreign friends?" revealed that their classmates had never before had experiences with immigrants, other languages, and cultures. These students concluded that their classmates' lack of experiences with other languages and cultures might affect their attitudes.

SC lessons were implemented in a mainstream classroom with immigrant students. An ESL/bilingual teacher worked with the social studies teacher and his fifth-grade class, which included six bilingual students. As part of the unit on settlement and exploration of the New World, students read, discussed, and carried out activities around the book *Guests* by Michael Dorris. *Guests* is a story about a Native-American boy and his first encounters with Europeans. Students discussed and wrote about rites of passage, gender roles and expectations, holidays, foods, and customs across cultures. One of the options for a final project for the unit was to write a critical autobiography. The social studies teacher as well as the students in the class learned a great deal about the bilingual students in the class. In turn, these students felt more confident about their English proficiency and became active classroom participants.

A family literacy project tested these lessons in a unique way. The instructor used the approach with adults in the class. The adults adapted the lessons to be used at home with their children. One mother who analyzed the linguistic and social situation began to understand why her children were developing English faster than herself. She also realized that her children were at greater risk to lose Spanish. As a result of the project, this mother modified her language policy at home. She increased the use of Spanish with her children to enhance their chances at bilingualism. She also looked for opportunities to practice English outside the home in order to improve her own proficiency (Pierce & Brisk, 2002).

SC lessons have not only been implemented with bilingual students. One mainstream teacher developed several units to analyze the negative influences of media on teenage girls. She worked with the soccer team of an affluent suburban school system. The young women on the team gained awareness of how their beliefs and behaviors are affected by the media. The strong grip of the media on teenage values is a well-documented situational factor in American society.

Students explored many pressing concerns in their lives while doing SC lessons. However, there was a need to develop a comprehensive structure to address all of the situational factors. In the original, open-ended approach, different important factors were ignored or avoided. In an effort to open the maximum possibility for covering situational factors, objectives were derived from the research on some aspects of the situational factors. Based on these objectives, lessons were written and tested for each of the five types of situational factors. This book includes the description of the implementation of the pilot lessons and instructions to guide implementation of lessons representing a wide variety of factors that have emerged from the research literature.

Classroom Context For Piloted Lessons

Five lessons, one from each of the situational factors, were piloted over the course of an academic year. The name of the approach was not changed until after this piloting. Consequently, in the lessons' descriptions, the teacher still uses the term "critical autobiographies."

Angela, a fifth-grade bilingual teacher, implemented five of the newly developed lessons over the course of a year. Angela works at a small urban school located in a residential neighborhood. The school has changed over the past decade to include a Spanish-transitional bilingual education program. It serves approximately 360 children with programs in early childhood and kindergarten through fifth-grade classes. In the past, the school was a neighborhood school, serving only students who lived nearby. But now, the families represent diverse racial and ethnic backgrounds and come from different neighborhoods throughout the city.

Angela's classroom is a busy place. The desks are arranged in clusters. Posters and decorations cover the walls. There are maps, classroom rules, homework rules, steps to problem solving, and guides to the writing process. Books in Spanish and English are everywhere on shelves, tables and displays. On the back wall there are bulletin boards with student work neatly displayed for each subject matter: math, social studies, writing, and language. There are also two computers with Internet access. Above the teacher's desk hangs a bright banner that proclaims, "Kids are special people."

Angela is an experienced teacher with a master' s degree in bilingual education. She has taught bilingual fifth-grade for 18 out of her 22 years of teaching experience. Angela works to foster teamwork, collaboration, and mutual respect in her classroom. In her teaching activities and style she employs a variety of techniques and approaches to reach all of the students in her class. Through her manner, verbal, and nonverbal signs, she shows the students that she values their contributions and encourages their learning.

In September there were 16 students in the class: 6 boys and 10 girls. Some were immigrant students and others were born in the United States but came from Spanish-speaking homes. Their families come from Puerto Rico, Central America and South America. The students in this year's class had a strong rapport. Some had been attending this school for several years, and they knew each other well. In the classroom, they conversed on a social and academic level in both languages. Many would transition out of bilingual education into mainstream classrooms at the end of the school year.

The enrollment of the class changed over the course of the year. In September the initial class included 16 students. By Christmas three had left. Five new students arrived during the last half of the year. Most of the new arrivals had very limited English. This changing classroom presented challenges as the students attempted to integrate.

Angela chose to implement five units, each addressing one situational factor in the students' lives. Each unit took approximately 3 days to implement. Activities were carried out during the 90-minute language arts block. Other classroom activities supported the implementation of the units. In preparation, Angela first practiced with them the skills of journal writing, speaking in oral presentations, and participating in class discussion. Angela introduced these skills in a nonthreatening context. Initially, she had students write, discuss, and present about literature before applying these skills to analyze their own lives. By the time the first unit was implemented, the class had developed a safe, open atmosphere.

Students participated in both Spanish and English. Their contributions were accepted and validated by the teacher and their peers. For example, the first day that Edison arrived at the classroom from Colombia, he was quickly integrated into the class discussion on education in other countries. He felt immediately included when the class used him as a resource for information about school in his country.

The first unit, language use, was implemented 6 weeks into the school year. By this time, Angela had gotten to know her students and had developed an atmosphere of trust in the classroom. In previous years, the students had not engaged in whole-class discussions on complex topics. They were more accustomed to a more regimented teaching and learning style. Angela had to model constructive participation and provide the students opportunities to practice discussion strategies. Before implementing the linguistic unit, she had students read and discuss a novel. This activity helped them to feel more comfortable with each other before delving into the more personal topic of language use.

These 3-day units did not consist of isolated lessons. Angela constantly referred to other related topics that the class had addressed. She used the units to reinforce skills learned in other units and in other disciplines. For example, students used graphing skills learned in math to graph their language use in the linguistic unit. They applied knowledge learned in a unit on the U. S. political system to better understand U.S. foreign policy in the political unit.

The 3-day units were implemented on a rough schedule of one every other month. This was not specifically planned. However, the units were naturally integrated with other topics and projects. Planned interruptions in the academic curriculum such as standardized testing also influenced the timing of the implementation.

Angela also coordinated the academic content of the units to reflect district standards. The students were aware of the high expectations Angela holds for them and their class work. The students had to work independently and in groups to accomplish their goals. They were expected to read and write daily and to integrate background knowledge into their work.

Using the Lessons

Each lesson includes the central objective, rationale, concepts to be taught, and relationships among the concepts and with the students. Activities and resources are suggested to help students relate these concepts and relationships to their own lives. Each lesson includes an extensive list of children's literature for different ages. These titles are summarized in a Appendix A. Reading these books is a productive activity to elicit discussion of relevant topics. These readings and discussion facilitate understanding of difficult or unexplored topics. Reflective pieces serve as a springboard for students to relate the situational factor to themselves and their families. The teacher encourages students to investigate solutions to complex issues. An annotated bibliography of relevant juvenile literature is also included in Appendix A. Teachers can draw from this bibliography to add or supplant titles suggested in the lessons. Frequently used instructional methodologies are described in more detail in Appendix B.

The lessons are flexible and can be adapted to grade level and students' needs. Teachers can choose individual lessons and implement them during the school year according to curricular requirements. It is not necessary to implement all lessons in one grade. Teachers in a school can coordinate to implement different lessons across grades.

Teachers can take advantage of timely events to connect the lessons with the world around them. As we see in chapter 4, the day Angela started the cultural lessons a new student from Colombia arrived in her class. The lesson focused on cultural differences between schools in the United States and those of her students' countries of origin. Angela took advantage of the presence of the new student and developed the whole lesson around his experiences.

Students keep a portfolio of their projects and writings (SC folders). The teacher reviews the contents to evaluate the students' understanding of the situational factors with respect to concepts, relationships among concepts, relationship to self, and potential solutions. Each lesson includes a rubric to check how much of the concepts, relationships, connections to self, and potential solutions the students have accomplished (see Appendix C for explanation of criteria used in the rubrics). Levels of achievement vary with experience and age. Young children rarely find all the relationships or find solutions. An analysis of the lessons piloted demonstrated that students reached different levels of understanding of each unit. Students successfully grasped essential concepts. They showed great enthusiasm in relating them to their own lives, but they did not always understand how a factor personally affected them. Prompting by the teacher helped them suggest some solutions. The cultural unit was more thoroughly understood, perhaps due to the presence of the new student. In this case, they could concretely study concepts, relations, and the search for solutions connected with the life of one of their classmates.

Whatever level students reach, these lessons are still beneficial because students begin to see the situational factors as a force outside themselves and helps them begin to understand their world. The students who participated in the pilot lessons became aware of their patterns of language use and the consequences on their language proficiency. They understood the demographic composition of their communities as opposed to the country as a whole. They understood the importance of bilingualism in relation to language use and needs in businesses and the world of work. They clearly analyzed the cultural differences between U. S. and other countries' schools and the effects on immigrant students in the United States. They were interested and amazed at the effects of foreign policies on immigrants in the United States. Through these lessons they learned much, from making and understanding graphs to the history of World War II.

Not only can these lessons be used to evaluate the content objectives related to the situational factors, but they can serve as evidence of students' language and literacy development. Teachers can analyze the students' work using reading and writing rubrics to gauge their literacy development. Activities in the lessons shed light on students' math and social studies knowledge.

The remaining chapters in this book provide the tools to implement SC lessons. The account of the piloted lessons gives a glimpse at a classroom using SC lessons. The review of the literature provides the theoretical knowledge for each situational factor. The lessons proper give clear guidelines for teachers new to the strategy. With experience, teachers can develop other lessons as appropriate for their students. Appendix E provides a lesson template to develop new lessons.

2

Linguistic Context

OVERVIEW

Teachers in U. S. schools are for the most part monolingual speakers of standard American English (Banks, 1991; Zeichner, 1993). Their personal experience with language is different from many of their students who speak a different language or a different variety of English. These teachers need to understand how language affects school performance, language development, and school staff's attitude toward such students.

This chapter explores the following linguistic variables:

- The nature of languages.
- Types of languages.
- Types of writing systems.
- Functions of language.
- Language alternation.

Bilingual learners must contend with all these linguistic factors. Educators' and families' cooperation and understanding can turn this reality into positive opportunities for learning and growing. The lesson on language use and proficiency included in this chapter reveals the variation of language proficiency levels and opportunities for language development bilingual students have. The discussions and analysis helped students express their feelings about initial inability in English and present loss of their heritage language. Students' use and proficiency became clearer to the teacher. Teachers often make assumptions about their students' language use and proficiency. Teachers' and families' knowledge of how these linguistic variables affecting the students facilitates planning support for their efforts.

Three lesson plans outlined in the last section of this chapter can help students explore some of the linguistic variables:

- Writing systems.
- The nature of languages.
- Language use and proficiency.

PART I: CLASSROOM IMPLEMENTATION

The linguistic unit 3, *Language Use and Proficiency,* was implemented early in the school year over a 3-day period. The students were becoming used to whole-class discussions or books and topics of interest. The lesson objective was:

> Students' use of language(s) in both the oral and written form. Students will understand how their proficiency relates to the amount of use in the context of home, neighborhood, school, and/or nation.

Day One

On the first day of the language lesson, Angela begins with the two semantic maps on the board. One circle is labeled "Spanish" and the other, "English." She poses a question to the class, "How many of you have thought about how much of each language you use? Where do you use the English language? When? Where?" The students begin brainstorming. As they answer, Angela writes their responses in the respective circles. "In school," Bernarda calls out. "In stores," adds Jenny. "Spanish in the house," says Alex. After each response Angela repeats aloud and writes on the chart.

The students continue responding eagerly. Angela keeps probing, "Have you ever thought about it? Where do you use each one?" Quietly Alex says, "Spanish in the house." "Yeah, in the home," Angela repeats, writing the comment on chart paper. Every child's contribution is added to the diagram until the circles are full.

Angela asks about the students' feelings related to language use: "Who feels more comfortable in English? *¿Se sienten más comfortable usando el inglés? ¿Por qué se sienten así?* [Do you feel more comfortable speaking English? Why do you feel that way?] How many feel comfortable using both?" "How many feel that they are improving one language and the other one they are sort of losing or forgetting?" In response to this question, many students raise their hands and say, "Yes." Angela continues this line of questioning: "Who feels they are losing one language?" Alex shyly nods.

Angela feels it is time to get straight to the heart of the problem. "Who only wants English? Who doesn't want to be bothered with Spanish anymore and prefers English only?" Only Cesar raises his hand. Jenny calls, "I want both." Angela accepts these two responses. She nods, yet does not voice her own opinion on the issue.

---

[1]See Appendix B for instructions on how to create semantic maps.

The next activity is the language use survey. Students will be expected to log their language use throughout a 24-hour period. By examining their own language use, the students will come to their own conclusions about language. Angela introduces the *Language Use Chart* (see Worksheet 1.4). She explains that the students will keep a record of their language use for 24 hours. She enthusiastically discusses the importance of being conscious of one's own behaviors and asks, "How many of you start speaking in Spanish sometimes and then switch to English?" Some students nod their heads.

Then Angela moves on to the next part of the lesson, the read aloud of the book, *I Hate English,* by Ellen Levine (see Appendix A for a description). She starts by asking students to make predictions about the book based on the cover and title. Jenny quickly comments, "When I was in first grade I hated English."

Angela adds this comment to a new sheet of the chart paper taped to the board. She turns to Jenny and asks, "Why?"

"Because it was hard," Jenny answers.

"How many can identify with this?" Angela asks the class. She pauses and then begins reading. As Angela reads, she continues to ask the students to predict. At times she begins a sentence and then abruptly stops and pauses while the students chime in with the last word. At other points in the text she stops to ask students if they identify with Mei Mei, the main character.

"Did you hear the part when she said, 'English is such a lonely language'? Where is she when she says English is such a lonely language?"

"In class," replies Jenny.

"In class." Angela pauses. "Have you ever felt that way? Did you ever feel..."

"Like you weren't there," finishes William.

"Like you weren't there?" Angela looks at William.

"Invisible," he adds.

"You were there," Angela states. "But you were invisible."

The room is quiet. "Okay, we'll continue." Angela continues on with the story. Although she picks up on the themes of loneliness and alienation, she does not dwell on them. Later, she will return to these negative feelings and show how they can be overcome.

As Angela reads, she pauses and looks around the classroom. Students interject with their ideas. At one point José notes, "At least Mei Mei is speaking English a little bit." This comment indicates that he is following the story and evaluating the character's changes.

At the end of the story, Angela shares one of her own experiences with language. Angela compares her story to the book, "I experienced a little like Mei Mei when I went to live for two years in Puerto Rico. They put me in second grade. The other kids called me 'la americana.' [the American]. And I was like Mei Mei when I returned to New York. I hated the sound of English."

Angela is willing to share stories from her own life with the students so that they can understand that she too has lived through similar situations. By giving the students a glimpse into her own life, she shows empathy for her students.

Angela ends this first lesson on a positive note. Drawing from the example of the story, she stresses an important theme. "What did Mei Mei speak of in English?" she asks. Jenny answers, "About China, Chinese New Year."

"That opened up her world," Angela explains. "She was able to share her feelings and her culture. Was she invisible then? No, because she made her teacher aware of her feelings." Angela wants to emphasize to the students that they are not alone and that through sharing their feelings, they can feel better.

While emphasizing the commonalties of the immigration experience, Angela also gives room for individual self-expression. She introduces individual journal-writing activities to encourage each student to reflect on his or her life. "Take out your journals. Respond to this question: Write about a time when you felt like Mei Mei in school with your friends, feeling invisible because of not knowing English well. Did you ever feel that people treated you differently because you speak another language?" Angela writes the question on chart paper for the students to refer to as they reflect. She also takes care to explain in Spanish.

At the conclusion of the lesson, Angela reviews the plan for the following day. She reminds the students to keep a record of their language on their language use surveys. She also mentions that they will share their journal responses with the class.

Day Two

The next day begins with the students sitting in their usual groups. Angela is standing in front of the room with three large poster papers taped to the board behind her. Angela asks for volunteers to share their journal entries.

Jenny is the first to volunteer, "I would."

"You would like to, Jenny. Let's hear Jenny."

Jenny goes to the front and stands behind the podium. Looking down at her paper she begins to read, "Write about a time when you felt like Mei Mei. When I first met my niece and nephew I felt sad because they speak so much English and I just know a little. They were speaking so much and I couldn't understand and I got mad because they keep speaking and I couldn't understand. From them I learned a lot and I thank them for that. From them I learned a lot and I would like to learn more English."

The students applaud. Angela asks for reactions to Jenny's writing and records student responses on the poster paper.

Bernarda raises her hand, "Mad."

Angela writes this comment on the paper. "She felt mad. Yeah. Mad. Right, Jenny, that's what you said?"

Jenny nods.

José reads next, "My brother didn't know English. He was sad when all his friends speak English. He did not know a single word. Some of his friends were arrogant with Christian. They made fun of him every day because he can't speak English. But one year passed. He could speak English. He could speak every little word. Then he was arrogant with the people who made fun of him."

As José reads, Angela writes main points of his essay on the chart paper. The students clap as José heads to his seat. Angela asks José about the actions that his brother took to change his negative situation into a positive one. José explains that his brother began to study and learn English.

One by one, the students step forward to share their stories. All of the students include their feelings in their reflections. The most frequently mentioned emotions include: sorrow, displacement, isolation, frustration, and even anger. After each one reads, Angela takes time to comment on their thoughts. She praises their work and affirms their right to feel upset by their experience. Angela extracts the ways that negative situations can be changed into positive ones.

Now Bernarda goes to front of room. She reads her essay:

When I went to Santo Domingo because I new more English than Spanish each time when I talk I scramble words like the two languages. Also I had a hard time, finding a friend because I wanted a friend that new English and Spanish that was hard to find. When I went to Santo Domingo I felt confused, invarest [embarassed], and shy. When I try to find a friend I was very nervous because my close [clothes] was different almost everything was different. But the worst part of all was that where I lived there weren't so much kids so there was always scilens [silence]. I fixed that problem because my brother came a long with me and he nows [knows] both.

Bernarda's feeling of alienation is echoed in the journal entries of her other classmates. For many children the feelings of frustration are manifested when they visit their heritage countries because they have lost some of their first language-skills. Angela senses this theme and helps the students realize that it is a common thread running through all their experiences, including her own. She helps students see the connection between language proficiency and opportunity to use the language.

When it is Alex's turn to share, Angela takes into account his shyness and gives him extra encouragement: "Go ahead Alex. You have a really powerful thing to share with us."

Alex reads from his journal:

When I went to Guatemala. The kids from Guatemala were talking in Spanish. And my mother helped me translate. When I went to the school in third grade, third grade was like 4th grade.

When the teacher gave us homework nobody in my house knew how to read. My mother was at work and my sister didn't know Spanish either. Sometimes I'd do the work put it in English and the teacher told me read and speak in Spanish. I took Spanish classes and that's why I can talk and read Spanish.

Angela smiles and says, "That happened to me, the same thing when I was in Puerto Rico. I spoke Spanish but I didn't know how to read and write it, a but I studied. Now I'm very thankful for the experience because that's how I learned how to read and write in Spanish."

The next step in the lesson is for the students to take out their language use charts that they completed for homework. The students form small groups to compare their language use. They have about 15 minutes to work in the groups. Angela instructs them to first add up how many hours they spoke each language during the day, then to share their figures with their group.

For example, one of the student's charts read as in Fig. 2. 1.

Time	Activities	Spanish	English
7 a.m.	Shower	X	X
8 a.m.	Talking		X
9 a.m.	Class		X
10 a.m.	Bathroom		X
11 a.m.	Class		X
Noon.	Lunch		X
1 p.m.	Class	X	
2 p.m.	Bus		X
3 p.m.	Phone		X
4 p.m.	Friends	X	X
5 p.m.	My Room		X
6 p.m.	Playground	X	X
7 p.m.	Outside		X

FIG. 2.1.   Sample language use chart.

After comparing their *Language Use Charts*, Angela reconvenes the class to discuss their findings. Alex indicates what he felt when he realized that he spoke more Spanish than the others. He actually reports that he was the "only one who spoke Spanish," which emphasized his self-conception of differentness, even within the bilingual classroom. His classmate, José, was quick to point out that he was not alone in using Spanish, but that he just spoke more than the others.

For homework, Angela asks the students to reflect on their language use in their journals. She writes the journal questions on the board, "What does your chart reveal in regards to quantity of language use? What were some of the activities where the most language was used? What surprised you? Does the ability of speaking change over time?"

Day Three

On the third day of the language use unit, Angela stands in front of the class and asks the students to take out their yellow folders where they keep all the work connected with the SC lessons.

Angela addresses the class, "Let's talk about settings. You know in stories we have settings. In school we have formal and informal settings. Where does Spanish come in?" She turns to the poster paper and writes, "settings: Home Spanish class, stores, community." She turns back to the class and says, "What I'd like to know now is your reactions to speaking one language more than another. John, why don't you read what you wrote? You were supposed to look over your language log and write about the extent of your language use."

John looks down at his journal and reads:

I think people speak English more so do I. I speak less Spanish and other languages to. Also its more complicated in Spanish and in english is not difficult. I read good in english and in Spanish it's hard. I write in english good but in spanish no so good.

The students seem to be feeling a sense of loss as they realize that they do not use Spanish as often as they had.

Angela senses the mood of the class and asks, "How do you feel about losing your language? Does that concern you? If you wrote about it, that means it does concern you." She pauses. "Anybody else? Sandra?"

Sandra reads from her journal:

I'm more comfortable speaking English because it is easier to pronounce. I'm losing my Spanish a little bit. I prefer reading in Spanish than in English because I read faster in Spanish.

Angela summarizes Sandra's comments: "So Sandra reveals to use that in some activities she prefers to do them in Spanish." Addressing Sandra she says, "Also you are conscious of losing the language?" Sandra nods. "And with friends you prefer English?" She nods again. "Do you ever speak in Spanish with your friends?"

"Sometimes," Sandra acknowledges.

The students are all engaged in the discussion. Some look a little uncomfortable, as if they are considering a personal question. It is clear that they have not articulated their thoughts on the issue within a classroom setting before. Angela continues, "What are some of the reasons why she prefers English?" She pauses, allowing time for the students to ponder the issue. "Spanish becomes complicated because you don't speak it as often." There is no response from the students so she tries a different angle. "When you speak with your parents at home what language do you speak? How many speak Spanish with their parents?" All raise hands.

José says, "I think people speak English more. I read good in English in Spanish I can't read that good."

Jenny raises her hand and says, "I like English because in this country you need English to get work and go to college."

Angela sees an opportunity to lead the conversation into a discussion of bilingualism. The students already seem to recognize the importance of knowing two languages. Angela's questions allow the students to explore the benefits of being bilingual. She does not give them the answers, but leads them to their own conclusions.

"Do you want to keep your Spanish?" she asks, "because you have an advantage. Uds. saben dos idiomas y tienen más oportunidades." [You know two languages and have more opportunities.]

William states, "My mom says that if you know two languages you can get raises faster."

John raises his hand and without waiting to be called on yells, "If you go to another country you can get a better job!"

"How many of your parents are learning English?" Angela asks.

"My father doesn't know English. My mom does," contributes José.

Jenny chimes in proudly, "My mom is learning English."

Angela smiles and asks, "How many of you help your mothers?"

Bernarda raises her hand: "I help my mother with her homework."

"What did you learn from this activity?" Angela inquires. "Do you think it was a good idea to do this activity. Was it important? What did you learn about yourself that you hadn't realized before?" Jenny has her hand raised. "Jenny?"

"It is important to know English well."

Angela writes this comment on the poster chart and repeats, "You feel it is important to know English well. Is it just English, or any language? Is it important to know Spanish well?"

Jenny agrees, "Yes."

Angela asks, "When you say 'learn the language well,' what does that include? Is it only important to speak it?"

Christopher says, "Write and read."

"Good," she switches to Spanish. "¿Que más aprendieron?" [What else did you learn?]

José says, "It is important to use both languages."

Angela also writes this on the chart. "It is important to value both languages? Good José. One more. Bernarda?"

"It is better to know both languages because when someone asks you a question you can answer right away," she says.

Angela adds to the chart, "advantage when faced with different situations. example in a business, jobs, stores..."

Alex, who has been quietly following the discussion, adds, "It is important because you can help your parents."

Angela praises him for his comment, saying, "That is a good one." She adds it to the chart. "How many have helped their parents?"

The students raise their hands.

The discussion has lasted for about 40 minutes. Angela reviews the conclusions the students have drawn. Their next assignment is to make a bar graph of the results of the language use logs (see Fig. 2. 2 for a sample graph).

The students move into groups to work on their graphs, a skill they had developed in math class.

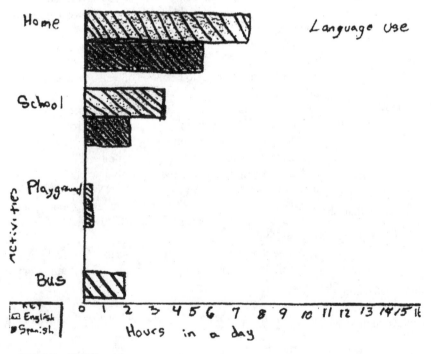

FIG. 2.2. Sample graph.

Lessons Learned

The students learned much about their language use and proficiency. The objective for the linguistic unit included two main concepts: language use and language proficiency. Students actively participated in activities related to language use. They logged their use of languages for 24 hours. They discussed and graphed the results revealing their bilingualism: "At the bus stop [I speak] in English. On the bus, Spanish and English. I see TV in English, radio in Spanish," noted Jenny.

The topic that engendered the richest discussion and reflections was the effects of limited proficiency when trying to function either in the United States or in their country of origin. Reading, responding, and discussing the responses to the book *I Hate English* revealed the anger, fear, and frustration that accompany limited language proficiency. José recalled the problems of his brother when they first arrived: "They [his friends] made fun of him every day because he can't speak English." Sandra, born in the United States, wrote about her experience visiting her relatives in Santo Domingo:

I felt really angry because none of my cousings (cousins) or anyone in my family knew English. I wanted to talk English so badly that when I said things in Spanish I felt like I didn't say anything at all.

This objective also requires students to establish the relationship between proficiency and use. They revealed that they had not made the connection between use and proficiency. When prompted by the teacher to look at their language use and make relationships with their proficiency, students just focused on proficiency. Sandra wrote:

I am more comfortable speaking English because it is easier to pronouns and I am losing my spanish a little bit. I prefer reading in spanish because I read spanish faster than English.

The teacher prodded them to find solutions to proficiency problems. A few offered some solutions to their lack of ability in one language or the other. José mentioned that he used the dictionary when he had difficulties with English as a new arrival. Sandra, frustrated with her lack of Spanish fluency when visiting relatives, mentioned that she spoke to her brother with whom she could use English. Bernarda, on the other hand, made the effort to communicate in Spanish. She claimed that with practice her language improved.

Although students did not reach all levels of understanding (see Fig. 2. 5 later in chapter) with respect to these linguistic factors, they discussed for the first time their deep feelings about their languages. Students discussed the value of bilingualism at an abstract level; they did not seem aware of what it would take to actually achieve high levels of bilingualsim.

Their teacher also gained a deeper knowledge of her students' linguistic profile. Their social and school context promoted the development of English but not that of the heritage language. Her students have found themselves in situations where they needed their heritage language to connect with family and function in their heritage country. Their frustrations and fears associated with the first intensive exposure to English were also revealed. The students' role in the family as often the most proficient in English was evident in some of their comments.

PART II: LINGUISTIC VARIABLES

Similarities and differences between the heritage language and the school language will influence performance in the school language. Differences in the type of languages can be a factor in learning a new language. In addition, other hidden variables play an important role in the promotion and development of the heritage and school languages among bilingual learners. The sociolinguistic category, writing system, and function of languages affect student performance and school policies and practices. Media, schools, and families promote languages to different degrees depending on whether they are considered world, national, or regional languages. Creoles, pidgins, dialects, and non-standard languages hold a fragile status within educational institutions. Schools and even families are often reluctant to promote literacy in heritage languages whose writing systems are considered difficult, such as Chinese.

Use of the languages at school, home, and the larger society supports the development or loss of languages among individuals. Language shift, the change from one language to another as the main medium of communication, occurs when a whole generation of individuals loses the heritage language in favor of a socially dominant language. This is prevalent in the United States, where most heritage languages are lost by the second immigrant generation.

Types of Languages

Languages can be classified by their historical relation or by their basic structural formation. Languages that belong to the same group tend to share characteristics. English belongs to the Germanic group with, among others, Dutch, Swedish, German, and Danish. Romance languages include French, Italian, Spanish, and Rumanian. Russian, Polish, Czech, and Bulgarian are among the Slavic languages whereas Finnish, Estonian, and Hungarian belong to the Finno-Ugric languages. There are relations across groups as between Germanic and Romance languages. English speakers take twice as long to learn Slavic and Finno-Ugric languages compared to learning Germanic and Romance languages, as evidenced by Foreign Service personnel attending the Foreign Service Institute to learn languages for their upcoming posts.[2] Similarly, comparisons of Dutch, French, and Greek stu-

---

[2] Foreign service data on ease of learning second languages provides good comparisons because the learners of the various languages are comparable in background and motivation.

dents learning English as a foreign language, showed that the Dutch students consistently outperformed the French and Greek speakers. Thus, language relatedness is considered a factor on ease of learning a second language.

In the study of language universals, languages have been classified with respect to their basic sentence structure rather than language genealogy. The major groups are SVO (subject, verb, object), SOV, and VSO. English, Spanish, Greek, and Finnish are SVO languages. Hebrew, Berber, Welsh, and Maori are VSO languages. German, Japanese, Turkish, and Quechua are SOV languages. The languages in each group share several characteristics

The characteristics of the native language influence both the ease and process of acquiring of a second language. Second-language learners use their native language as data to help produce the new language. This transfer can be positive or negative depending on the similarities and differences between the languages. Comparison of languages is not enough to predict errors because other influences affect second-language development.[3]

Sociolinguistic Category[4]

English, Spanish, Chinese, and French are presently world languages because they are used in many nations and they are important languages of international organizations. Most of the world literature is printed in English or Spanish. Most nations include a number of regional languages, that is, languages serving a region or ethnic group. For example, Inuit is a regional language in the United States used by some Alaskan Eskimos. The language most widely used in a country is considered its national language, such as English in the United States. The language used in government and legal documents is called official. English is the official language of 68 nations, whereas 30 nations claim French, 22 Arabic, and 20 Spanish as their official languages. Over 60 nations have more than one official language (Central Intelligence Agency, 2000). For example, in Israel, Arabic and Hebrew are official languages. In India, where both Hindi and English are considered national official languages, there are also 14 regional official languages.

The language "used as an institutionalized norm in a community" is considered a standard language, which is the variety used in the media, schools, and other official and cultural institutions. Varieties that do not conform to these norms are considered nonstandard. North Mandarin, spoken in Beijing, is considered standard Chinese, while all other Chinese languages are considered nonstandard dialects.

Certain languages are classified as dialects, Creoles, and pidgins. A dialect is a geographical or social variety of a language. Dialects used by low socioeconomic-status groups are some times called patois. These usually do not have a written form. The distinction between dialect and language is as much social as

---

[3]See Gass and Selinker (2001) for a discussion of various theories of second language acquisition.
[4]This topic is explored in Lesson Two.

linguistic. In linguistic terms a dialect is considered a variety of a language with certain differences yet mutually comprehensible. Different countries in Latin America use different dialects of Spanish that have some structural and lexical differences, yet people can communicate with ease. In many countries throughout the world several languages coexisted preceding the establishment of modern nations. The language used in the political and economic center of the new country became the literary and later the national language . Other languages became "dialects," often mutually incomprehensible. Such is the case of Sicilian in Italy, Cantonese in China, and Bavarian in Germany. The social designation of dialect lowered the status of these languages and the power of their speakers.

The active contact among people of different languages gave birth to pidgin languages. As people wanted to trade and communicate, they developed pidgins with limited vocabulary, reduced grammatical structure, and narrower range of functions. People do not speak them as native languages but millions use them in their daily lives. In Papua New Guinea, where more than 700 distinct languages are spoken, Tok Pisin, a local pidgin, is the most widely used language to facilitate communication among this nation's 3 million speakers. Pidgins appear and some also die when people cease their contact. During the Vietnam War a pidgin English developed. It disappeared with the end of the war.

When pidgins become the native language of a community, they are called Creoles. Their vocabulary, grammar, and functions develop to serve all the linguistic needs of the community. Haitian and Cape Verdean Creoles are widely used in communities throughout the eastern United States by immigrants from Haiti and Cape Verde. These Creoles have developed writing systems that are widely used in their communities.

Sociolinguistic categories change over time. For example, Portuguese was a world language in the 16th century when the maritime Portuguese dominated lands and trade throughout the world. With the decline of the Soviet Union, Russian lost the status of official language in a number of countries. In Estonia, as they declared Estonian the official language, it also became the main school language, displacing Russian.

Types of Writing Systems[5]

Writing systems can be logographic, syllabic, or alphabetic. In logographic systems, such as Chinese and Japanese Kanji, symbols represent words. Most Chinese characters have two parts, one that represents meaning and another that represents pronunciation. Some characters represent abstract ideas, and yet others combine characters to represent a new idea. For example, woman + woman = quarrel . Although the complete Chinese dictionary includes more than 50,000 characters, Chinese students learn about 3,000 in their elementary years (Shu & Anderson, 1997).

---

[5]This topic is studied in Lesson One.

Each character represents a syllable in syllabic systems, such as Japanese Katakana, Korean, and Cherokee. Syllabaries usually contain more than 50 symbols. Syllabic systems are relatively easy to acquire. Few reading disabilities have been reported among children who learn to read through syllabic systems (Tzeng, 1983).

In alphabetic systems there is a direct correspondence between graphemes (symbols) and phonemes (sounds). There are more than 25 different alphabets with very different-looking symbols. Most alphabets have around 25 symbols. The smallest alphabet is Rotokas with 11 letters and the largest is Khmer, with 74 letters. English, Spanish, and many European languages use the Modern Roman alphabet. Some languages, such as Finnish and Spanish, have transparent spelling with most sounds represented by just one symbol. English and Gaelic on the other extreme are very irregular. Hebrew indicates vowels with diacritics, which are not always written.

Children learning to read and write in English as a second language may encounter very different challenges. A Spanish speaker must learn new sound–symbol correspondence. The differences in the vowels are particularly confusing. The letter *i* in Spanish corresponds to the vowel sound in *Pete;* the letter *e* corresponds roughly to the sound in *pet*. Thus, for a Spanish speaker Pete and pet are not representatives of the so-called "long e" and "short e" but two different vowel sounds. Arabic and Hebrew speakers learning English must learn not only a completely different alphabet but must also learn to read from left to right. A Chinese speaker must learn a completely new writing system. Having a totally different alphabet or writing system from English (such as Chinese or Arabic) is more cognitively demanding than for learners who already know the Roman alphabet. For Spanish, Portuguese, and other users of the Roman alphabet, the task is more confusing because the same letter represents different sounds in each language.

Function of Language[6]

People who function in more than one language use these languages in different contexts and with varying frequency. In different contexts, they may feel pressure to use one or the other language. They also may use these languages only orally or also in written form (W. Mackey, 1968).

In the United States many languages are commonly spoken and used. English is the language of the government, education, business, and in the world of work. English is the predominant language of the media. It is the language of signs, directions, and most written expression in the environment. Other languages are spoken mostly in small communities, usually in addition to English. They are used in the home, ethnic neighborhoods, religious institutions, and local media. There is, however, little public use of these languages outside the immediate ethnic community. Many members of ethnic groups do not know or use their heritage language. "[Fif-

---

[6]This topic is explored in Lesson Three.

teen] % of California's Hispanics do not even speak Spanish" (Hodgkinson, 2001, p. 3). The majority of students in Angela's class used more English than Spanish.

Although English is also the international language of computer communication, the Internet facilitates access to newspapers and other resources in the heritage language. Some schools promote the use of two languages in bilingual programs. Programs differ in the amount, length of time, and pressure to use English and the heritage language. ESL and short-term Transitional Bilingual Education (TBE) programs pressure students to develop English and discourage the heritage language. Long-term TBE, Dual Language, Two-way, and Canadian Immersion programs encourage students to use both languages. The school context where the program finds itself also varies in the promotion of each language. The Rachel Carson School in Chicago, with only a TBE program, promotes the use of English and Spanish in the whole school (Portraits of Success, 2002). The English-speaking teachers resented the French Immersion bilingual program in their school. Even if some of them knew French they refused to use it when communicating with their bilingual colleagues (Cleghorn & Genesee, 1984).

Bilinguals use different languages depending on the setting and the addressee. Children often use the heritage language with older relatives whereas they use English with contemporaries. Church services may be in the heritage language, but Sunday school is often conducted in English because the younger generation is typically not fluent enough in the heritage language.

Limited use of a language is particularly harmful for the development of those heritage languages that are highly contextual. Development of the nuances of these languages depends on opportunity to use them in different contexts. Japanese, for example, uses very different terms when the speakers are of different age and social standing. Children who are not exposed to the language in different situations and different speakers do not learn the full range of the language. A Japanese student recalled moving back to Japan and being unwilling to speak to her school principal for fear of using improper language. Korean children in the United States report abandoning Korean after adults scolded them for not being addressed using the proper form of the language.[7]

Language Alternation

Bilinguals, when communicating with other bilinguals, frequently alternate languages. Such codeswitching is more common in oral than in written language. A number of linguistic constraints determine when and how the switch occurs (Grosjean, 1982; Romaine, 1995). The syntax, morphology, and lexicon of the languages play a role on possible switches. Codeswitching occurs at the discourse, sentence, or word level in the communication between bilinguals. A person may be talking to somebody in one language but switch to a different one when switching

---

[7]This phenomenon was reported in several child studies of Korean bilingual students done by students in my courses.

topics or when a different person joins the conversation. Bilingual mothers and teachers often employ codeswitching to call children's attention. Angela addressed her class mostly in English. Her students were quite fluent in the language and were getting ready to be mainstreamed to English-medium classes. However, around March, when she started implementing the lesson on cultural factors (see chap. 4) a new student arrived from Colombia. Angela constantly codeswitched to make sure that Carlos understood the class content.

Language switches may occur between (intersentential) or within (intrasentential) sentences. Topic or a number of stylistic reasons drive bilinguals to switch languages. For example, a bilingual 7-year-old boy telling a joke said: "Les voy a contar un chiste. Um... there was a boy so dumb... Esto saque de Boy's Life...." In the first intersentential codeswitch, he used Spanish to set the stage—"I'm going to tell a joke—" while he started telling the joke in English. Then he went back to Spanish to clarify the source of his joke: "I took it from *Boy's Life.*" This sentence also has an intrasentential codeswitch because the source title was in English. His codeswitching was a sophisticated strategy to distinguish the joke from needed clarifications.

Children often insert a word in the other language when they cannot remember or do not know the word in the other language. Miki, a Japanese 3-year-old learning English, switched to Japanese for words such as *clown, drums,* and *blocks.* These consonant clusters are particularly difficult for Japanese speakers. To avoid making a mistake, he just said the word in Japanese

In the United States, there are communities where codeswitching is the normal form of communication. In East Harlem, the Puerto Rican community has developed well-documented norms for the use of Spanish and English. Most tasks in the community can be carried out in either language. Of important consideration is the language proficiency of the participants. Children are encouraged to use the dominant language of the addressee. Typically children speak to each other in English except when addressing or in the presence of an adult. Adults tend to be more proficient in Spanish.

Influence of the Linguistic Context on Development of Bilingual Learners

Bilingual learners need to develop the language of the school to succeed in education. Preservation of the heritage language is considered an important asset in the formation of identity and in the ability to integrate to the new social context . For students going to school in the United States, learning academic English and preserving their heritage language is no small feat.

Oral and written language development of bilingual learners is affected in many ways by their linguistic context. The sociolinguistic categories of languages influence the way languages are regarded in our society and the relative status they hold in comparison to English. It is not surprising that standard English predominates in schools and other situations, given its status as world, national, and official language.

The type of languages students speak and the type of writing system used by the languages will influence the ease of acquisition of English. The greater the difference, the more likely that families and school will neglect the development of the heritage language. Often these students develop limited oral language skills in their heritage language whereas they become fluent and monoliterate in English.

The function and amount of use of a language influence proficiency of specific languages and language skills. Our society offers opportunities to use English in a wide variety of contexts. Heritage languages are mostly relegated to use at home or ethnic neighborhoods. When the language is used only in casual conversations, the student will develop the informal oral register of the language. Practice of the written language in academic settings is needed to develop the language for successful schooling.

Opportunity to use languages stimulates motivation to learn and to practice them (Graham & Brown, 1996). Intensive exposure to English helps develop English proficiency among students who are native speakers of other languages. As the heritage language erodes due to its limited use, speakers become less motivated to search for such opportunities and their families, school, and churches accommodate increasing use of English and contribute to the loss of the heritage language. Persistent language loss among young members of an ethnic group results in language shift for the whole community. Other social, cultural, political, and economic variables contribute to the maintenance or erosion of heritage language use within an ethnic community.

Families and educators realize that if they want their children to achieve bilingualism, they must provide opportunities for use of the two languages in both oral and written form. Students need plenty of exposure to social English through activities that integrate bilingual students with native speakers of American English. A demanding curriculum that explicitly teaches English academic skills is a precondition to success in the educational system (Chamot & O'Malley, 1994). Exposure to the heritage language through the Internet, connections with students in other countries,[8] and as a medium of instruction in schools helps develop these languages beyond the familiar uses.

Families do not always have access to written material in the heritage language. Their children develop oral skills but do not acquire literacy unless the schools have bilingual programs or they attend special weekend schools for the promotion of ethnic languages. In some cases the language is not written. Thus, although students may be bilingual, they are not necessarily biliterate.

Language alternation is a little-understood bilingual behavior. Codeswitching is regarded often as poor language practice. Adults often may worry that code-

---

[8]For example the project Orillas connects classrooms in the United States with classrooms throughout the world. The program's web page address is http://orillas.upr.clu.edu/ The e-mail address is orillas-info@igc.org

switching is evidence that children are confused. Codeswitching is, in fact, a sophisticated form of language use. It requires knowledge of two languages and of linguistic and sociolinguistic rules. As children develop language, they also develop their ability to codeswitch.

The present linguistic context in the United States strongly supports standard American English and not much else. Excluded are other languages, or language varieties. From a purely linguistic viewpoint this social stance is unacceptable. No language or language variety is "in any sense inherently inferior to the standard variety in grammar, accent, or phonology" (Corson, 2001, p. 67).

Suggestions for Additional Reading

- Corson, D. (2001). *Language diversity and education.* Mahwah, NJ: Lawrence Erlbaum Associates.
- Zentella, A. C. (1997). *Growing up bilingual.* Oxford, England: Blackwell.

PART III: DOING ANALYSIS
OF THE LINGUISTIC CONTEXT

Teachers and students study their linguistic context to understand their own language abilities, and their advantage or struggles associated with their own proficiency in English. Teachers who are native speakers of standard American English must realize that their own triumphs as students were facilitated by their knowledge of this variety of English. Their students have to struggle much harder because their own linguistic context is much more complex.

This section includes three units addressing linguistic factors. It is important to read the general instructions on lesson implementation included in the Introduction before implementing any of the lessons. The first one explores writing systems, the second addresses the relative importance of various languages in the world, and the third covers the relationship between language use and proficiency. A description of the implementation of the third unit is included at the beginning of the chapter. Students explored the uses of languages and reflected on their struggles with the development of English and the loss of the native language.

Teachers can choose among these lessons and adapt them to the age and grade level of their students and linguistic composition of the class. Mevlida, a second-grade Bosnian teacher, adapted the opening discussion of the lesson on language use. She prepared an attractive sheet with icons representing school, home, and other places frequented by her students. Next to each icon she wrote: I use ____. She asked the students to fill in the blank with the word Bosnian and/or English. A discussion followed.

Regardless of lesson plan, the teacher must be ready to follow students' cues when issues are raised in connection with the lesson. While discussing their worksheets on language use, Mevlida's students commented on the difficulty of learning English. Their comments reflected alarming hopelessness over learning the language. Instead of continuing with the prepared lesson, Mevlida discussed the specific difficulties faced by Bosnian speakers when learning English. She also asked students to survey their work from the beginning of the year to analyze how much progress they had made. They were pleasantly surprised.

Linguistic Lesson 1: Writing Systems

> **Objective:** Study the variety and complexity of writing systems (including heritage languages represented in the classroom) in order to understand levels of difficulty of acquisition of different scripts.

Rationale: Bilinguals can learn more than one writing system but, depending on the nature of the system and the similarities and differences among them, they pose different challenges. Similar systems such as English and Spanish use comparable symbols but they represent different sounds, causing some confusion. Different systems such as English and Chinese do not cause confusion but the learner needs to learn a whole new set of symbols. The types of symbols pose different degrees of difficulty. Alphabetic systems such as English, Spanish, or Russian are learned faster than logographic systems such as Chinese. Motivation to teach and learn writing systems may be influenced by these differences. Students need to understand that confusion or motivation to learn or teach various languages is not related to the value of the language or their own ability but to the nature of the writing system.

Time: Three to 4 days (60–90 minutes per day).

Materials:

- Books (see descriptions in Appendix A): *Talking Walls* (available in Spanish) by Mary Knight Burns.
- Alternate books: *Abuela, America Too, How My Family Lives in America,* and *Dumpling Soup.*
- Worksheet 2.1 *Forms of Writing.*
- Worksheet 2.2 *Poster.*
- Large world map.
- Internet: http://www.yahooligans.com/Around_the_World/languages/
- Newspapers, magazines, and other resources depicting different writing systems, such as Chinese, Japanese, Russian, French and others.
- Transparencies of various alphabet systems.
- Chart paper.
- Overhead projector.

Overview of Activities

- Introduction to writing systems.
- Reading and discussion of the book *Talking Walls.*
- Writing-system demonstration by invited guest
- Writing systems in our communities
- Group investigations of different writing systems.
- Compare/contrast writing systems.
- Exploring names with different writing systems.
- Big book of various writing systems.

Choose one or more of the suggested activities depending on the age of your students and the availability of resources.

Introduction to Writing Systems

1. The day before reading *Talking Walls,* give students a 5 x 8 card and ask them to bring them in the following day with the word *wall* written in a language other than English. Ask them to write the name of the language on the back of the card. They can ask parents, relatives, or neighbors for assistance. You may bring examples yourself to add variety to the possible writing systems your students may bring. It is good to have different writing systems such as Chinese, Japanese, Korean, Russian, Greek, Khmer, or Gudgarati.
2. The following day, ask students to show their cards to the class, read the word, and give the name of the language.
3. Put the cards up on the wall. Discuss the differences and similarities of the writing systems.
4. Use a world map to connect the card to the country where the language is spoken.

Reading and Discussion of the Book *Talking Walls*

1. Show the cover of the book *Talking Walls* to the class. Ask students to describe what they see. What writing systems do they recognize?
2. Open the book to the second page and ask what one word is represented in English? Write the word *wall* on chart paper. Inform students that the words written on these pages are all different writing systems for the word *wall.* Ask students if they can find the words on the cards they brought.
3. Read sections in the book. Choose those that have a connection to the heritage languages in your classroom or others that may have connections with your curriculum.
4. Before reading the section, introduce vocabulary and discuss the part of the world that section covers (refer to the world map).

Writing-System Demonstration by Invited Guest

Invite a guest to introduce a writing system to students or have students survey someone in their school who knows a different writing system. Choose a writing system of the native language of students in the class that is not taught in school.

Writing Systems in Our Communities

1. Provide disposable cameras and have students take pictures representing different writing systems in their communities.
2. Ask students, working in groups, to describe their picture. Have them individually write descriptions of their picture.
3. Create a bulletin board displaying the photos taken by students along with a written description explaining the picture.

Group Investigations of Different Writing Systems

1. Tell students that they will be detectives investigating different writing systems. They will do it using a version of the game "Show and Tell."
2. Using an overhead projector, display transparencies illustrating a particular writing system at a time.
3. Initiate the game of "Show and Tell" by asking students to name the countries in which each writing system is used. You may wish to provide clues to assist students with their guesses.
4. Have students plot the countries identified on large world map.
5. Display a sign-up sheet labeled *The Writing Systems of Countries*. Have students form groups of two to three and write on the sheet the three writing systems they wish to investigate.
6. Display various writing systems' resource materials such as foreign-language newspapers, magazines, and encyclopedias for students to use in their investigation. Refer students to previous activities, that is, photographs, *Talking Walls,* invited guest presentation. You may also have students conduct searches at their public library.
7. If you have computers and Internet access, have students conduct a search using the following search engine: http://www.yahooligans.com/ Around_the_World/ languages/. Have students print several samples of writing systems.
8. Distribute Worksheet 2.1 *Forms of Writing.* Ask students to complete the worksheet by providing information using various sources.
9. Have students design a poster illustrating the three writing systems studied and present it to the class. They can use Worksheet 2.2 to sketch their poster.
10. Display posters in the classroom.

Compare/Contrast Writing Systems

1. Using the posters and other materials in the class, have students to compare and contrast various writing systems with English.
2. Have students discuss the difficulties with learning more than one writing system, the level of difficulty of various writing systems, confusion involved in learning different systems, and writing systems taught in school.
3. Have them speculate how long they think it would take to learn various writing systems.
4. Have them reflect and write about their own experiences learning more than one writing system and their own motivation to learn them.

Exploring Our Name With Different Writing Systems

Provide students with a copy of an alphabet system different from their own heritage language and have them write their names using this alphabet.

Book of Writing Systems

Have students design a big book with the same word or sentence as written in different languages. For example, hello (English), hola (Spanish).

Outcomes

	1	2	3	4
Concepts: Different writing systems. (Include systems of the heritage languages of students in the class.)				
Relationships: Type of writing system and difficulty and length of time it will take to learn.				
Connection to self: Difficulty of own heritage language writing system and differences with English affect ability to write in the heritage language.				

Key (for further explanation, see Appendix C)
Each concept, relationship, and connection to self covered in the lessons can be graded with respect to the following levels of understanding:
1. Misguided notion or no recognition.
2. Passive understanding.
3. Expresses some understanding of concept or relationship.
4. Expresses full understanding of concept or relationship.

Proposing a solution	1	2	3

Key: Solutions proposed can be noted with respect to whether student:
1. Does not propose a solution.
2. Engages in a solution proposed by the teacher.
3. Proposes a solution.

FIG. 2.3.   Linguistic context rubric, Lesson 1.

Linguistic Lesson 2: The Nature of Languages

> **Objective:** Classification of languages (including all those represented in the class) as world, national, regional, dialects, Creoles, official, standard, nonstandard, written, and/or oral only.

Rationale: Languages are more or less important in a particular society at a particular time. This relative importance promotes use and motivation to teach and learn particular languages. Among the factors influencing standing of languages are: spread of use (world, national, regional); use in government business (official); specific classification as a language, dialect, pidgin or Creole; defined system (standardize vs. nonstandardized); and whether or not it has a writing system. Students need to understand that all languages and dialects or varieties are perfectly adequate for communication. Within countries around the world, languages vary in importance. In Israel, Hebrew is considered an essential symbol of national identity. This standing changes over time. Latin was a major language in Europe. Presently only a few people in Italy still use a variety of it as a daily language.

Time: Four to 5 days (60–90 minutes a day).

Materials:

- Book: *Who Belongs Here: An American Story* by Margy Burns Knight (available in Spanish).
- Alternate books: *F is Fabuloso, Isla, My Name is Maria Isabel, Working Cotton.*
- World map (Worksheet 2.3).
- Copies of a small map for each student.
- Audio recordings of five different languages.
- Internet addresses: *http://www.sil.org/ethnologue* and *http://www.yahooligans.com/Around the_World/Languages/*
- Atlas.
- Chart paper.
- Graph paper.

Overview of Activities

- School language survey
- World and regional languages
- Nature of languages in the school
- Survey on teaching a second language
- Dialect survey

School Language Survey

1. Tell students that they will be conducting an investigation to find out what languages are spoken by students in their classroom and other classrooms and by school personnel.
2. Have students design a school language survey form by generating a list of questions. The following question may be included:
   - What languages are used in different "regions": classrooms, cafeteria, playground, hallways, and bus?
   - What languages are spoken by people of authority?
   - What is the school's official language?
   - Do different teachers speak differently?
   - Which language is more important?
   - How do people who are not speakers of the important language feel?
   - What countries are the majority of speakers from?
   - What other countries are represented?
3. Distribute the *School Language Survey.*
4. Have students work on the survey either individually or in teams. Then conduct the survey, tabulate the results, and write a summary of their findings.
5. Have students discuss the survey results with the class.

World and Regional Languages

1. With the whole group, introduce the lesson by playing brief recordings of examples of five different languages. Ask students to guess what languages are being spoken. Write student responses on chart paper. Ask students to name other languages and add them to the generated list.
2. Display a large world map and provide students with their own copies (Worksheet 2.3 *World Map*). Review generated languages list and ask students to identify the countries that use the languages in the list. Label the countries on the large map and write the name of language(s) spoken.
3. Have students select a language and conduct research on the country or countries where that language is spoken. If you have computers and access to the Internet use the following address: *http://www.yahooligans.com /Around_the_World/Languages/*
4. Have students share their findings, adding information to the large map.
5. Explain that world languages are those that are used widely in many countries. National language is the most widely used in a particular country. Regional languages are those used in a section of a country or countries.
6. Have students identify the languages for their respective countries. Have them determine whether their heritage language is a world, national, or regional language.

Nature of Languages in the School

1. Introduce students to the concepts of world, national, regional, dialects, Creoles, official, and standard languages by thinking of the school as a nation. They will define the nature of languages in the school.
2. Ask students to first define the nature of languages spoken in the classroom. Make a chart where you can include the different languages of the classroom. Determine whether they are: (a) used all over the school or only in certain classrooms, or by a group of students in a classroom (world, national, or regional); (b) dialects or Creoles; (c) used for all documents in the classroom (official vs. nonofficial); (d) written always in the same way (standard vs. nonstandard). Write students' responses on the chart.
3. Expand the chart to include all languages in the school using the data from the School Language Survey.
4. Have students reflect on the nature and importance of various languages in the school.
5. Have them reflect in writing responding to the prompt:

   What is the nature of your heritage language in the school?
   Is it important or not? Is it necessary to know it to communicate in the school? How do you feel about it?

Survey on Teaching a Second Language

1. Ask students to conduct a survey on language preferences in their school or neighborhood. They can pose the following question: The school is thinking of teaching a second language to all students. Which one of these languages (Spanish, French, Chinese, Japanese, Portuguese, Greek, Latin, or Russian) would you like to learn and why? (The specific languages can be changed depending on your own school).
2. Have students discuss the results and reasons given by those polled. The following guided questions are suggested:
   • Why were certain languages favored over others?
   • What is the nature of the most favored languages?
   • How important in the society are the favored languages?
3. Have students reflect in writing responding to the following prompt: Was your heritage language one of the most favored? Why or why not?

Dialect Survey

1. Ask students to conduct a survey on teaching Spanish. They can pose the following question: The school is going to offer Spanish classes, would you prefer to have a teacher from Spain, Puerto Rico, the Dominican Republic,

Mexico, Colombia, or Argentina teaching and why? (The specific language and dialects can be changed depending on your own school).

2. Have students discuss the results and reasons given in the survey. The following guided questions are suggested:
   - What country received the majority/minority of votes?
   - Which countries were not selected?
   - Is there a pattern in the reasons given for their selections?
   - Were there any surprises with the results?
3. Have students reflect in writing responding to the following prompt: Was your heritage dialect one of the most favored? Why or why not?

Outcomes

	1	2	3	4
Concepts: (check the level for each concept) • Selected countries in the world and languages spoken in different countries. • Nature of languages (selected items): world, national, regional, dialects, Creoles, official, standard, and written languages.				
Relationships: Nature of language and its relative importance in a specific country at a specific time in history.				
Connection to self: Nature of heritage language, relative importance of heritage language at present in the United States.				

Key (for further explanation, see Appendix C)
Each concept, relationship, and connection to self covered in the lessons can be graded with respect to the following levels of understanding:
1. Misguided notion or no recognition.
2. Passive understanding.
3. Expresses some understanding of concept or relationship.
4. Expresses full understanding of concept or relationship.

Proposing a solution	1	2	3

Key: Solutions proposed can be noted with respect to whether student:
1. Does not propose a solution.
2. Engages in a solution proposed by the teacher.
3. Proposes a solution.

FIG. 2.4.   Linguistic context rubric, Lesson 2.

Linguistic Lesson 3: Language Use and Proficiency

Objective: Students' use of language(s) in both the oral and written form. Students will understand how their proficiency relates to the amount of use in the context of home, neighborhood, school, and/or nation.

Rationale: Language use greatly influences development. More specifically, the language skills that develop will be those that students have opportunities to practice. If the students use only the oral form they will develop oral language. To develop literacy they need opportunities to read and write. Children often blame themselves for lack of ability in a language, for difficulties learning a language, or for forgetting a language they knew. They do not realize that their language skills fluctuate relative to opportunities for practice. For example, students from Vietnam are fluent in Vietnamese but they may not read or write it if they did not go to school. Life in the United States usually provides more opportunities to use English, enhancing the chances of developing English while they forget their Vietnamese. The arrival of new relatives increases the use of Vietnamese and so on. Students need to become aware of the uses of the languages—both oral and written—in their environment in order to understand that there is a logical explanation for their language development and language loss.

Time: Three to 4 days (60–90 minutes per day).

Materials:

- Book: *I Hate English* by E. Levine.
- Alternate books: *I Speak English to My Mother, Molly's Pilgrim, A Day's Work.*
- Language Use Chart (Worksheet 2.4).
- Chart paper.
- Small notepads.
- Graph paper.

Overview of Activities

- Brainstorm about language use (Venn diagram or table).
- Reading and discussion of the book *I Hate English.*
- Language Use Chart.
- Graphs based on Language Use Charts.
- Reflections on the main topics of the unit.

Brainstorm About Language Use

1. Working with the whole class, determine students' use of English and heritage language in their daily lives. On chart paper create a Venn diagram or semantic maps (see Appendix B) reflecting students' responses. Do several if there are several heritage languages in the classroom. Ask about which language they use. Ask where and when the languages are used. Write in the appropriate place on Venn diagram. For example, if students say they use English at the *store* write the word *store,* and so on. After students volunteer ideas, ask questions related to areas not mentioned.

Areas to Explore

Home
Neighborhood
Church
School
Media (T.V., Radio, Newspapers, Internet)

---

2. Within each of these contexts both languages may be used. Ask for more detail. For example, with whom do you use English? With whom do you use your heritage language at home?

   While doing the Venn diagrams, incorporate discussion of proficiency and whether they use language orally, or for reading or writing in each place.

Reading and Discussion of the Book *I Hate English*

1. Prior to reading the book aloud, write the title of the book and the author's name on chart paper. Show the book cover to the class and ask the students to predict what the story will be about. Write students' responses on chart paper. For example, students may infer that the main character dislikes English, or that she is from an Asian country, and so on. Through students' predictions lead a discussion on when they may have encountered similar feelings about English/or their heritage languages.
2. Read the story aloud. Pause at certain instances in the story to probe students' understanding and how it relates to their own experiences. At the conclusion of the read aloud, ask students to share their reaction to the story. Some of the points that are important to raise are: feelings felt when students did not know

a language well, what helped in difficult situations, changes over time, perception of themselves relative to language ability, and so on.

3. Ask students to respond in their journals to the following prompt (see Appendix B, Response to Literature Journals):

> Write about a time in which you felt invisible for not knowing English well like the main character Mei Mei. How did you turn this into a positive experience?

Suggest to your students that they describe their reactions to the story using examples from the book, to explain how what they read relates to their own experiences, or to those of someone they know.

4. Respond briefly in writing to the journal entries.
5. Have students read aloud their journal responses to the class. Ask the class for reactions after each individual reads. Compare essays with the contents of the book. This activity takes time because all students get a turn. The discussion is essential for teasing out the issues relevant to the objective of this lesson.

Alternative: If the class is very large, select a group of students to share with the whole class. Choose students who cover different important topics related to language use and proficiency. Have the rest of the students share in small groups.

Language Use Charts

1. Bring copies of a Language Use Chart (see Fig. 2.1) that has been filled to reflect your own language use in a 24-hour period.
2. Describe how you recorded the extent of your language use beginning on the previous day. Ask students the following: What categories are present in the chart? What information does this chart provide? And so on.
3. Provide students with a blank *Language Use Chart* (Worksheet 2.4). Ask students to record the extent of use of English and their heritage languages for a 24-hour period. Have students start immediately and continue throughout the day until the following morning when you meet again for this lesson.
4. The following day invite students to form groups to share the results of their Language Use Chart completed for homework. Have them tally the results. Write on chart paper some questions to assist the group while looking at their results:
   - Was one language used more than the other was in your group?
   - What activity was the language used more often for within your group or was it about the same?
   - What information does the tally tell us about your groups' language use?
   - Is there a pattern found in your group?
   Circulate around groups and provide assistance.

Graphs Based on Language Use Charts

1. Ask students to look at their *Language Use Charts* and tallies and think of ways to represent their individual language use. If students don't know how to make a graph, use this opportunity to teach them.
2. Distribute graph paper to students. Have students chose two colors to represent the languages used. On the X axis students will write the hours in the day and on the Y axis the list of activities. The graph has a key indicating the color for English and the one for the heritage language. Students create their bar graphs using the results from individual charts.
3. Have students give a brief presentation and showcase their graph (see Fig. 2. 2).

Outcomes

	1	2	3	4
Concepts: (check the level for each concept) • Language use. • Language proficiency.				
Relationships: Language use influences proficiency in both the oral and written languages.				
Connection to self: Level of proficiency in each language (oral and written) and how it relates to how much they use each language.				

Key (for further explanation, see Appendix C)
Each concept, relationship, and connection to self covered in the lessons can be graded with respect to the following levels of understanding:
1. Misguided notion or no recognition.
2. Passive understanding.
3. Expresses some understanding of concept or relationship.
4. Expresses full understanding of concept or relationship.

Proposing a solution	1	2	3

Key: Solutions proposed can be noted with respect to whether student:
1. Does not propose a solution.
2. Engages in a solution proposed by the teacher.
3. Proposes a solution.

FIG. 2.5. Linguistic context rubric, Lesson 3.

Worksheet 2.1. Forms of Writing.

Provide information on the distinguishing characteristics for each of the three writing systems researched.

Name of Writing System: _____

Characteristics

Name of Writing System: _____

Characteristics

Name of Writing System: _____

Characteristics

Worksheet 2.2. Poster.

In the space below sketch a poster showcasing three writing systems you have studied.

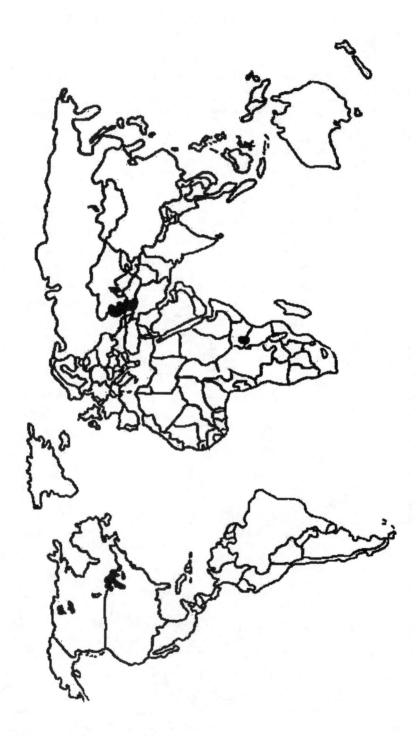

Worksheet 2.4.   Language Use Chart.

Time	Activities	Heritage language Oral/Reading/Writing	English Oral/Reading/Writing
7 a.m.			
8 a.m.			
9 a.m.			
10 a.m.			
11 a.m.			
Noon			
1 p.m.			
2 p.m.			
3 p.m.			
4 p.m.			
5 p.m.			
6 p.m.			
7 p.m.			
8 p.m.			
9 p.m.			
10 p.m.			
11 p.m. to 6 a.m			

3

Economic Context

OVERVIEW

Present immigration includes families with high education and economic levels as well as large numbers of poor families. Bilingual students cluster in urban centers vexed with economic, political, and social problems. Such problems affect the educational support families and schools provide for students. Economic factors are also connected to language proficiency and education level. In addition to mastery of English, in the present global economy proficiency in another language is a valuable asset. In the lesson on "Language and Careers," students in Angela's class discovered the multilingualism in their communities, the business opportunities for various ethnic groups, and the usefulness of languages in the world of work.

The second part of this chapter includes the analysis of the following economic variables:

- Financial resources of families and schools.
- Economic impact of serving populations with particular needs.
- Economic mobility and career opportunities.

The effects of economic variables cannot be easily remedied. Students and teachers need to realize the potential effects of poverty, the present educational demands to achieve economic mobility, and the role played by proficiency in English and the heritage language. Support mechanisms and high expectations are means for balancing negative economic variables. Part III offers two lessons that help explore economic variables:

- Careers, languages, and school achievement
- Educational demands of modern society

PART I:CLASSROOM IMPLEMENTATION

The economic unit on *Languages and Careers* is implemented over three consecutive mornings, 4 weeks after the students have completed the linguistic lesson.

The objective for this lesson is as follows:

Students will determine the economic viability of their languages and of English in their communities and nation. Students will relate language proficiency with career opportunities and social mobility.

Angela is a little apprehensive about starting the first economic lesson. "I don't know how this is going to fly," she confides.

Day One

Angela has the blackboard set up with three large blank pieces of chart paper and two maps of Boston. Angela instructs the students to take out their SC folders and to move their desks forward.

First, Angela asks the students to think back to the novel they had been reading for class, *Felita,* by Nicholasa Mohr. The students talk about the different resources that Felita had in her neighborhood including: stores, laundromats, and diverse people. Angela then asks the students to go up to the maps of Boston and to mark their own neighborhood with a sticker. The students jump up to find their homes on the map.

Angela looks at the clusters of stickers and draws some conclusions. "What conclusions can we make? We have someone out in East Boston. We have a large group of people who live in the Jamaica Plain area. We have people who live in the Roxbury area. Why do you think we are doing this? It is interesting to see. Are all the neighborhoods the same?" She makes a chart on the board indicating neighborhoods and number of students living in each one.

Next, Angela hands out a K-W-L chart (see Appendix B). She asks the students to close their eyes and visualize their communities. They are asked to list all the places they find in their neighborhood. "Close your eyes and visualize your neighborhood. You go by your neighborhood every day. I don't just mean the block where you live, your whole neighborhood. What does it offer you? What characteristics do you find there? For example, do you have a laundromat? Write under 'know' in your chart."

As the students write, Angela walks around classroom offering encouragement and ideas. "What kind of people live in your community?" she asks. The students talk quietly as they make their lists, sharing ideas.

Angela instructs the students to pair up with someone from a different community and share what they know about their neighborhoods. She gives them 5–10 minutes to share similarities and differences.

When the time is up, Angela calls for attention and asks the groups to report on their findings. She asks them about access to transportation and records their responses on the chart paper. Sandra brings up the point that her neighborhood has "integrated people." This prompts Angela to ask about the different ethnic groups. Students mention different groups: Latinos, Asians and Northern Europeans.

For homework, Angela asks the students to "be detectives" in their communities. Using the K-W-L charts, they can fill in the categories, "What I Want to Know" and "What I Learned." They are to walk through their neighborhoods and write down a list of agencies and services that they find. If possible, the students are to collect brochures to bring in to school. Angela tries to motivate the students for this activity by saying, "You already reflected on your community. Today you are going to verify it. It should be a fun activity. You will find it is very diverse."

Day Two

The next day in class, Sandra and Bernarda rush up to show Angela the research they had done on their neighborhoods (see Fig. 3.1).

Angela matches their enthusiasm, "Great. I'm really excited. Hold on to these." When everyone is settled in their seats, she asks the class what they had discovered. José speaks up first, "I found a restaurant." Students start volunteering their discoveries: fast-food restaurants, car washes, schools, hospitals, community centers, and shelters. Angela writes them all down on chart paper.

What I Know	What I Want to K now	What I learned
• Jamaica Pond • osco • Parks • Brigams Hospital • Basketball court • Laundry Mat • Integrated People • Childrens Hospital • Hennegain school and the Kennedy • Nail Salon • 2 train stations • Franklin Park 200 • Many stores • Bank Boston • Gasoline Station	• I want to find out if only caucasian people owned the businesses. • If everyone spoke only English and Spanish	• I learned that there are more businesses than I thought. • All the people are not caucasian • And, that the people speak all the languages not only English and Spanish.

FIG. 3.1.   K-W-L chart.

"How about newspapers?" Angela asks. "How about in the *bodegas*? Do you notice what kinds of newspapers are sold there?" Students list names of newspapers: *The Boston Herald, The Boston Globe, The Allston/Brighton Tab.*

Angela then asks, "How many people noticed different languages?"

One student answers, "There is a restaurant in my neighborhood where the Chinese man speaks Spanish."

Angela then asks, "What does that tell you when you are in a business and you see diverse people owning their own business? Are there career opportunities? Is it important to have two languages? You guys have definite advantages, don't you think?" The students nod and answer yes.

Angela takes out some brochures that one of the students had brought in. She reads aloud, "When you need help with your banking just call 1-800-su banco." It's in Spanish. "Cuando nescesita ayuda con sus transaciones llama 1-800-su banco. [When you need help with your transactions call 1-800-your bank.] It is providing a service."

Angela continues to explain the next project. Pointing at the brochure she says, "You are going to do something like this but you are going to showcase your neighborhood." She hands out a graphic organizer for first draft of the brochure. "This is your outline. Describe your neighborhood on a brochure. Pretend you want people to visit your neighborhood. So write a description of your neighborhood. Use the list of features from your notebook. Once you do your sample and fill in your information, I'll give you the drawing paper."

Jenny walks over to Angela with the first draft of her brochure, looking for feedback. Angela skims the draft and asks Jenny to read it aloud. Jenny reads for the class, "Come, come to this community. It has everything you are looking for. It's going to be the best day of your life. You could eat any food you like. Come, it's going to be the best day of your life. Trust me, you will love Roxbury. For more information call 277-0534."

The students clap as Jenny finishes reading.

Day Three

Angela gives the students 2 days to work on the brochures. The students can work independently, in small groups, or for homework. On the last day of the economics unit, Angela calls the class together to have the students present their final products. She has the students share in front of the class, allowing them to practice their public speaking. She stresses the themes of diversity and acceptance. Angela also focuses on the skills of comparing and contrasting and making conclusions.

The first group is from Allston and Brighton (see Fig. 3.2 for their brochure). José, William and Maria stand in front of the classroom. José moves forward to read first, "Come to Allston. This is where you can find anything guaranteed. Don't know how to get here? Call 783-1871 to get your way here. For a free brochure call. For more information call. Hope to see you there." José shows the panels of the bro-

Brochure Outline

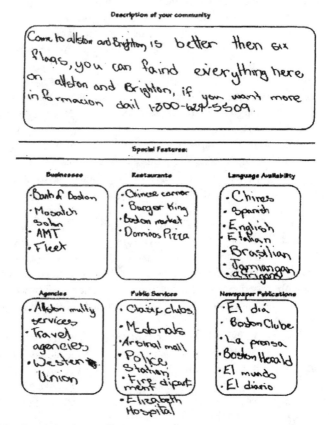

FIG. 3.2.   Sample brochure outline.

chure where he had listed public services, businesses, restaurants, newspapers, and languages available.

As each student reads aloud his or her brochure, the class listens carefully, then applauds. Angela asks each student, "What did you learn from your neighborhood?" The answers vary. José concludes that there are many opportunities in his neighborhood. "Anyone can make it," he claims.

William states, "I learned there are a lot of languages that I never heard."

Alex and Sandra both found that their communities are changing. Sandra reports, "I've been living in Jamaica Plain for five years. The language has changed. Before it used to be English and a little Spanish. Now it's all mixed up."

Finally, Jenny challenged her own assumptions about her neighborhood: "I thought there were a lot of English people. Now I see there are other people too."

Students who initially had trouble describing their neighborhood in a positive light were able to find positive characteristics that they had not previously considered. As the unit concluded, they reflected on the benefits of linguistic and ethnic diversity. One of the students wrote:

What I learn was that the people from different countries are getting a chance to own a business. For example, China Garden it is owned by Chinese. One Sub Way owned by an Italian. Back in the days while people had businesses.

Lessons Learned

This lesson encouraged students to bring community knowledge into the classroom. Students were able to conduct research in their neighborhoods and share their findings with their classmates. They discovered the resources and strengths of their multicultural environments. Many of the discussions and students' products centered around the themes of neighborhood and the variety of languages: "I learned there are a lot of languages that I never heard," remarked one of the students. The children expressed their perceptions of their neighborhoods and some even changed those perceptions.

Students also recognized and appreciated the ability to speak more than one language. The students discovered numerous opportunities to use different languages in real-life situations. This discovery showed the students the value of bilingualism.

The role of the teacher was key in making the connection between bilingualism and career opportunities. The teacher prompted the students by asking: "Is it important to know two languages? Are there career opportunities? You guys have definite advantages, don't you think?" The students replied affirmatively. This was an indication that they had grasped the relationship between knowledge of languages and career opportunities.

This unit allowed for the teacher to learn about the students' lives outside of school. The teacher learned about the neighborhoods of the students, and some information about the jobs of the students' parents. This knowledge can be important for teachers who would like to learn about the real-world experiences of children.

PART II: ECONOMIC VARIABLES

There is a two-way relationship between economics and education. The economic level of the family and school district affects educational success and quality of education provided to students. In turn, education influences economic mobility and career opportunities. The emergence of special programs to serve bilingual populations demands resources of districts. Education and language proficiency are tied to economic possibilities. Economic factors may not seem relevant to youngsters in schools because the direct impact of these factors is not experienced until later in life. However, students' understanding of how education affects their career options can influence school performance. Students need to understand that economic mobility in the modern era is increasingly dependent on education.

Economic variables are closely connected with political and social variables. For example, the financial support of schools depends on political pressures carried out by communities. Furthermore, many social problems are exacerbated by poverty.

Financial Resources of Families and Schools

The present immigrant population falls on the two extremes of the economic spectrum. Large numbers of low-skilled laborers with limited education have entered the country in the past decade. They command low-paying jobs in insecure and unpleasant working conditions and come with less education than native populations. However, many of the new immigrants are well-educated professionals. Immigration in the 1990s included more than 30% professionals. College-educated immigrants are in comparable proportion to native populations. Initially, because of language and lack of familiarity with the American world of work, they are often unable to secure high-paying jobs. Eventually their education and professional training allows them to gain entry into better-paying jobs. Educational background and better economic conditions support the success of their children in school (A. Portes & Rumbaut, 1996; C. Suárez-Orozco & M. M. Suárez-Orozco, 2001). Complications brought about by political or social factors may interfere with immigrants' social and economic mobility. Illegal immigrants or dark-skinned people face more hardship because they can secure good jobs or suffer prejudice (A. Portes & Rumbaut, 2001).

Financial situations of families impact children's education. Families with financial resources are better prepared to provide educational support for their children. If their children are having difficulty in school, they can help them or hire tutors. Two international studies on science and on mathematics achievement concluded that:

> "Students from homes with a high level of educational resources (more than 100 books; all three study aids: computer, study desk, and dictionary; and at least one parent finished university) had higher science [and math] achievement than students from homes with fewer resources...." (Martin et al. 2000, p. 5; Mullis et al. 2000, p. 5)

These families can also afford to live in more costly neighborhoods that support school districts with better resources. These neighborhoods are safer. Children can play outside and interact with English speakers. Families with less financial resources make great sacrifices to provide for their children for essentials and for educational opportunities. However, they are limited in the experiences and resources that they can offer their children. In spite of their efforts, the general conditions are not favorable. They often live in unsafe neighborhoods, where they don't allow their children out of their apartments except to go to school. They are often forced to move in search of jobs. Their children suffer from these frequent changes of school (McQuillan, & Englert, 2001). In the case of high school students, work, motherhood, and other life pressures get in the way of their education.

Some teachers perceive poor families as "illiterate and disinterested." (Silva, 1998, p. 229). Such an attitude affects how these children are educated. Staff develops low expectation for these students, which in turn results in less challenging curriculum and instruction. Research with these families showed that, contrary to teachers' perceptions, the families were interested and had high hopes for their children's education (Delgado-Gaitan, 1990; Valdés, 1996).

The economic level of school districts affects students' performance (K. J. Payne & Biddles, 1999). Increase in per-pupil expenditures correlates positively with student achievement (Koski & Levin, 2000). The TIMMS 1999 international studies on science (Martin, et al. 2000) and mathematics (Mullis, et al. 2000) achievement reported that well- resourced schools "generally had higher average science [and math] achievement than those in schools where across-the-board shortages affected instructional capacity" (p. 9). These shortages included inadequacies in school buildings, instructional space, instructional materials, supplies, audiovisual resources, library materials, science laboratory equipment, computers, and computer software. Schools with more resources also provide for students who are struggling, therefore increasing their chances to succeed. Scholarships help a small number of students from poorer neighborhoods attend wealthier schools. Expectations are another common difference between schools in affluent as opposed to poorer neighborhoods. The former assumes their students will go on to college, thus raising their expectations with respect to their performance in high school. Alva (1991) found that Latino students attending schools that included college preparatory programs performed better and were at lower risk of dropping out.

Inequity in funding across public schools is pronounced in the United States (K. J. Payne & Biddles, 1999). Inner-city schools receive much less funding than their suburban counterparts. "Denial of 'means of competition' is perhaps the single most consistent outcome of the education offered to poor children in the schools of our large cities." Poor education limits job opportunities and economic mobility, keeping families in a vicious circle of poverty and limited education. Immigrants and language- minority students, who tend to cluster in the inner city, are deeply affected.

Poverty among families affects the stability of schools. Students attending schools with a great number of other poor students are doubly affected (Flaxman, Burnett &

Ascher, 1995). There is a high negative correlation between concentrated poverty and student achievement. Schools with a high level of poor families evidenced higher dropout rates, lower rates of attendance, lower grades, lower test scores, and fewer students enrolled in AP (Advanced Placement) courses. The opposite was true for schools with students in a better financial situation (McQuillan & Englert, 2001).

Lack of family and school resources not always equates with limited educational success. Community support often makes up for lack of resources. Large and inter-connected social networks that provide resources to their members promote economic growth. These networks help second-generation immigrants succeed, particularly if members in this network posses educational and financial resources (A. Portes, 1995b; A. Portes & Rumbaut, 2001).

A high school in Alaska staffed mostly with volunteers, in a building with extremely limited resources, graduated many successful students. They were among the most accomplished Eskimo students at the University of Alaska (Kleinfeld, 1979). The quality of their education was based on forming thoughtful bicultural students with the ability to think as educated individuals and a solid understanding of their identity as Eskimos and as American citizens.

Economic Impact of Serving Populations With Particular Needs

Development of special programs, such as ESL and bilingual education, for bilingual students is seen as an economic threat to the staff, as a financial burden to the district, and as a job program for ethnic minorities.

Recruiting qualified personnel to serve the increasing numbers of bilingual students may, in a level-funded school district, reduce the job opportunities for current personnel unfamiliar with the languages and cultures of the students. In addition, school committees claim that providing education in the home languages increases the costs of education beyond their school systems' budgets. Because of the dramatic increase of bilingual students, many school districts find themselves with a large percentage of bilingual students and a small percentage of bilingual teachers. Therefore, either new teachers need to be hired or existing teachers may have to re-tool to work with the bilingual students. In California, where bilingual students with limited English proficiency represent a quarter of the student body, the teachers union adamantly opposed a new certification system passed by the State Commission on Teacher Credentialing. The certification requires all teachers working with bilingual students to undergo training in cross-cultural, language, and academic development (CLAD) (California Commission on Teacher Credentialing, 2001; Schnalberg, 1995). Fears and opposition to such measures as a threat to mainstream teachers' job security are to a degree unwarranted. Great number of teachers still work with bilingual learners with limited English proficiency without having obtained the proper credentials.

Opponents of bilingual education perceived this educational program just as a job program for members of ethnic communities. Bilingual education has indeed opened career opportunities to adults from ethnic communities because of their language skills. Their presence in schools has benefited the students and allows professionals to use their social capital. Economically successful adults provide support to their ethnic communities with added benefits to their children. (A. Portes & Rumbaut, 2001). Bilingual programs also benefit those English speakers with skills in other languages, particularly Spanish. The majority of teachers in bilingual education Spanish programs are not native speakers of the language (Guerrero, 1997).

School districts claim that bilingual education costs more. This claim is hard to prove and much debated. Though materials in the native language and the cost of busing children to schools that offer programs in their language add to costs, bilingual teachers, as teachers with less seniority, actually command lower salaries. School accountings make it difficult to determine exactly expenses just for the bilingual program. In Massachusetts a law requires that the state provide school districts with student in bilingual programs with additional funding for each bilingual student. Because the money awarded is not earmarked for bilingual education, districts are free to spend the additional funds any way they choose. Although bilingual education adds to the state budget, it does not mean that the added expense actually funds bilingual education.

Whether the added cost of bilingual education is real or only perceived, the negative effects on students are the same. School personnel and boards lament the presence of these students and begrudgingly serve them. This unwelcoming school climate creates substantial barriers for bilingual students. In a community in Massachusetts with 80% Spanish-speaking students, the school committee chair saw her role as a guardian of the school budget to avoid tax increases. Education took a back seat. Proposals to improve services for bilingual students were judged for their costs rather than their educational merits. Demoralized bilingual administrators and teachers abandoned the school system curtailing the already limited services for bilingual students.

Federal funding has often helped bilingual education programs even in hostile districts. Once the funds are gone, some programs have enjoyed continued support from the districts, whereas others have lost personnel and resources or have been dismantled. Federal funding often supported professional development, material acquisition, and assessment of students. When the federal funding expired, districts often failed to provide such essential support for the programs (Cahnmann, 1998). Districts routinely fund such activities for monolingual programs.

Economic Mobility and Career Opportunities.

"My Mom wants me to have a good education and wants me to know Spanish and English real good, so I have better opportunities to get a job" (Cazabon, Nicoladis & Lambert, 1998, p. 3). Diana synthesizes the conditions for economic advancement in modern society. The opportunities for economic and social mobility that existed earlier in the century have greatly diminished. In the past, education and language proficiency was less crucial for economic success. "Persons who, in another age, could nonetheless scratch out an income by the bending of the back and patient labor of the hands—may find no work at all" (Kozol, 1985, p. 58). Today, well-paid blue-collar positions are quickly disappearing. Corporations can only retain those workers who can be retrained. This retraining requires high levels of literacy. High school education is now a minimum requirement for most productive work. Students need to acquire sufficient education to move from entry-level jobs to professional jobs if they can hope for socioeconomic mobility (A. Portes & Zhou, 1993).

Proficiency in Standard English opens the door to educational and employment opportunities. Immigrants fluent in English earn twice as much as those with limited or no fluency (A. Portes & Rumbaut, 2001). Proficiency in the heritage language is also economically beneficial. In the present market, companies look for workers with knowledge of languages and ability to work with people of diverse cultural backgrounds. In some communities, hospitals, government offices, and businesses hire bilinguals to service their customers. In some cases the heritage language is essential to function in established ethnic communities with plenty of opportunities for employment (Fradd & Boswell, 1996; Gibson, 1993; A. Portes & Zhou, 1993). Students in Angela's class were surprised at the variety of languages used in their neighborhoods' businesses.

Career opportunities and the prospect of economic mobility motivate achievement in school. Students are driven by a determination to improve their families' economic situation. Parents strongly believe that education holds the key to their children's future. (M. M. Suráres-Orozco, 1987). Many parents have high hopes for the education of their children (Delgado-Gaitan, 1990).

For many ethnic minorities, however, the "American dream" of hard work translating to economic prosperity is a myth. Ogbu and Matute-Bianchi (1986) believe that groups that have been historically marginalized by society, such as Mexican-Americans, Native Americans, and Puerto Ricans, doubt that education makes a difference to their economic conditions. These groups have statistics and experience to disprove the theory that correlates economic and educational achievement. Hispanic men with a college education make only $10,000 more than White men with a high school degree. White men with a college degree make $20,000 more than their high school counterparts (Women's Policy Research, 1997). Hispanics with doctorates earn less than their non-Hispanic colleagues (Veltman, 1983). Even within Hispanic groups, there are differences in employment prospects. Mexican immigrants are at a greater disadvantage than Cuban immigrants when seeking employment prospects (A. Portes, 1995a). Immigrants with limited educational and financial resources, limited knowledge of English, and dark skin color are often assimilated to segments of the American society with limited possibilities of socio-economic mobility. These immigrants settle in poor neighborhoods with poor schools in a path of "downward assimilation" (A. Portes & Rumbaut, 2001, p. 59).

The families of these students question whether schools make a real effort to educate their children. They get discouraged when even with an education their children's situation is not better than their own. Teachers, on the other hand, often perceive only that these students and their families are not interested in education or in pursuing socioeconomic mobility. They compare these students with those who succeed and conclude that students' and families' apathy causes the failure rather than sociohistorical factors.

Influences of the Economic Context on Development of Bilingual Learners

Economic factors affect families and their children. These factors are intertwined with the other factors, particularly social, in a complex net. Students are lifted to high levels of school achievement or fall in a vicious circle of poverty and poor education with little hope for educational achievement or economic mobility (K. J. Payne & Biddles, 1999). Poor children live in poor neighborhoods, which offer limited resources and in some cases may be unsafe. Children raised in higher income neighborhoods come to school with the literacy preparation needed to succeed in school. Both the family and the community resources support this preparation. Neuman and Celano (2001) compared the resources in four communities, two low-income and two middle income. In each category one of the communities had a large concentration of people of ethnic variety. The middle income communities surpassed their low-income counterparts in literacy resources such as amount of reading material available for purchase, quality and quantity of street signs, public places conducive to reading and writing, and availability and quality of books in day-care centers, schools, and public libraries. Although parents showed equal motivation in wanting their children to succeed, the environment offered differential opportunities. Schools, for the most part, exacerbate these trends. Exceptional schools in poor neighborhoods have acted as positive filters, breaking the cycle and enhancing the chances for social and economic mobility.

Even if the opportunities were there, the unsafe neighborhoods prevent children from accessing public places. Miguel Angel's Mexican American-family lived across the street from a crack house in San Diego. His poor and hardworking parents had high ambitions for him. Miguel Angel applied himself in school but felt frustrated by his inability to freely move around after a close encounter with a gang (A. Portes & Rumbaut, 2001).

Local politics often affect economic decisions regarding programs for bilingual students. Schools that believe in the economic advantages of knowing more than one language and adequately preparing all students for the demands of the future will see fit to meet the needs of bilingual students. On the other hand, schools that perceive bilingual students as an economic burden unconsciously or consciously renege on their commitment to these students. No consideration is given to the negative social and economic consequences of limited education.

Suggestions for Additional Reading

- Kozol, J. (1992). *Savage inequalities: Children in America's schools.* New York: Harper Perennial.
- Neuman, S. B., & Celano, D. (2001). Access to print in low-income and middle-income communities: An ecological study of four neighborhoods. *Reading Research Quarterly, 36* (1), 8–26.
- Portes, A., & Rumbaut, R. G. (2001). *Legacies: The story of the immigrant second generation.* Berkeley: University of California Press.

PART III: DOING ANALYSIS
OF THE ECONOMIC CONTEXT

The following two units address economic factors. The first one explores the relationship between careers, proficiency in English and other languages, and school achievement. This lesson covers a number of topics usually included in the social studies curriculum such as characteristics of the neighborhood, careers, and skills required for various vocational preferences. The second lesson is also a good social studies unit. It explores more closely the connection between careers and education. The lesson includes a study of the industrial development by exploring how educational background required in the world of work has increased over time.

Economic Lesson 1: Careers, Languages, and School Achievement

> **Objective:** Students will determine the economic viability of their languages and of English in their communities and nation. They will understand how knowledge of languages influences career opportunities and social mobility. They will understand that the extent of knowledge and preparation required for success has increased over time.

Rationale: Factual knowledge of the language needs in the world of work helps students understand the purpose for learning English and their heritage language. Specifically they need to understand the value of reading, writing, and speaking, in formal and informal styles. Students understand that there are pragmatic rather than just affective reasons for knowing languages. Although affect is a powerful force in language development, it can also be a factor in rejecting languages. Therefore, a practical approach can help students move beyond emotional perspectives. Students must understand that over the generations, academic and linguistic demands have greatly increased. When students understand the linguistic and academic preparation needed to succeed in school and in a career they will be motivated to develop both their heritage language and English.

Time: Four to 5 days (60–to 90-minutes sessions).

Materials:

- *Felita* (available in English) by Nicholasa Mohr (see Appendix A).
- Alternate books: *Abuela, The Always Prayer Shawl, Don't Forget, El Chino,* and *The Folks in the Valley: A Pennsylvania Dutch ABC* (see Appendix A for description).
- K-W-L chart (see Appendix B for explanation of use).
- Brochure outline (Worksheet 3.1).
- Career Requirements (Worksheet 3.2).
- Maps of cities and towns.
- Telephone yellow pages.
- Chart paper.
- Notebook.
- Drawing paper.
- Colored stickers.

Overview of Activities[1]

- Reading and discussion of the book *Felita.*
- Location of students' neighborhoods (or streets).
- Languages and careers in students' neighborhoods (or streets).
- Neighborhood (or street) brochures.
- Possible future careers.
- Interview with a professional.
- Summary and reflection.

Reading and Discussion of the Book *Felita*

1. Read the first chapter aloud as students follow along in their own book, or a photocopied version. Translated written or taped copies can be provided for students with limited English proficiency. As you read, ask students to compare their own neighborhood to Felita's.
2. After reading aloud the first chapter, distribute large drawing paper and suggest students illustrate Felita's community. Ask students to review the first chapter and identify the people and places. For example, students can draw maps or pictures of the community. Students can include streets, buildings, stores, and streets of the community.
3. Display illustrations of Felita's community on wall or blackboard.

---

[1]After piloting this lesson, it was decided that more activities were needed to help students understand better the connection between language proficiency and career opportunities.

4. Use the map display of Felita's community to initiate a discussion about the various things that make up her community. Ask students the following questions:
   - Who lives in Felita's neighborhood?
   - What types of businesses are there?
   - Who owns these businesses?
   - Is her neighborhood integrated?
   - What languages are spoken?
5. Have students write in their *Response Journal* (See Appendix B) reflecting on their reaction to the first chapter.

Location of Students' Neighborhoods (or Streets)

1. Display a large map of your respective city or town on the blackboard and have students read the map. (This lesson assumes map skills. If the students don't have these skills, use the lesson as a way to teach map skills.) Provide students with color-coded stickers. Have each place a sticker on the neighborhood where he or she lives. (If all students live in the same neighborhood focus on streets.)
2. With the whole class, generate and write a list on chart paper as you ask students to name the street or area represented. Create a tally chart of the number of students represented in each street or area.

Languages and Careers in Students' Neighborhoods (or Streets)

1. Provide each student with a K-W-L chart (see Figure 3.1 for an example) as you display a larger version on the blackboard. Ask students to close their eyes and visualize their respective neighborhoods. Suggest that students reflect and write everything they know in the "What I Know" about their respective areas. Brainstorm questions that will assist in their descriptions. The following guided questions are suggested:
   - How does it look?
   - What features distinguish your neighborhood?
   - What languages do you hear?
   - What ethnic backgrounds are represented?
   - What types of business and services are provided?
   - What languages are used in these businesses?
   - What professions are represented?
2. Upon completion of preceding activity, pair students representing different neighborhoods to share their descriptions. Encourage students to compare and contrast their respective neighborhoods and place an asterisk next to the things that are similar.

3. Using the large K-W-L chart, initiate a discussion and ask students to share what they know. Write responses on the chart under "What I know."

4. Ask students to look at the second column of the K-W-L Chart entitled, "What I Want to Know." Encourage students to write questions about what they would like to learn about their respective neighborhoods. Have students share their questions and write them on the large knowledge chart display.

5. Distribute notebooks for students to use as they conduct a survey of their neighborhoods. Suggest to students to use the notebooks like a detective. They can write things they see as they explore their neighborhood as part of the daily homework assignment. Suggest they use the questions as a reminder of what to investigate.

6. The following day, using the K-W-L chart, have students refer to their investigative notebooks. Initiate a discussion on what students learned about their respective neighborhoods. Have students review their questions on the "What I want to Know" column. Students share their findings about their neighborhoods. Write students' responses in the column "What I Learned."

7. Conduct a class discussion on languages and careers using the following questions as a guide:
   • To what extent were your heritage language and English utilized in your neighborhoods?
   • What was the prevalence of different languages in the neighborhoods?
   • Who owns the businesses?
   • What can you say about services provided in your respective neighborhoods?
   • What do these patterns suggest in terms of career opportunities?
   • How many of your parents work within your neighborhoods?
   • What are the differences among the various neighborhoods? Why?
   • What do these patterns or findings tell us?

Neighborhood (or Street) Brochures

1. Distribute and review a blank *Brochure Outline* (Worksheet 3.1). Have students transfer the information collected from their investigation logs and K-W-L Charts to the brochure outline. Have students fill in the various sections of the outline providing the following:
   • Descriptions of their neighborhoods.
   • Special features of their neighborhoods: (a) Stores, supermarkets, agencies, public services, (b) Language spoken, (c) Hospitals, (d) Media and (e) Professions.

2. Once students have completed their outlines, provide large drawing paper and have students design their first-draft brochures showcasing their respective neighborhoods. Students who have access to community tele-

phone yellow pages can use these as a reference and bring them to class to share with others.

3. Students will complete their final drafts of their brochures for homework. They will then prepare a class presentation.

4. The following day, organize the class presentation of brochures by listing the names of the different neighborhoods (or streets) on the blackboard. As each neighborhood (or street) is announced, have students present their brochures to the class.

5. Ask probing questions to elicit further discussion of students' presentations, such as:
   - What did you learn about your neighborhood?
   - What discoveries were surprising to you?
   - How long have you lived in this neighborhood?
   - What changes have you seen in your neighborhood over time (in relation to people, languages, businesses, and career opportunities)?
   - What did you learn by doing this activity?

6. Design a bulletin board showcasing the brochures.

Possible Future Careers

1. Ask students to brainstorm careers they are interested in pursuing in the future. Write students' responses on chart paper.

2. Initiate a discussion with the whole class by reviewing the generated list of careers. The following guided questions are suggested:
   - How can you prepare for your particular career?
   - Which careers require a high school diploma, college degree, master's degree, or additional training?
   - Which careers require the knowledge of languages other than English?
   - What are some of the specific skills or talents required for your particular career?
   - Which careers require knowledge of computer skills?
   - Which careers are found in your neighborhoods?
   Write students' responses on chart paper.

3. Tell students they will be using classified ads of a Sunday newspaper in order to find out the skills, education, and language required for a career of their choice.

4. Provide students with a blank *Career Requirements Worksheet* (Worksheet 3.2) and distribute copies of the classified ads of the newspaper. Explain to students how the jobs in the classified ads are organized according to career fields. For example, a career in nursing would be listed under the field of Health Care. A career in teaching would be listed under the field of Education.

5. Have students read through the job description for their chosen career and write the information in the worksheet. You may wish to provide assistance as students work independently.
6. Have students discuss the results of their investigation. The following questions can be used as a prompt:
   - What are the skills and knowledge required?
   - What were the educational and linguistic requirements for your selected career?
   - What kind of preparation do such careers demand?

Interview With a Professional

You may want to provide students the opportunity to interview a community professional:

1. Locate a professional (doctor, lawyer, or other adult) willing to visit your class and talk about his or her profession.
2. Tell students about your potential guest. Have them write three to five questions they would like to ask the guest.
3. Invite your guest to come to your class and dialogue with your students.
4. Introduce the guest speaker to the class. The guest speaker may wish to give a brief talk to students about his or her background and work experience in the neighborhood.
5. Encourage students to ask their prepared questions.
6. Write the guest's responses on chart paper.
7. Ask students to reflect on what they have learned through their investigation of career opportunities. Write the students' responses on chart paper.
8. Have the students reflect on the importance of education for meeting career goals.

Summary and Reflection

Have students reflect in writing on the following prompt: What career are you interested in pursuing in the future? What are some of the things you need to do in order to prepare you for reaching your career goal?

Outcomes

	1	2	3	4
Concepts: (Check the level for each concept) • Demographic composition of community. • Reasons why people migrate.				
Relationships: (Check the level for each relationship) • Influence of social variables on the opportunity to interact with English speakers and with people of the heritage language. • Influence of interaction with English speakers on the development of English. • Influence of interaction with heritage-language speakers on the development of the language.				
Connection to self: Personal experience with English and heritage-language speakers. How the contact helps with English development and with maintenance of the heritage language.				

Key (for further explanation, see Appendix C)
Each concept, relationship, and connection to self covered in the lessons can be graded with respect to the following levels of understanding:
1. Misguided notion or no recognition.
2. Passive understanding.
3. Expresses some understanding of concept or relationship.
4. Expresses full understanding of concept or relationship.

Proposing a Solution	1	2	3

Key
Solutions proposed can be noted with respect to whether student:
1. Does not propose a solution.
2. Engages in a solution proposed by the teacher.
3. Proposes a solution.

FIG. 3.3.   Social context rubric, Lesson 2.

Economic Lesson 2: Educational Demands of Modern Society

Objective: Students will understand how current educational and career demands differ from those of their parents and grandparents.

Rationale: In the manufacturing society of the early 20th century, immigrants could succeed in the world of work with limited education and literacy skills. This is no longer the case. The literacy demands, command of English, and educational background required in most modern jobs are very high. In addition, working with and among a multilingual population requires proficiency in other languages and the ability to function with people of diverse cultural backgrounds. Students must understand that they need to reach a much higher level of education than previous generations if they want to succeed. They also should value their native-language skills and develop high levels of literacy in English.

Time: Two days (60–90 minutes a day)

Materials:

- The book *A Day's Work* by Eve Bunting (see Appendix A)
- Alternate books: *Coming to America: The Story of Immigration, I Speak English to My Mom, Tea With Milk* (see Appendix A).
- Alternate books for middle and high school students: *Bill Peet, Esperanza Rising, Wild Swans: The Daughters of China, Working Cotton* (see Appendix A).
- Parent and/or Grandparent Interview Questions (Worksheet 3.3).
- Changes in Educational Demands (Worksheet 3.4).
- Chart paper.

Overview of Activities

- Reading and discussion of the book *A Day's Work.*
- Differences in job demands over time.
- Intergenerational educational demands.
- Interview with parents and grandparents about educational and career demands.
- Summary and reflection.

Reading and Discussion of the Book *A Day's Work*

1. Prior to reading the book aloud, write the title of the book and the author's name on chart paper. Show the book cover to the class and ask students to predict what the story will be about. Write students' response on chart paper. For example, students may infer there's a boy and his grandfather sitting on a curb near a large trash can. They appear to be waiting to go to work and so on. Through students' predictions, lead a discussion about the relationship between the two characters and the types of work they will be doing.
2. Read the story aloud. Pause at certain intervals in the story to probe students' understanding. Ask students to relate to their own experiences. At the conclusion of the read aloud, ask students to share their reaction to the story. Some

of the points that are important to raise are: demands of English proficiency and careers for people in the generations of students' parents and grandparents, advantages of being a bilingual person, and levels of educational preparation across generations.

3. Ask students to respond in their journals—in class or as homework—to the following prompt:

> Francisco helped his grandfather who did not speak English, find a job as a gardener. Write about your parents' or grandparents' jobs. Do their jobs require knowledge of English? How are the jobs similar or different to Francisco's grandfather? What do you think are some of the advantages of being a bilingual person?

Suggest to the students to use examples from the book in their responses.

4. Respond briefly in writing to their journal.

5. Have students read aloud their journal responses to the class. Ask the class for their reaction after each individual reads. Compare essays to the content of the book. This activity takes time because each student gets a turn. The discussion is essential for teasing out the issues relevant to the objective of this lesson.

> Alternative: If the class is very large, select a group of students to share with the whole class. Choose students that covered different important topics related to language ability, job requirements, and careers over three generations.

Differences in Job Demands Over Time

1. Inform students that educational demands for participation in the workplace are quite different today than in the time of their grandparents. Ask students to name jobs that did not exist during their grandparents' or parents' generations. Write students' responses on chart paper.

2. Brainstorm with the whole class and create a list of the skill requirements for each job.

Intergenerational Educational Demands

1. Display a large *Venn Diagram* (see Appendix B) on chart paper with the headings *Grandparents/Grandchildren Schooling* as illustrated in Worksheet 3.4. Inform students that they will be conducting an investigation by comparing and contrasting the educational demands of the two groups.

2. Ask students to list the educational demands for grandparents and grandchildren. Allow students time to work independently.

3. Upon completing the preceding activity, ask students to choose one response and write it on the large Venn diagram display.

4. Review the responses for each category (grandparents and grandchildren) with the whole class. Initiate a discussion using some of the following questions:
   - What are some changes in educational demands over time between the two groups?
   - What do you think caused these changes?
   - What were some limitations with regard to career opportunities for grandparents?
   - What advantages do you have with your academic preparation?

5. *(Optional)* Have students write a brief summary describing the similarities and differences based on the information provided in the Venn diagram.

Interview with Parents and Grandparents About Educational and Career Demands

1. Tell students that they will be interviewing their parents or grandparents to learn about the educational requirements and career demands during their generation.

2. With the whole class generate a list of interview questions. Some of the following questions are suggested:
   - What was the highest level of schooling you completed?
   - What were the required courses?
   - Were there any vocational courses offered? What were they?
   - Did you have a language course requirement?
   - What were your career aspirations?
   - What did you do for a living?
   - What were the job opportunities when you entered the workforce?
   - What types of service occupations existed?
   - What skills did you need in order to get a job?
   - What jobs do you see as important in modern society?
   - What advice would you give our young generation to prepare for the future?
   - Do you consider it an advantage to be a bilingual person?

3. Provide students with a copy of interview questions (Worksheet 3.3) and have students conduct their interviews for the homework assignment.

4. The following day, invite students to share the results of their interviews. The following guided questions are suggested:
   - What was the highest level of education completed?
   - What were the similarities/differences in subjects taught?

- What were some of the skill requirements in the workplace?
- What types of career choices did they have?
- What limited them from getting the job they wanted?
- How do the educational requirements compare to yours?
- What commonalties and differences are found among grandparents?
- What valuable advice did they give for your future?
- What valuable lesson did you learn from interviewing your parent or grandparent?

5. Provide students with the Venn diagram entitled *Changes in Educational Demands* (Worksheet 3.4) and have students complete it using the information collected in their interviews.
6. Ask students to create a book about their parents or grandparents and themselves based on the information from their interviews. Tell students they will present these books to their families.

Summary and Reflection

Students reflect in writing responding to the prompt:

How do the present educational demands compare to those of your parents or grandparents?

What will you need to do to succeed with the current demands in the world or work compared to those of your grandparents?

Outcomes

	1	2	3	4
Concepts: (check the level for each concept) • Jobs that exist now did not exist in the past. • Educational requirements for specific jobs, for example, computer specialist, medical technician, machine operator, and social worker. • Language abilities and careers change over time.				
Relationships: • Educational background and job requirements.				
Connection to self: (check the level for each) • Academic and linguistic preparation and economic success over three generations. • Advantages of a bilingual-bicultural person in today's society.				

Key (for further explanation, see Appendix C)
Each concept, relationship, and connection to self covered in the lessons can be graded with respect to the following levels of understanding:
1. Misguided notion or no recognition.
2. Passive understanding.
3. Expresses some understanding of concept or relationship.
4. Expresses full understanding of concept or relationship.

Proposing a Solution	1	2	3

Key
Solutions proposed can be noted with respect to whether the student:
1. Does not propose a solution.
2. Engages in a solution proposed by the teacher.
3. Proposes a solution.

FIG. 3.4.   Economic context rubric, Lesson 2.

Worksheet 3.1.　Brochure Outline.

Description of Your Neighborhood

Special Features

Businesses	Restaurants	Language Availability	Professions
Agencies	Public Services	Newspapers Publications	Medical

Worksheet 3.2.   Career Requirements.

Complete each section with the information provided in the classified ads in a newspaper.

Job Title/Career Field Category   Employer's Name

Educational Requirements   Language Requirements

Description of Job Responsibilities

Specific Skills or Experience Requirements

Salary

Worksheet 3.3.　Parent and/or Grandparent Interview Questions.

Name _____　Date _____

1. What was the highest level of schooling you completed?

2. What courses were required?

3. Which vocational courses were offered?

4. Did you have a language course requirement?

5. What were your career aspirations?

6. What did you do for a living?

7. What were the job opportunities when you were starting in the work force?

8. What types of service occupations existed?

9. What skills did you need to have to get a job?

10. What jobs do you think are important in today's modern society?

11. What advice would you give our young generations to prepare for the future?

12. Do you consider it an advantage to be a bilingual person?

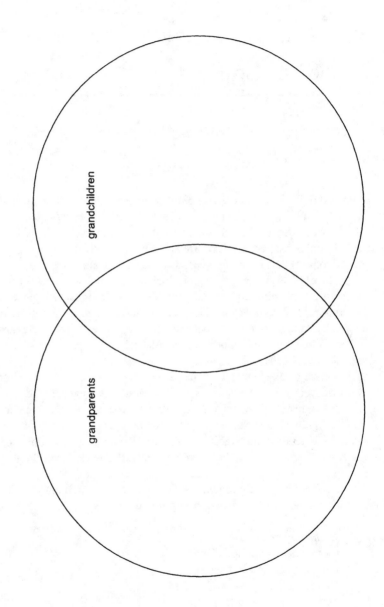

grandchildren

grandparents

4

Social Context

OVERVIEW

A myriad of social factors affects children in general. For bilingual students these interact with language, ethnicity, and culture. Girls are constrained by gender and cultural views. Social factors influence the opportunities students have and the way students are perceived. Students are at the mercy of socially constructed attitudes toward some of their characteristics, whether gender, ethnicity, rage, language, dialect, or level of language proficiency. Social circumstances differ for different ethnic groups, explaining differential attitudes toward bilingual students. Most social factors are closely connected with others. Status of languages often drives attitudes toward the language and its speakers. Economic level influences expectations of students. Governmental support of particular ethnic groups colors societal attitudes toward those groups.

The study of the social factors helps students understand their environment and even discover their own positive or negative attitudes. Angela's students, who lived in a world where "Spanish was king," were amazed at both the number of English speakers in the United States as well as the multilingual nature of this country. In trying to understand how their environment provided opportunities to interact in one language or the other, they developed factual knowledge of the society where they live.

The second part of this chapter synthesizes the research on social factors. The following topics are relevant for bilingual students:

- Demographics.
- Connections with homeland.
- Language and dialect status.
- Gender, ethnicity, race, and class.
- Sociohistorical events.
- Support systems.

Social attitudes are pervasive in schools. Children are confused and hurt by them. Analysis of these variables help students put in perspective unfair treatment. Kathryn's seventh-grade students were convinced that students in their school hated Hispanics. A survey of students and analysis of the results demonstrated to them that poor attitudes were confined to only a small group of students. Ignoring this group, students in Kathryn's class set out to make friends among others. Their study allowed them to see that ethnic prejudices were not generalized.

A set of three lessons suggests ways to cope with social variables:

- History of ethnic groups.
- Demographics and language development.
- Language, ethnicity, class, race, and gender attitudes.

PART I: CLASSROOM IMPLEMENTATION

It has been 3 weeks since Angela did the economic unit and she is ready to start the social unit on *Demographics and Language*. Again, she is apprehensive about how the students will respond to the lesson. But she has carefully prepared for the class by doing research on the demographics of the Boston area. The objective for this unit follows:

> Students will know, to varying degrees, the history behind the demographic composition of their communities, state, and/or nation to understand how demographic variables influence opportunities for interaction with English speakers.

Angela has prepared a four-page reference handout with information from several sources. The handout includes an article from the *Boston Globe* entitled "Non-English Speaker Rise in US." This article features a pie graph showing the percentages of people who speak other languages in Massachusetts. Also included in the packet is "Language Information From the 1990 Census." This article includes a table with the numbers of people who speak a language other than English at home in each state. Angela passes out this information to each student as she starts class.

Day One

Angela begins the class by reviewing with the students the previous work they had done for the SC lessons. She wants to activate their background knowledge about the purpose of the units. First, she asks the class about the activities they remembered doing in the language use and economics units. Then she asks them what they learned from the activities. The students are able to recall the projects from the lessons. They mention making the language use graphs, the brochures, and the neighborhood investigations. When Angela asks the class what they learned, the students reply that they were struck by how their neighborhoods had changed in ethnic composition.

Angela uses this cue to swing the discussion to the handouts. She asked the students to turn their attention to the article, "Non-English Speakers Rise in US."

"Look in the handout," Angela instructs. "Look at the graphs. What kind of graph is this? We did these last Friday."

Sandra calls out, "Pie graph!"

Angela writes on the board "pie graph." The students are able to analyze the figure, showing that they remember the concept of the pie graph and what it represents.

Angela continues, "This pie graph shows the native languages of people living in Massachusetts by percentage. What is the largest language, after English, spoken in Massachusetts?"

The students do not seem surprised to note that it is Spanish. Next, Angela asks them to turn to the graph on the following page. "Let's look at the next one on the next page. What is different on this graph compared with the one you just looked at?"

"It has all the states," answers one student.

"Right and it is focusing on who?" Angela inquires.

"Children."

"Right. Let's look at children in 1990."

The students remark that there are "high numbers" of children who speak a language other than English at home.

Angela asks, "High numbers, where? In all the states?"

As the students start to analyze the chart, they realize that the states with the largest population of home speakers of non-English languages are California, Florida, and Texas. Angela writes this list on the board.

Angela tries to get the students to think about the reason behind the statistics, "Why is there so much Spanish there?"

The students think quietly. But no one tries to answer. *"¿Qué país está bien cerca?"* [What country is really close?] Angela probes. "Don't forget that Mexico is right to the south."

Angela then switches the discussion to the next table in the handout, "Estimated Numbers of Home Speakers of Non-English Languages." This table lists the total number of speakers for 35 major languages in the United States. It also breaks the information down by three age groups. Angela asks the students to look at the variety of languages that are spoken. The students reflect on this list for a while and begin to realize that, although there is a large population of Spanish speakers, many other languages are also spoken in this country.

This first part of the lesson has taken just 15 minutes. Now Angela tries to get the students to think about demographic changes over time. "Why do people move to places like California and Texas?"

"Jobs," says Alex.

Angela nods. "Looking for opportunity."

"Freedom," adds Alex.

"Right. Looking for freedom," Angela agrees. She decides to use a personal example to illustrate this point. "There used to be more people coming from Europe. My mother, when she moved to New York, she was 16 years old. She remembers that there weren't that many Spanish people. My mother says she lived in an area where the woman upstairs was German and the woman downstairs was Polish. My mother learned a lot from them." The students listen attentively to this personal account. "The women would talk to her and taught her a lot. They helped her out with learning more English. What did we discuss when we first started this lesson? With English you can get a better job. What is the biggest group coming here now?"

"Spanish," says Alex.

"They are coming for all the same reasons." At this point, the door opens and Mrs. O'Connor, the Title I teacher, walks in. She stands to the side, listening.

Ms. O'Connor is listening intently to the conversation and seems willing to participate so Angela includes her. "As homework, interview someone who has lived in your community for a long time. Maybe Ms. O'Connor can tell us how this neighborhood has changed?" She turns to her.

Ms. O'Connor eagerly begins her story:

> I live in This neighborhood and I moved into This neighborhood in the 1960s. I moved here when I was in seventh grade. I lived down on Faneil Street. Anyway, when I moved in the projects there were mostly Irish people. There were a few Black families, very few. There were few people of other ethnicities. It didn't start to change until the 1980s. And more Hispanic families came in. Actually, more Black families moved in first.

Angela writes on poster paper: This neighborhood 1960s, Irish-White, European descent, 1980s-Blacks.

Ms. O'Connor continues:

> It also matters what community you are in, who you know. You tend to stay in neighborhoods where people are like you. We are Catholic and we went to church together. I knew mostly English speakers. My mother was an exception. She spoke French. We knew some Irish who spoke in Gaelic.

Angela explains the rest of the lesson quickly to her. "We are going to go in groups of four to the computer. I have it set up to a Web site of the Census Bureau. I would like them to investigate language groups."

Ms. O'Connor thinks of more information to share with the class and she continues to reminisce:

> In the late 60s when I started to teach in East Boston, many of the children spoke Italian. We had kids who mostly spoke Italian. Then we had Southeast Asian, Vietnamese, and Cambodian. Now there is a heavy population of Hispanic families. That has

changed a lot demographically. We are going to see if you guys can find information about Boston.

Sandra announces, "My mom learned Italian a year ago."

Angela adds to the chart: "East Boston-Italian, Asian." Then she finishes giving the assignment, "During the Thanksgiving holiday if you could find someone who is a fixture in your neighborhood, you could interview them. Okay, now we are going to go on the computers. I want Alex, John, José, Veronica, Sandra, and Bernarda to go up." The students jump up eagerly and rush to sit at the computers. Angela motions to the first computer. "Three can work here, but you guys have to look carefully for information." She turns to Ms. O'Connor and says, "I bookmarked it for them. If they go to 'language use,' go to the bookmark."

Veronica, Sandra, and Bernarda are at one computer; José, Alex, and Juan are at the other. At this point the class is 40 minutes into the lesson. Angela is over at the computers showing the students how to use the Web site.

Angela points to the screen of the girls' computer and says, "This is really interesting. Table 5."

The girls look at Web site. They print out Table 5.

Angela announces to class, "Feel free to go through the Web site."

Ms. O'Connor is working with the group of boys. She says to them, "This looks good, 'Language spoken at home by persons 5 and older by state.' Print that one." Then she stands up and says to all the students, "When we came to this neighborhood, my mom had an accent. When she used to go to school to speak with the teachers, we felt they looked down on her because she didn't speak English well."

Angela explains to Ms. O'Connor, "What I want them to do is to get the information, understand the different statistics, and make their own graphs and timelines."

It has taken the students 15 minutes on the computers to find the information. Angela turns to address the class and says, "We are able to get information from the Census Bureau. They provide information on Massachusetts. It mentions that Boston is a diverse mix of neighborhoods from the North End to Bay Village. I'm going to make copies of this Web site information that the boys found. It will show you so much information but we are going to focus on the demographics. We're going to *pasandose la informacion. La estadística puede ser un gráfico enseñando la población, los cambios. Les voy a preguntar que es lo que tienen que hacer.* [We're going to copy the information. The statistics can be made in the form of a graph showing the population and the changes. I'm going to ask you what you have to do.] I'm going to give you this graph for one ethnic group. It could be for Hispanics. *El census lo toman cada 10 años. El gobierno va a tu casa y les hacen preguntas. Es importante porque con esta información hacen cambios.* [They take the census every 10 years. The government goes to your house and asks questions. It is important because, with this information, they make changes.] Any questions? Okay. Did you enjoy this lesson?"

The students nod their heads. The lesson has taken just over 1 hour.

Day Two

To begin the second day of the social unit, Angela stands in front of the class and says, "I want just your yellow folders on your desks. Who would like to explain for those who were absent what we did yesterday?"

Sandra volunteers, "We were studying the changes that are happening in some communities."

"What did we look at specifically?" Angela asks. She turns to write on the chart paper taped to the blackboard. "What did we do? Study the changes that have taken place in communities."

Sandra continues, "Language."

Angela writes, "Language, culture, ethnic groups, population." She says, "We are trying to identify the changes." She turns to William. "You said your mother saw things were different when she first moved to This neighborhood. How long ago was that?"

William answers quickly, "Eleven years ago."

"What was the contact between different groups? How has it changed? What groups were coming 20 or 30 years ago? Where were they coming from? Let me go back a little bit. Ms. O'Connor was kind enough to contribute to us yesterday. She pointed out that in the 1960s the high concentration was Irish and I think she also said Italian. They were White Europeans. What other countries are in Europe?"

William guesses, "England?"

Angela nods.

"I would say in the 1930s or early 1940s my mother moved to New York. What group did I tell you she met?"

José says, "Polish."

"Right."

José remembers a second group, "German."

Angela begins to write these on chart paper, "New York: Polish, German, small group of Puerto Ricans." She says, "My mother was 18 or 19 years old. She was already starting a family because they married young then. Also I think there were parts that were Jewish. Then Ms. O'Connor said that in the 1980s she started to see the Blacks moving in. Then she talked about East Boston. We are talking about how your communities have evolved. There is more diversity. Do you know what diversity means?"

The students don't respond.

Angela continues, "That there is not just one group. There are more groups. Now if you go to your packet with your census material.... Yesterday we got on the Internet and we looked up the census. What is the census?" She pauses.

Sandra raises her hand, "They do something every 10 years."

"It is a questionnaire," Angela explains. "What do they get out of this?"

"To find out how many people have come," says Sandra.

"What do you call this?" Angela asks, "St ..."

José calls, "Statistics!"

"Right." Angela reminds the class of a previous activity they had done for math with statistics. "What did we find out yesterday from the statistics?"

John says, "The numbers are getting bigger."

"Look at your charts." The students look at the charts obtained from the Internet the previous day.

"They also have some predictions for the year 2000. They make these predictions through estimation. We've done this before. When I ask you to figure out in your heads. Remember when we did this in *matemática.*[mathematics] *Vamos a calcular.* [Let's calculate.] It doesn't have to be exact. What are they predicting in the year 2000?" She writes: 2000- 628, 382. "Why are they predicting this? What happens every few seconds?"

"Babies are born," says Alex.

"Right. Not only does the census talk about race. Where is the highest concentration of population for this state? Suffolk County. Look at the ages. What is the highest concentration of ages, 15–44. There is also race and ethnicity. What can you see by looking at this? Discuss it and really think. I'm going to give you a couple of minutes. You pair up or work in a group of three. What does this mean?"

Christopher moves over to work with William. They get started with Sandra as recorder. William tells Sandra to copy some information onto a chart they are making, "*Oye,* put that the Spanish population will grow bigger."

John says, "Put that the White people will grow more."

Ms. O'Connor joins the class. Angela says to her, "What I've decided to do is have them interpret this table and make a graph." At this point, the class has been in session for 30 minutes and the students have been working in their groups for 10 minutes. Angela turns to the class and says, "Let's hear what you have to say."

As a representative of the first group goes up in front of the class to present, Angela tapes a chart paper to board. John reads his group's list of conclusions:

> There are more White people than any other. Indian Eskimo or Aleut have the smallest population. We thought that Hispanics would have the highest amount of population. We predict that in 10 years the population of Hispanics will grow. We think the Indian population will grow smaller and smaller by the years. Whites have a larger population by 102,000 compared to the Black.

"I am impressed," Angela remarks. "Are there any questions?" She looks around the class, then turns to the next group. "In this group who is going to present?"

Doris steps forward and reads, "There is more White people in the population. There is less Indians Eskimo in the population. The Hispanic origin is third.

We think that the numbers mean how many people are in the world."

"Good," says Angela. "Now Julia." Julia goes up to present. After Julia speaks, Angela remarks, "That was very good. You showed me you could interpret the data. You showed that you understood the number of people in the in the world and in Suffolk County." She turns back to the class and says:

I found out that the science teacher grew up in this neighborhood. Tomorrow he has agreed to be interviewed by you. I want you for homework tonight to make a list of questions. Focus on the groups of people who have lived here throughout the years. Also focus on the interaction between these groups. I want you to come up with creative questions that you can ask. What do you want the science teacher to share with you on how the community has changed?

Angela pauses, holds up a sheet of paper, and continues:

The second activity which you are going to choose is: "Historical Perspective of Our Communities." We are going to do this on graph paper first. You decide, you can put a title. You can do race and ethnicity. You can put race on the horizontal axis. Since you are doing a linear graph, look at how the number population grows. This activity is very similar to the graphing activity we did in math class yesterday.

She holds up the worksheet entitled *"Interpretación de gráficas lineales"* [interpretation of graphic lines] that the students had done yesterday. "Get started on that for the next 10 minutes."

There are only about 10 minutes left in the language arts time block so the students quickly take out graph paper and rulers and start working.

Day Three

On the final day of the social unit, Angela asks the students to recap the main conclusions from the demographic statistics. After they review the information, she explains, "The reason we are going over this is because we want to understand how our communities are changing."

Mr. Kelly, the science teacher, enters the room. He is a tall, middle-aged man. His demeanor shows that he is comfortable with the students. He also appears pleased to share some observations about his life history.

Angela welcomes him to the classroom. "We have Mr. Kelly with us today. Last night for homework we had to make some questions for him. How many have their questions?" Students take out questions that they have developed for homework. As they listen to the teacher they jot down answers.

Mr. Kelly smiles at the class and says, "I'm going to let you ask me the questions because I don't know what you want to know." As he speaks, Angela takes notes on the two paper charts taped to the blackboard. "I lived in this area. We first lived in Fanueil Projects. My father worked for the police department and at that time if you were a city employee, you could get a nice, inexpensive apartment in the projects. Then we moved to Brock Street. We lived in an apartment there until I went to college. Then we moved across town. Now elementary schools are K–5. I used to go to this school when it was until eighth grade."

When he pauses, Sandra is ready with the first question. "Have you seen any differences in the businesses?"

"Yes. There are lots of differences. We used to have a Woolworth's and we used to have drugstores. There you could go and get sodas. The restaurants were different. Every area used to have a nice grocery store where we used to walk and get food. Not everybody had a car. The library I'm really upset about. You know the new library? It used to be a nice Victorian house. Now it is a modern, kind of ugly building."

He calls on Bernarda for the next question. "What kind of races were there?"

"In the 1950s and early 60s there were a lot of Italians and people from Ireland. There weren't too many Black families in the area. I do remember one Black family in the Fanueil Street Projects. I don't remember any Hispanic families. Mostly from Europe. A lot of people from Italy."

Jenny asks, "Why did you came here for?"

"I was only 4 years old. I went where my family went. Back then in the projects the rent was on a sliding scale so when you made more, you paid more to live there."

"Has the population of Hispanics increased?" asks Sandra.

"Yes. There is much more of a mix of cultures that live in this area now."

José raises his hand and asks, "Is there anything that you had back then that you don't have now?"

Mr. Kelly smiles nostalgically. "Hmm. Let me think. Back then we had a lot more friends and people to play games. That is sort of missing. It seems to be much more organized. Now you have to belong to a group. Back then you'd show up at the park and have kids to play with. We used to walk around much more back then."

"What are most of the things you liked about the people?" inquires Bernarda.

"Back then the people were very friendly. I had friends I could play sports with. Growing up in the projects there were a lot of kids."

The students are listening intently. They take notes on the answers to the interview. They show interest in the evolution of the neighborhood and Mr. Kelly's childhood. The students continue to fire away questions at a fast pace. The interview has only been going on for less than 15 minutes, but the students have asked many questions in that short time.

José has another question, "Did the laws change?"

"No, I don't think so."

"Would you like to live somewhere else?" asks Jenny.

"No, I like Boston. Now we live in West Medford. I like it here."

Sandra asks, "Are the traditions the same as long ago?"

"I think the traditions depend on your family. Celebrations have changed. They never had a parade in this neighborhood. They didn't have the Christmas tree lighting."

John asks, "Did you have to change your culture when you came here?"

"No, my family had been in the United States for generations," Mr. Kelly explains.

Sandra, looking perplexed, asks, "Did you come from someplace else and move here?"

"No, I was born in Boston and stayed here all my life." At this, the students raise their eyebrows in disbelief.

"Was it easier or more difficult back then?" asks John.

"It seemed much easier back then. I think today young people have more pressures." He looks up at the clock in surprise. "These are great questions. I'm sorry I have to go. I am very impressed. I hope we can talk more about them later. We'll see you during science class."

The students call, "Thank you," as he turns to leave.

As the science teacher spoke, Angela had filled several charts with details.

Angela addresses the class, "We'll have to hold the rest of our questions for later. What is the focus of what we have been talking about?"

Sandra, who had been quiet during the interview, says, "Finding out how neighborhoods have changed."

Angela nods. "Bernarda had a good question about the ethnic groups. What did we find yesterday that our neighborhoods were very... what did we find? That word that starts with a d- ..." She pauses. "Diverse? Right. Mr. Kelly said that back when he was a boy, there was only one Black family."

Angela moves on to the homework. She had assigned students to write reflections on Tables 4 and 5 from the census web page. Table 4 shows the number of speakers for different languages in the 50 states. Bernarda's reflection reads:

What I see in the paper is that there are a lot of states or should I say countries. What I think the paper is trying to show me is that how many people are in each state like their races or there color of skin. Or also maybe it is trying to show me how many people speak those languages in each state or country.

"How many did table number 5? How many did number 4? Anybody? No? Let's do five then." Table 5 shows the number of speakers for each language and their English-language ability. "Who would like to share what they wrote? John?"

John reads from his paper, "There are more Spanish in the state. There is a high level of people who speak English well in the Spanish group."

Angela repeats this fact and calls on José.

José adds, "This represents how well people from different cultures speak English. The people who speak English the best are the Spanish."

Sandra says, "I was surprised. The main thing this table shows us is that many Spanish people can speak English well." Sandra reads aloud her reflections:

This graph shows us that Spanish is speaked more in the U.S.A. than anything else. I didn't know all these languages were spoken in the U.S.A. I'm surprised. The language that was least spoken was Amharic. I was very surprised, I thought that Spanish would rule, would be the highest. I predict that in ten years the number of Spanish peo-

ple will grow and so would the Chinese. Another thing this chart shows us is that not only how many people are able to speak a language but if they speak well, very well, not well or no.

Angela nods, then says, "Let's go back to your first comment. That is an interesting comment. Were you surprised to see that the group that has the highest concentration of speaking English well is Spanish? How many were as surprised as Sandra?" Jenny, Julia, and Sonia raise their hands. "We are focusing on English ability. What would contribute to the numbers of speaking English well? Why would it be that high? There is no wrong or right answer. It is what you interpret."

John has a thought. "There are more Hispanic people and they want to speak English."

Alex also contributes. "There are a lot of countries that speak Spanish."

"Good point. Anybody else? What else did we do yesterday?"

"We were also working on our linear graphs." José proclaims with confidence, "That was easy."

"Then maybe, José, you can help the other people. José? Do you want to help people?" Angela directs the class, "Some of you will be working on your graphs for Tables 4 and 5. Others can work on their questions for Mr. Kelly."

The entire lesson has taken just 45 minutes. The students take out their graphs and questions while talking quietly. The students' written questions reflect to a degree the students' own experience. For example, Bernarda develops questions concerning issues with safety and people getting along:

What are most of the things that you liked about the people?

How was that community, lonely, quiet, or crowded?

Did the people from other races fight with each other?

Did your mother let you go outside?

Before was the community dangerous or not dangerous?

Would you ever like to move back?

Lessons Learned

The social lesson on demographics remained at the basic concepts phase. This lesson elicited a number of other relevant issues such as language attitudes, race, and cultural and linguistic changes.

Angela was able to draw on resources from within the school by inviting different teachers from the community to speak with the class. These interactions served to bridge the gap between the school and the community. Students realized that their teachers had grown up in the community. These teachers provided firsthand knowledge of the demographic changes in the area.

Information from the teacher interviews was analyzed in conjunction with statistical information from the U.S. Census Bureau Web site. Angela developed independence in her students by asking them to use the Internet to research demographic changes and to analyze this information. The students were able to analyze the statistics by drawing on skills learned in mathematics. They then reflected on the numbers by making connections to their own personal worlds.

Demographic and linguistic realities of the United States seemed quite surprising for these students. They were so engaged in their discoveries that Angela never had the opportunity to explore further connections between demographics and language proficiency.

PART II: SOCIAL VARIABLES

Demographic composition of a community affects contact with people of different language and cultures, impacts the nature of the student body in schools, and may affect attitudes toward ethnic and linguistic diversity. Size and cohesiveness of the ethnic community assist families' cultural adjustment and impact language proficiency and social integration. Ties to the homeland and expected length of stay influence motivation to learn English and maintain the home language.

Social variables such as status of languages and dialects, class, race, gender, demographic characteristics, and sociohistorical events shape social attitudes and perceptions. These attitudes and perceptions affect treatment of language-minority and immigrant children in schools. A positive reception of certain ethnic groups in U.S. society has been shown to have a positive effect in the school performance of their children. Discrimination, or even perceived discrimination, has negative effects (P. R. Portes, 1999).

Community networks and institutions such as churches often provide much needed support to language minorities and immigrants. Families that reach for such support are more successful in coping with the new social environment.

Attitudes often change over time. The most recent immigrants and the language they speak often occupy the lowest social strata. Lowell, an industrial center in Massachusetts, has witnessed waves of immigrants from Northern Europe, Southeastern Europe, and more recently, Latin America and Asia. As new immigrants, each group endured similar types of negative attitudes (Crawford, 1992). Gender perceptions are slowly changing. Whereas early reports demonstrated differential expectations in math and science for female students, the American Association of University Women (AAUW) is reporting more even treatment of girls in schools (AAUW, 1992).

Demographics

The United States is populated by a variety of linguistic and ethnic groups. They are spread all over the country, although certain states such as California, Texas,

Florida, and New York attract the largest numbers. Nearly 2 million Native-American and Alaskan natives live throughout the country and speak about 175 languages (McCarty & Watahomogie, 1998). Larger concentrations are found in the reservations in the western part of the country. Colonizers, immigrants, and refugees from other countries have been arriving on the American shores for more than two centuries. Initially, they came mostly from Europe. Since the second half of the 20th century, the largest numbers have come from Latin America and Asia. People of German ancestry constitute the largest group in the country with more than 46.5 million, followed by Spanish with 35.3 million, Irish 33 million, and English 28 million. Half of the foreign-born immigrants presently come from Latin America, more than a third originate in Asia, and the rest come from Europe and other parts of the world (U.S. Census Bureau, 2000). The Spanish immigration has increased considerably in the last decade from being 9% to 12.5% of the country's population. Close to 60% of the Spanish-background people are of Mexican origin. Spanish-background people have settled throughout the United States, with the largest concentrations living in the West and Southwest (Guzman, 2001).

Asians have settled throughout the United States, with the largest concentrations living in Hawaii and California. They constitute 3.6% of the population of the United States. Of those 3.6%, 25% are Chinese, 19% are Filipino, 16% Asian Indian, 11% Vietnamese, 11% Korean, 8% Japanese, and 13% other Asian (U.S. Census Bureau, 2000).

Traditionally minority populations have settled in cities. In the future, "the inner suburban ring ... will see a major increase in student diversity—more minorities, more immigrants, more students learning English as a second language (ESL), and more students from poverty" (Hodgkinson, 2001).

Settlement of people of different language backgrounds affects schools. Depending on personnel's language ability and students' English proficiency, the impact on the schools can be substantial (Dentler, 1997). A large number of the school-age children who speak a language other than English at home are bilingual with varying degrees of ability in English. Whereas more than 18% of the school-age population reports speaking a language other than English at home, 12.8% also claim to know English very well. Others, 5.4%, noted that they speak English with difficulty (Crawford, 2001). It is estimated that nearly 4,416,580 students with limited English proficiency were enrolled in public schools (Pre-K through Grade 12) for the 1999–2000 school year. This is approximately 9.3% of the total public school student enrollment and a 27.9% increase over the reported 1997–1998 school year (National Clearinghouse for Bilingual Education [NCBE], 2002a). In 1999–2000, limited-English-proficient students nationwide spoke over 400 languages. Spanish is the most common language group with nearly 77% whereas the others that followed include Vietnamese (2.34%), Hmong (2.21%), Haitian Creole (1.09%), Korean (1.06%), and Cantonese (1.00%). All other languages accounted for less than 1% of the bilingual student population with limited English proficiency (NCBE, 2002b).

Connections With Homeland

Facility to return to or visit the homeland, length of residence in the United States, and length of expected stay influence English-language proficiency and motivation to maintain the heritage language. These factors combined promote different degrees of bilingualism.

Puerto Ricans and Latin American families expose their children to the heritage language and culture with frequent trips or visits from relatives. Such is not the case of Southeast Asian refugees, for whom travel is complicated by distance and political problems. Cambodians immigrated in large numbers in the late 1970s. They have settled permanently with little intention to return. Ties to their heritage culture are maintained more through religion than language. Time and distance reduce heritage language proficiency and interest in language maintenance among younger generations. For instance, Hornberger (1992) reported that the Cambodian Buddhist Temple in Philadelphia, a major institution for Cambodian refugees, stopped Khmer language classes for children. Connections with the homeland have led the Puerto Rican community to create institutions to promote Spanish, no such institutions support Khmer or other Southeast Asian languages.

The longer the residence, the greater the proficiency in English of people in the workforce (Chiswick, 1978). Schumann (1978) encountered some exceptions to this rule. A complex set of psychological and social factors gets in the way of English proficiency for some immigrant workers. Even after years of residence, some workers' proficiency in English continued to be rudimentary. Among other factors, attitudes toward English and American culture and career aspirations, interfered with individuals' second-language development.

Many immigrants come with the intention of staying permanently or for a long time. Others expect to be in the United States for only a few years while completing studies, representing their company, or saving enough money to return and live a comfortable life. Schumann (1978) reported that laborers who plan on a temporary stay have little motivation to learn the language whereas professionals have a high motivation. The latter believe in the advantage of knowing English. As the international language of the moment, fluency in English is a valuable asset. These professionals want their children not only to learn as much English as possible but to maintain their heritage language so that, upon return, they can continue their schooling without delays.

Language and Dialects Status

Different languages, dialects, and their speakers hold different status in society:

> Standard English has become the dominant language in mainstream US society, and speakers of Standard English are attributed more prestige as a result of their proficiency in English.... This "language prejudice" means that other languages and

speakers of those languages are marginalized in mainstream US institutions and society. (Freeman, 1998, p. 10)

Differential status of languages affects students' attitudes toward their own native languages: "When asked which language they [Spanish-speaking students] spoke better, they usually said Spanish, but when asked which language they liked better they usually said English" (Ben-Zeev, 1977, p. 34). The differences experienced by subgroups of languages other than English are often mitigated by a sense of solidarity that evolves in these communities to resist complete dominance by English (Corson, 2001).

In spite of its lower status Spanish is seen as a practical language to learn by English speakers, who prefer it over the more prestigious French. In recent years, more high school students are choosing Spanish over French, German, Italian, and the classical languages. In 1994, 27.2% were enrolled in Spanish classes whereas only 9.3% were enrolled in French, 2.8% in German, and .4% in Italian (American Council on the Teaching of Foreign Languages, 2002).

Dialects or varieties within languages also are perceived as more or less desirable. Language variety is "any standard or non-standard form of a language, whether a geographical or social dialect, a patois, a creole or some other code of a language" (Corson, 2001, p. 67). Each variety contains all of the elements for a valid linguistic form, such as phonology, grammar, and vocabulary. In the social context, however, varieties are granted different status. What is called the standard language is the variety of the people with power. Society considers it the correct form of the language and it is the variety used in schools. In the United States Standard English is considered the most desirable whereas the various forms of African American Vernacular English, sometimes called Ebonics, are less desirable. Similarly, the southern and the Boston dialects are held in lower status in our society than midwestern and middle-class northeastern dialects.

Similar differential status exists among other languages. Portuguese-speaking Brazilians, Cape Verdeans, Continental Portuguese, and Azoreans make distinctions among themselves and the variety they speak. Portuguese speakers regard Brazilian dialect as having the highest status (Macedo, 1981). The Spanish variety spoken by South Americans enjoys higher status than the one used by Puerto Ricans and Mexican Americans. Negative language attitudes extend to people's accents when speaking English. Maria de los Angeles, a fair-skinned Cuban immigrant, easily blended among her classmates in a Chicago school. Instant rejection appeared when she addressed her classmates in her heavily accented English (A. Portes & Rumbaut, 2001).

Gender, Ethnicity, Race, and Class

Attitudes toward gender, ethnic group, race, and class together or independently affect students and their families. In the case of immigrant families, their own cultural values sometimes intensify existing attitudes or perceptions; other times they clash with those in the host society.

Gender, ethnicity, and often both affect teachers' interaction with students in the classroom and family's expectations and control of girls. Differences in treatment of female and male students have been observed with respect to teachers' responses to verbal participation, inequality of assistance, subtle gender bias in teachers' language, and nonverbal messages (LaFrance, 1991). Teachers tend to interact more with boys than with girls. They call on girls less frequently to answer questions, even if they volunteer more often (AAUW, 1992; Orenstein, 1994). In the case of immigrants and language minorities, gender bias is aggravated by the fact that these groups already have less status. In science classes in the United States, immigrant girls experienced poor treatment (Corson, 1998). Even in all-girls schools, there are still differences in the treatment of students of minority ethnic groups. Pacific Island girls were asked a lower percentage of questions than European-background or Pakeha girls in a New Zealand school. Pacific Island students' culture does not promote individualism. Such students cringed when asked questions individually. The teachers' instructional approach was more suited to the middle-class European-background students. Rather than modifying their approach, teachers asked the Pacific Islanders less questions, with negative effects on their education (Jones, 1988).

Cazden (1990) reported decreased teacher–student interactions when teachers of European background in New Zealand worked with Maori students of any gender. Similarly, immigrant students in a science class in the United States experienced interaction of inferior quality with the teacher. "[T]he questions were primarily procedural rather than content based questions requiring higher reasoning" (Verplaetse, 2000 p. 31).

Theoretically "he" is used as a generic pronoun but females interpret it as masculine referent. Classroom studies have demonstrated the negative effect of teachers' use of the masculine generic pronoun (LaFrance, 1991). Immigrant students have experienced similar language biases in their own languages. In Spanish and French the masculine is also considered the generic pronoun.

Adolescence among girls is marked by a loss of confidence in their academic abilities, concern about their bodies, and development of a general sense of inadequacy (AAUW, 1992; Orenstein, 1994). Many of these feelings emerge as a result of social attitudes around expectations for girls. Often girls are not expected to do well in such subjects as math and science (Orenstein, 1994).

Attitudes toward gender that characterize many immigrant families are added to those that affect all female students in U.S. schools with respect to abilities and interests. Both teachers and families have different expectations for girls and boys. Some ethnic groups are concerned that boys do well in school so that they can succeed professionally later on. Girls are more burdened with family and household responsibilities with less concern for their school performance. Girls are also often directed to different career paths from boys. However, one cannot generalize for all ethnic groups. Chinese parents expect all their children to do well in school (Siu, 1992).

In some cases, these differential expectations of girls were incorrect perceptions that the teachers had of the girls' culture. Teachers believe families want the girls to marry rather than pursue careers. However, the families' main purpose for immigration is often to provide all of their children with the educational opportunities they never had. They are very eager for their girls to succeed academically and professionally (Tsolidis, 1990, as cited in Corson, 2001).

Control over teenage girls limits their contacts and possibilities. Socializing restrictions often limits immigrant girls' contact with English-speaking friends, therefore reducing their opportunities to practice English and become acculturated into American society. Parental restrictions on girls limit their educational options. Gibson (1993) reported on a Punjabi community where girls' academic performance declined during high school. There was no college at commuting distance and the parents would not let them move. These girls saw no point in succeeding in high school with no prospect of attending college.

Race is a complex and unclear abstraction. "Race has always been an arbitrary label that was wrapped in pseudoscientific doctrine to legitimize socioeconomic and political power" (R. Payne, 1998, pp. 31-32). "The world of biology has found the concept of race virtually useless" (Ladson-Billings & Tate, 1995, p. 49). Nevertheless, views toward race negatively affect certain students in schools (Kozol, 1992).

Gender, class, and ethnicity combine with race to aggravate or amerliorate the effects of race. African-American girls are affected more by attitudes toward race than by gender. Unlike their White and Latino counterparts, female African-American students tended to be more assertive in class (Orenstein, 1994). Gender and class have an effect on teenage pregnancy among African-American girls. For poor girls having a child is often a desirable outcome reached as a result of a set of complex social issues. Mistrust in the power of education, competition among peers, and early maturity makes having children desirable and the consequence of dropping out of school irrelevant (Kelley, 1995).

Negative attitudes toward native-born minorities due to race are extended to immigrants who are not White. Gibson (1993) reported on the difficulties Punjabi Sikh students experienced in California. Their classmates abused them verbally and physically. Nevertheless, these Punjabi students regularly outperformed academically their White tormentors.

The latest census figures show that:

> Most poor children in the United States are white, but a higher percentage of black and Hispanic kids are poor. Being black is no longer a universal handicap; over one-quarter of black households have a higher income than the white average, and rates of blacks who go to college and own homes continue to grow. (Hodgkinson, 2001, p. 3)

Race and class are factors that influence tracking of students in schools. The amount of time dedicated to learning was noticeable in higher as opposed to lower tracks (Oakes, 1985). "While there is certainly no automatic placement of poor and minority students in low tracks ... in virtually every study that has considered the question, poor and minority students have been found in disproportionately large percentages in the bottom groups" (Oakes, 1985, p. 64).

The effect of class on students' success in school is a disputed factor. A national study identified high-performing schools with a majority of low-income students (Ali & Jerald, 2001). Others maintain that the percentage is too small to show any significant trend (Krashen, 2002). The root of contradictory results lies in the inter-connection of factors. Attitudes to lower-class students compounded with attitudes toward ethnic groups and race as well as scarcity of resources in schools influence the opportunities for academic success.

Fernandez and Nielsen (1986) found that the correlation between academic achievement and socioeconomic level is more significant for Whites than Hispanics. However, low socioeconomic status is often compounded by other factors such as the lack of support and a low level of English language and literacy (P. R. Portes, 1999). Immigrants have more difficulties when they move from rural to urban communities because their lifestyle changes dramatically.

Lower-class children have historically been discriminated against in schools. Todd, a child-labor inspector in Chicago at the turn of the 20th century reported on poor children's negative school experiences. She noted that poor children preferred factory jobs to school because "nothing that a factory sets them to do is so hard, so terrifying, as learning" (Deschenes, Cuban, & Tyack, 2001, p. 526). Most of these children were immigrants.

Prejudice toward certain ethnic groups exists regardless of class or race. Colombians are burdened with the association with the drug trade. Mistrust of Colombians is even prevalent among themselves (A. Portes & Rumbaut, 2001). Some Haitian immigrants who are mostly Black have experienced prejudice from African Americans. In Miami's inner-city schools African-American adolescents "make fun of French and Creole and of the Haitians' accent" (A. Portes, 1995, p. 249). Some immigrant students suffer from prejudice by second- and third-generation members of their own ethnic group. Portes' (1995) study of several generations of Mexican students illustrates such phenomena. Immigrant students acquired English and maintain high proficiency in Spanish as well as close ties to their Mexican culture. They achieved success in school. Doing well in school was unacceptable to their American-born counterparts. Second- and third-generation students were in conflict with White society and tended to equate academic success with being White. As a result they "referred derisively to successful Mexican students as 'schoolboys' and 'school girls' or as 'wannabes'" (p. 255).

Sociohistorical Events

The United States is a multiethnic country. A great variety of indigenous populations inhabited its territories when the Europeans arrived. The colonizers represented Europeans of several nations and languages, including Spanish, English, French, German, Dutch, Swedish, and Russian. Immigrants, refugees, and sojourners have increased the variety of languages and ethnic groups. Some languages and their speakers are held in higher regard than others.

Sociohistorical events mold and change societal attitudes toward various ethnic groups. The status and perceptions toward Chinese immigrants are very different today than last century. Presently, the Chinese enjoy a high status and are perceived as high-achievers. However, in the 19th century severe prejudice prohibited Chinese immigration. The only Chinese allowed entrance were officials, teachers, students, merchants, and visitors (McKay & Wong, 1988). These well-educated immigrants established themselves and changed the reputation of the Chinese (Siu, 1992).

Prejudice often coincides with numbers. When immigrants arrive in large numbers they are often seen as an economic threat to the local labor force. At the turn of the 20th century, the country witnessed the largest proportion of immigration. This mass immigration coincided with legislation that closed the doors to most Asian immigrants. The new immigration law of 1985 opened the door to the largest immigration in absolute numbers that this country has witnessed. Nearly 1 million immigrants a year entered the United States in the 1990s (U.S. Census Bureau, 2000). A resurgence of anti-immigration sentiment is evident in numerous legislation proposals and organizations that try to curtail the rights of immigrants.

Multiple cases of attacks, vandalism, harassment, and discrimination toward Arab-Americans followed the terrorist attacks of September 11th (Zogby, 2001). Furthermore, immigration from Mexico has been affected due to the terrorist attacks. Gedda (2001) reported that "since September 11, the administration has been making it more difficult for foreigners to enter the country. For Mexicans, this has meant more stringent searches at border crossings."

Certain factors can reduce the discrimination and violence against immigrants and minorities that follow such a national crisis. The president and the FBI acted quickly and proactively to prevent racial discrimination and hate crimes. Additionally, the media "worked with [the Arab American Institute Foundation] to produce public service radio and newspaper ads that focused on warning against anti-Arab and anti-Muslim hate and bias" (Zogby, 2001, p. 4).

Support Systems

Society sometimes provides support systems that allow language-minority and immigrant families to cope with a social environment that is often unwelcoming. Informal community networks and community-based institutions organize to provide such support. When families leave their countries, they also abandon a familiar and supportive network. As they settle in this new foreign environment, some seek established communities of their own ethnic group where they feel welcomed. Other groups are dispersed throughout the country. Mexican, Cubans, Chinese, Korean, Vietnamese, Laotian, Cambodian, Dominican, and Haitians tend to concentrate. Colombians, Filipinos, and Jamaicans are more dispersed (A. Portes & Rumbaut, 2001).

Cohesive ethnic communities provide a great deal of help to their members. These communities support heritage-language use, give immigrants a better chance to use the skills they brought, support the family as an institution, and help parents maintain their authority (A. Portes & Rumbaut, 2001). But living in their own ethnic community diminishes the need to use and learn English (Schumann, 1978) and hinders social integration with English-speaking Americans. The dilemma lies between seeking support and enhancing the children's chances for social integration. Many families move away from their ethnic neighborhoods to English-speaking neighborhoods, often at tremendous emotional and social cost to the adults. Parents want to provide social mobility, opportunities to develop English, and American friends for their children. However, living in a neighborhood surrounded by English speakers does not guarantee social integration. Rodriguez (1982) recollected how his family lived on their own island with little contact with the neighbors. It was not until he was in third grade, when he became fluent in English and avoided Spanish, that he made some friends in the neighborhood. Poor experiences force families to move back to their ethnic communities. A Cuban family who had encountered prejudice in Chicago decided to move to Miami where social acceptance and economic mobility are possible (A. Portes & Rumbaut, 2001).

Upon immigration families lose the support of the extended family and the natural connection with schools where the personnel speaks their language. Churches often fill this vacuum. Their programs provide a safe haven for children after school when parents are working and cannot afford day care. Parents from other cultures are confused and fearful of the freedoms teenage children have in the United States. They often do not allow them out of the house except to go to school. Girls are particularly vulnerable to restrictions. Chaperoned programs for teenagers offered by churches allow for a social life that is acceptable to such parents.

Nevarez-La Torre (1997) described a church-based program that successfully provides assistance and support to the Latino community in Harrisburg, Pennsylvania. Personnel that speak English and Spanish offer a variety of social and educational programs. The most popular is the after-school program where participants have time for homework, tutoring in reading and/or math, snack, movie, storytelling, and play. "*El Hogar*" (The home), as it is called, also provides families with connections to other institutions, such as schools, welfare, and potential employers. "*El Hogar* offers a safety net of support and, at the same time is effective because people have trust in it" (Nevarez-La Torre, 1997, p. 65).

Canda and Phaobtong (1992) studied Cambodian communities settled in the Midwest. The temples became the pivotal institution of their ethnic communities. The services provided by the temple include material, psychological, social, and spiritual support. "People who need temporary shelter, clothing, food, or other material assistance are aided by the temple staff, who draw on the store of donated material support" (p. 64). Psychological support comes in the form of counseling provided by the monks. "Often the monks listen sensitively and then authoritatively provide advice based on Buddhist and ethnic moral principles" (p. 64). Educational activities offered on weekends provide social support. These programs "teach traditional language, arts, and religion to youth" (p. 64). With respect to spiritual support, temples and monks provide several religious services that include community festivals linked to the traditional calendar.

Influences of the Social Context on Development of Bilingual Learners

Demographic and sociocultural factors affect the quality of schooling and students' experiences. Increases in immigration and language-minority groups means that these students are not only in the inner cities but are also in most school districts across the nation. Many school districts are unprepared to work with such students. Some districts provide ESL or bilingual education programs but more than half of the students in schools in the United States receive no specific support. Moreover, their teachers have not received professional development that addresses the needs of such students (Beykont, 2002). Personal resilience and outside support may help some. However large numbers of these students are being underserved.

Class and cultural differences have contributed to negative attitudes toward ethnic minority students in schools. Detrimental school policies toward such students emerged from schools' poor concept of these students and their inability to teach them. At the turn of the century a large percentage of immigrant students were retained (Cohen, 1970). By the 1950s large numbers of Mexican Americans and other Latino students found themselves in classes for the mentally retarded (Deschenes, 2001). To this day Latino, Native-American, and African-American students continue to be overrepresented in special education and underrepresented in gifted classes when compared with White and Asian students (Donovan & Cross, 2002; U.S. Department of Education, 2000).

Another problem brought about by low socioeconomic level is that poor immigrants share neighborhoods with English speakers whose language incorporates nonstandard English. Consequently, the bilingual students may not properly learn standard forms of English, which impedes later social mobility.

Attitudes toward languages, dialects, and ethnic groups open opportunities for some but not for others. Negative attitude toward the language and dialect students speak often affect teachers' expectations and student performance. Varieties other than the standard are not considered correct, and students are often admonished for using them. Because language variety is tied to the identity of a group, students may personalize this rejection of their language. "Linguistically diverse students ... feel anonymous and distant from the school's goals" (Corson, 2001, p. 26).

Societal attitudes toward languages and dialects has had a devastating effect on programs that have proven to support students who come to school speaking languages or dialects different from Standard English. Negative public and media reaction to the use of Ebonics crushed such initiatives in spite of the fact that the research showed substantial gains in the development of literacy among speakers of that language variety (Rickford, 1999). Similarly, the research on bilingual education has proven the academic value of using students' heritage language for extended periods alongside English (Ramirez, 1992; Thomas & Collier, 2002). Politicians, the media, and the unaffected public press for short-term or no use of the heritage language.

Societal pressures force immigrants to make difficult choices between heritage language and English as well as between ethnic and American culture. Although English proficiency is essential to succeed in the American society, accompanying loss of the native language and culture does not correlate with success. "Maintenance of the native language and fidelity to their culture of origin is independent, to a great extent, of their assimilation into American culture" (P. R. Portes, 1999, p. 497).

Gender, ethnicity, race, and class often define students' status in the classroom. "Within schools, the quantity and quality of participation correlates with variables of gender, race, and/or social class" (Cazden, 1990, p. 292). Depreciation by teachers and other students contribute to bilingual students' poor performance in school (P. R. Portes, 1999; Ramirez, 1985). Differential attitudes within an ethnic group also affect students' performance. McCollum (1993) observed that a Spanish-speaking teacher's negative attitude toward the Spanish dialect of Chicano students curtailed these students' desire to learn Spanish.

Social factors have a powerful effect on classroom interactions, quality of teaching, teacher expectations, and other important characteristics of environments conducive to learning. Regardless of the students' and their families' aspirations, negative learning experiences make learning more difficult and often thwart these students' educational careers. Achievement gaps and drop-out rates among different groups of students continue to plague our educational landscape (Lee, 2002).

Suggestions for Additional Reading

- Corson, D. (2001). *Language diversity and education*. Mahwah, NJ: Lawrence Erlbaum Associates.
- Deschenes, S., Cuban, L., & Tyack, D. (2001). Mismatch: Historical perspectives on schools and students who don't fit them. *Teacher's College Record, 103*(4), 525–547.
- Orenstein, P. (1994). *School girls*. New York: Anchor Books.

PART II: DOING ANALYSIS OF THE SOCIAL CONTEXT

Three lessons address the numerous social factors. Teachers may choose to implement part of the lessons, depending on which issues they feel are important for their particular group of students. The first lesson covers the history and settlement of different ethnic groups. It is important to address those groups included in the class, but students should have the choice of studying other groups as well. Ethnic communities and their presence in the country are the topic of the second lesson. Part of this lesson was tested by Angela in her class. The last lesson includes some of the most sensitive social issues. Using the recommended literature helps students and teachers tackle such topics as attitudes toward language, dialect, class, gender, ethnicity, and race. These topics are very important to students but often schools and families avoid them.

Social Lesson 1: History of Ethnic Groups

Objective: Students will know the history of the settlement of their ethnic groups. Students will understand that sociohistorical events shape the reception of their ethnic groups and the attitudes toward them.

Rationale: Attitudes toward ethnic groups are often colored by events connected with the history of the groups' establishment in the United States. Students must understand that these attitudes are not related to them as individuals but are the result of the complex interaction of a number of factors that favor certain groups and not others. These attitudes in many cases change with time. For example, Cubans no longer enjoy as warm a welcome as they received in the early stages of Castro's regime.

Time: Three to 4 days (60–90 minutes per day).

Materials:

- *Coming To America* by Betsy Maestro (see Appendix A).
- Alternate Books: *A Picnic in October, Faraway Home, Journey Home, Maranthe's Story: Painted Words/Spoken Memories, The Silence in the Mountains, F Is for Fabuloso, Esperanza Rising, Gold Dust, Dream Freedom, Becoming a Citizen: Adopting a New Home* (see Appendix A).
- Immigration Research Project Outline (Worksheet 4.1).
- Internet:
     http://www.yahooligans.com/
     http://www.ins.gov/graphics/aboutins/statistics/310.htm
     http://www.immigrationforum.org/
     http://www.census.gov/dmd/www/teachers.html (special site for teachers)
     http://factfinder.census.gov/servlet/BasicFactsServlet?_lang=en
- Map of the United States.
- Books.
- Encyclopedias.
- Periodicals.
- Newspaper articles.

- Chart paper.
- Drawing paper.
- Color stickers.

Overview of Activities

- Demographic composition of the United States.
- Demographic census information.
- Reflections on demographic information.
- Discussion of the book *Coming to America*.
- Waves of Immigration Timeline.
- History of settlement or immigration of our heritage group.

Demographic Composition of the United States

1. Display current maps showing the distribution population of the United States. These maps are obtainable from the Bureau of the Census Web site (http://factfinder.census.gov/servlet/BasicFactsServlet?_lang=en) or current social studies textbooks.
2. Lead whole-class discussion about the information one can obtain by examining these maps.
   (a) List students' responses on chart paper.
   (b) Identify the number of ethnic groups.
   (c) Discuss why groups decide to settle in certain places.

Interpretation and Discussion of Demographic Census Information

1. Ask students to describe the role of the Census Bureau. Why is collecting this information important?
2. Distribute graphs and tables of census statistics obtainable from Web addresses listed earlier. Select graphs and tables that show various language groups in the country, distribution in various states, proficiency in English, and others.
3. Initiate a discussion with the whole class. The following guided questions are suggested:
   - How is the information organized in the table or graph?
   - What is the title of the graph/table?
   - What information is represented?
   - What do the statistics reveal about language and population?
   - Why do you think there is a higher concentration of people in certain areas of the United States?
   - What are the changes from the last census?

4. Using samples of demographic information for your state or nation, have students formulate predictions:
   - What population estimates are being projected for the next census?
   - Where is the highest /lowest concentration of population for your state?
   - What is the highest/lowest concentration of ages?
   - What does this section tell us about race and ethnicity?
5. Select a table from the census on either language or population and have students in groups of four discuss, write, and interpret the information represented. Each group designates a recorder and presenter. The recorder will write the group's interpretation of the table. The designated presenter will share the findings with the class. Write their interpretations and predictions on chart paper.

Reflections on Demographic Information

Have students reflect in writing on the various census tables and charts studied. Ask students to describe what data, if any, surprised them. What were some of the interesting statistics about English proficiency of non-native speakers, and other information obtained through the census.

Reading and Discussion of the Book *Coming to America*

1. Prior to reading the book aloud, write the title of the book and author on chart paper. Show the cover to the class and ask students to predict what the book will be about. Write students' responses on chart paper. For example, students may infer there are large group of immigrants from various countries waving at the Statue of Liberty. They appear to be waving and hugging each other as they reach America. Through students' predictions lead a discussion about what information they will learn about immigrants from this account.
2. Read the book aloud. Pause at certain intervals in the story to probe students' understanding. Ask students to relate to their own experiences. At the conclusion of the read aloud, ask students to share their reaction to the story. Some of the points that are important to raise are: the status of immigrants and refugees in the United States today, reasons for coming to America, where immigrants settled and languages they spoke, changes of the waves of immigration, adjustments to a new way of life, and acquisition of English.
3. Ask students to respond to the following prompt in their journals using the Responses to Literature technique (see Appendix B):

   What can you say about the origin of people that settled in the United States?
   Did you find people of your heritage in this book?

4. Respond briefly in writing to their journal entries.

5. Have students share their responses to *Coming to America*. Ask the class for their reactions after each individual reads. Compare essays to the content of the book. This activity takes time because each student gets a turn. The discussion is essential for teasing out the issues relevant to the objectives of this lesson.

Alternative: If the class is very large, select a group of students to share with the whole class. Choose students whose families represent different ethnic groups.

Waves of Immigration Timeline

1. Have the class create timelines of the waves of immigration using information from the book *Coming to America.*
2. With the whole class, generate a list of various periods of waves of immigration and groups who came to America.
3. Provide students with drawing paper and have students select a time period to represent on their timeline.
4. Display timelines in the classroom.

History of Settlement or Immigration of Our Heritage Group

1. Tell students that they will be investigating the history of immigration of their heritage group to the United States.
2. With the whole class, generate a list of questions about their heritage groups and write these questions on chart paper. Some of the following questions are suggested:
   - What is the name of your heritage group and country?
   - Why did they come to America?
   - Where did they settle?
   - What language/dialect do they speak?
   - What documentation was required to enter the United States?
   - What were the immigration laws during their arrival to the United States?
   - What are some problems experienced by your group in the United States?
3. Distribute and review with students the worksheet entitled "Immigration Research Project Outline" (Worksheet 4.1).
4. Have students conduct their research investigation using various resources such as books, encyclopedias, and periodicals.
5. The following Web site addresses are suggested:
   http://www.yahooligans.com/
   http://www. Ins.gov.
   http://www. immigrationforum.org
6. Have students write a summary of their research and present their findings to the class.

Summary and Reflection

Ask the students about the reception their ethnic group received in the United States and how it compares with the reception they have had in school. Students can write a reflection on this comparison.

Outcomes

These activities are geared to achieve the following outcomes. The teacher will keep a record for each student using the rubric in Fig. 4.1 as a guideline.

	1	2	3	4
Concepts: (Check the level for each concept) • The multiethnic nature of the United States. • The history of their ethnic group including when and why they came, who came (socio-economic background, race, and other characteristics), number of immigrants, and reception that was afforded to them.				
Relationships: • Students will relate the history of their ethnic groups with the attitudes toward that ethnic group.				
Connection to self: • Students will explore how the social attitudes toward their ethnic group affects how they are being treated in the world outside their own ethnic group.				

Key (for further explanation, see Appendix C)
Each concept, relationship, and connection to self covered in the lessons can be graded with respect to the following levels of understanding:
1. Misguided notion or no recognition.
2. Passive understanding.
3. Expresses some understanding of concept or relationship.
4. Expresses full understanding of concept or relationship.

Proposing a Solution	1	2	3

Key
Solutions proposed can be noted with respect to whether student:
1. Does not propose a solution.
2. Engages in a solution proposed by the teacher.
3. Proposes a solution.

FIG. 4.1.   Social context rubric, Lesson 1.

Social Lesson 2: Demographics and Language Development

Objective: Students will understand that motivation to learn English and maintain the heritage language is related to a number of demographic and social variables including:
- Demographic composition and cohesiveness of communities.
- Reasons for being in the United States.
- Proximity to the country of origin.
- Length of stay in the United States.

Rationale: The demographic composition of the community defines the amount of contact students and their families have with English speakers and people of their own ethnic group. Some ethnic groups may form close communities with intense interaction among the members of the group. These communities offer a strong network of support. Often stores and churches cater to these groups, offering services in their native language. In these neighborhoods, contact with English speakers may be limited. Some immigrants may choose to live in more mixed communities, where the lingua franca is English. Other factors such as length of intended stay in the United States, proximity to the country of origin, and reasons for coming will also influence the motivation to develop English-speaking skills.

Time: Three days (60–90 minutes a day).

Materials:

- Internet:
    http://www.census.gov/
    http://www.ins.gov/graphics/aboutins/statistics/lprest.htm
    http://www.immigrationforum.org/
- Local Web pages with information on own community.
- *Some Factors That Affect Learning English and Maintaining the Heritage Language* (Worksheet 4.2).
- Current newspaper or magazine articles on demographic topics.
- Maps (population, census).
- Learning logs (see Appendix B).
- Graph and chart paper.

Overview of Activities

- Ethnic composition of our neighborhood(s).
- Interviews with community representatives.
- Summary and reflections.
- Use of English and the heritage language in my neighborhood.

Ethnic Composition of Our Neighborhood(s)

Ask students to describe the composition of their community (or communities). The following guided questions are suggested:

- How long has your family lived in your neighborhood?
- What ethnic groups live in your community?
- What languages are spoken within your community?
- Why did your family leave your heritage country (if they are immigrants)?
- How long does your family plan to stay?
- Do you have people from your heritage country living within your community? If so, how does this make you feel?
- Have you experienced any difficulties within your community with regard to use of your heritage language?
- How would you describe the level of interactions with English speakers within your community?
- Have there been any changes in the population?
- What changes in the world explain changes in the composition of your neighborhood?

Interviews of Community Representative

1. Invite speakers representing different experiences to speak to students. Experiences can be contrasted in these ways:
   - Representatives could live in a community with lots of speakers from the heritage language that provide a strong cohesive support network, or they could live in a community with mostly English speakers.
   - Representatives are in the United States for different reasons. For example, they might be immigrants, refugees, foreign students, indigenous, original colonizer, and so on.
   - Some immigrants come from a country bordering the United States. Others come from a country very far from the United States.
   - Some plan to live in the United States forever. Others plan to return to country of origin.

Possible speakers can be found among the school staff, students' families, or within the neighborhood at large.

2. For homework, have students write five questions to ask the guest speaker. Direct them to some of the questions used in the initial activity. Ask students to think of questions about the following topics:
   - Heritage country of the speaker.
   - Ethnic composition of the community where speaker lives.
   - Languages spoken.
   - Reasons why the speaker lives in the United States.
   - Planned length of stay.
   - Speaker's motivation to learn English and to maintain heritage language.

   Encourage your students to think of additional questions in any subject. They are likely to raise relevant topics covered in other lessons.

3. Introduce guest speaker and have students ask prepared questions.

4. Write responses to questions on chart paper.

5. After each speaker, encourage students to reflect on the information presented. The following guiding question is suggested:
   What did you learn about:
   - Heritage country of the speaker?
   - Ethnic composition of the community where speaker lives?
   - Languages spoken in his/her neighborhood?
   - Reasons why the speaker lives in the United States?
   - Planned length of stay?
   - Speaker's motivation to learn English and to maintain heritage language?

Summary and Reflections

After the students have interviewed two or more speakers, have them reflect on what factors helped motivate the speakers to learn (or not) English and maintain (or not) their heritage language. Choose one of the following two activities:

A. Written Reflection

1. Have students reflect in writing to the prompt: Do the speakers know English and their heritage language or not? What do you think help or did not help them?

2. Discuss with the whole class their reflections

B. Matrix of Factors

1. Create a matrix of factors that help/do not help people learn English and maintain their heritage language (Worksheet 4.2). Draw a large matrix on the board and give copies to students.

2. Ask students to form groups of four and discuss what helped their speakers learn (or not) English and maintain (or not) their heritage language.
3. Discuss the results as a whole class.

Use of English and the Heritage Language in My Neighborhood

1. Have students brainstorm on the places they went during the past week in their neighborhood and the people they encountered.
2. Have them indicate the ethnic background and language of the people in their community.
3. Write their responses on chart paper using a chart like that in Fig. 4.2.

Places	People	
	Language Group	Ethnic

FIG. 4.2   Languages of the neighborhood.

4. Have them discuss if the English they hear in the neighborhood is similar or different from the one they hear in the school.
5. Have them write a reflection paper using the following prompt: What opportunities does your neighborhood give you to practice your heritage language and the type of English used in your school? How do you think this influences your motivation to become good in English and in your heritage language?

Outcomes

These activities are geared to achieve the following outcomes. The teacher will keep a record for each student using the rubric in Fig. 4.3 as a guideline.

	1	2	3	4
Concepts: (Check the level for each concept) • Demographic composition of community. • Reasons why people migrate.				
Relationships: (Check the level for each relationship) • Influence of social variables on the opportunity to interact with English speakers and with people of the heritage language. • Influence of interaction with English speakers on the development of English. • Influence of interaction with Heritage language speakers on the development of the language				
Connection to self: Personal experience with English and Heritage language speakers. How the contact helps with English development and with maintenance of the Heritage language.				

Key (for further explanation see Appendix III)
Each concept , relationship, and connection to self covered in the lessons can be graded with respect to the following levels of understanding:
1. Misguided notion or no recognition
2. Passive understanding.
3. Expresses some understanding of concept or relationship.
4. Expresses full understanding of concept or relationship.

Proposing a Solution	1	2	3

Key
Solutions proposed can be noted with respect to whether students:
1. Does not propose a solution.
2. Engages in a solution proposed by the teacher.
3. Proposes a solution.

FIG. 4.3 Social context rubric, Lesson 2.

Social Lesson 3: Language, Ethnicity, Class, Race, and Gender Attitudes

Objective: Students will investigate attitudes toward languages, dialects, ethnic groups, race, gender, and socioeconomic level in the context of the home, school, community, and/or nation. The students will understand that these attitudes vary from one place to another or from one time in history to another.

Rationale: Communities evince attitudes toward language, dialects, ethnic groups, race, gender, and socioeconomic levels. These attitudes vary and may be more favorable to certain languages, ethnic groups, gender, and so on. These attitudes change over time and from community to community. Members of the community are affected by these attitudes. Students must understand that these attitudes are not personal but are formed over time for a variety of reasons. It is important to realize that they exist, whether they are right or wrong. These attitudes are different in the United States and in other countries.

Time: Three to 4 days (60–90 minutes per day).

Materials:

- *Felita* by Nicolasa Mohr.
- *School Survey* (Worksheet 4.3).
- Graphic organizer (see Appendix B).
- Learning logs (see Appendix B).
- Chart paper.

Overview of Activities

- Reading and discussion of the book *Felita*.
- Survey on social interactions in school.

Reading and Discussion of the book Felita

The first three chapters of the book will be thoroughly discussed in class to elicit ideas, reflections, and connections to self with respect to attitudes toward language, dialect, ethnic background, and socioeconomic level. The students will read the remainder of the book independently.

1. Prior to reading the first chapter aloud, write the title and author of the book on chart paper. Show the book cover to class and ask students to predict what the story will be about. Write students' responses on chart paper. For example, students may infer that a girl plays hopscotch on the street, as friends look on. Ask the students where they think the story takes place.
2. Read aloud chapter 1, "The Last Day." Pause at certain intervals in the story to probe students' understanding. Ask students to relate to their own experience. At the conclusion of the read aloud, ask students to share their reaction to the story. The following guided questions are suggested:
   - Why is Felita unhappy about her family moving to a new neighborhood?
   - Why have Felita's parents decided to move to the new neighborhood?

- Why do you think Felita's parents consider the new neighborhood a "better neighborhood?"
- What opportunities are they hoping to find there?
- How does Felita feel about an all-White neighborhood?
- What do you think Felita will miss most about her neighborhood?

3. Have students respond to the chapter in their journals. They should explain how the story relates to their own experiences, or to those of someone they know.

4. Respond briefly in writing to their journal entries.

5. Share responses to chapter 1 of the book *Felita*. Have students read aloud their journal responses. Ask the class for their reactions after each individual reads. Compare essays to the content of the book. This activity takes time because each student gets a turn. The discussion is essential for teasing the issues relevant to the objective of this lesson.

   Alternative: If the class is very large, select a group of students to share with the whole class. Choose students that cover different important topics related to attitudes toward language, dialect, ethnic background, and socio-economic level

6. Prior to reading chapter 2, write the title "Trouble" on chart paper. Ask students to predict what the chapter will be about. Write students' responses on chart paper. For example, students may infer that there may be problems for the Maldonado family in the new neighborhood. Through students' predictions, lead a discussion about the kinds of problems the Maldonado family may encounter in the new neighborhood.

7. Have students read the chapter independently.

8. After the independent reading, ask students to share their reactions to the chapter. The following guided questions are suggested:

- How would you describe the new neighborhood?
- Why do you think Felita was reluctant to go outside to play?
- How does Felita's mother convince her to give the new neighborhood a chance?
- How do you think Felita feels when asked to play hopscotch by a group of girls in the new neighborhood?
- How would you describe the attitudes of the girls as they talked with Felita while they played?
- What causes the girls' attitudes to change toward Felita?
- What were some prejudicial statements made about Felita's heritage background?
- Why do you think the White parents did not want their children playing with Felita?
- How did Felita feel after being verbally attacked by her neighbors?
- Why is Felita upset about not fighting back?
- What advice does Felita's mother provide?

- How does the Maldonado family react when Felita's brother is beaten up?
- Why does Felita's father refuse to move even though two of his children have been attacked?
- Why do you think Felita's father was not supported by the landlord or superintendent with his complaints?
- What occurs to change Felita's father's mind about moving back to the old neighborhood?
- Do you think the Maldonados made the right decision to move back to the old neighborhood? Why or why not?

9. Have students respond to the chapter in their journals. They should explain how the story relates to their own experiences, or to those of someone they know.
10. Teachers can respond briefly to their journal entries in writing.
11. As with the previous chapter, have students (or a group) share their responses to the chapter.
12. Prior to reading chapter 3, write the title "Abuelita" on chart paper. Ask students to predict what the chapter will be about. Write students' responses on chart paper. For example, students may contribute that "Abuelita" is the Spanish name for grandmother. Through students' predictions lead a discussion about the importance of Felita's relationship with her grandmother.
13. Have students read the chapter independently.
14. Ask students to share their reactions to the chapter. The following guided questions are suggested:
    - Why does Felita want to stay over Abuelita's house?
    - How does Abuelita help Felita talk about what's troubling her?
    - Why do you think Felita feels ashamed for not standing up to the neighborhood bullies who attacked her?
    - Abuelita tells Felita that "the most important thing is for her to feel strong inside." How do you think this might help Felita understand the conflict with her neighbors?
    - What advice does Abuelita give Felita about standing up for herself in the future?
    - What are some things Felita can say when someone makes fun of her Spanish language, skin color, or says that she should go back to her country?
    - What important lesson do you think Abuelita taught Felita about what to do when confronted with prejudiced and racist attitudes?
15. As with the other two chapters, have students respond in their journals and have them share their responses. Respond briefly in writing to each student.
16. Have students read chapters 4 through 7 independently and respond in their journals describing their reactions to the chapter. They should explain how the story relates to their own experiences, or to those of someone they know.

Survey on Social Interactions in School

This activity will help students work on solutions to potential social problems in the school:

1. Ask students to conduct a survey in their school to improve the social interactions among the diverse student population.
2. Initiate a whole-class discussion and brainstorm possible questions to include in the survey (see Worksheet 4.3). The following prompts are suggested:
   - Who do you mostly interact with in school?
   - Tell me about your friends with respect to the following: ethnic background, race, and language.
   - What language is used in your daily social interactions among your peers?
   - Have you encountered negative attitudes for speaking in your heritage language? If so, how did it make you feel?
   - How would you describe the school social climate?
   - How does the school address the needs of students who are learning English as a second language?
   - What activities would you like to see organized to promote positive social interaction among the diverse student population?
3. Have students discuss the results and reasons given by those polled. The following guided questions are suggested:
   - What were the major concerns with relation to social interaction among students?
   - What is the level of interaction among students?
   - What activities were considered important in improving social interactions among students?
4. Have students reflect in writing on the importance of organizing activities that promote social interaction among the diverse school population.

Outcomes

These activities are geared to achieve the following outcomes. The teacher will keep a record for each student using the rubric in Fig. 4.4 as a guideline:

	1	2	3	4
Concepts (Check the level for each concept) • Language, dialect, ethnic group, race, gender, and social class. • Feelings and attitudes toward language, dialect, ethnic group, race, gender, and social class.				
Relationships: Attitudes and treatment of people of a particular language, dialect, ethnic group, race, gender, and socioeconomic level				
Connection to self: Effects of these attitudes on personal treatment given language, ethnicity, race, gender, and socioeconomic level.				

Key (for further explanation see Appendix III)

Each concept, relationship, and connection to self covered in the lessons can be graded with respect to the following levels of understanding:
1. Misguided notion or no recognition
2. Passive understanding.
3. Expresses some understanding of concept or relationship.
4. Expresses full understanding of concept or relationship.

Proposing a Solution	1	2	3

Key

Solutions proposed can be noted with respect to whether students:
1. Does not propose a solution.
2. Engages in a solution proposed by the teacher.
3. Proposes a solution.

FIG. 4.4   Social context rubric, Lesson 3.

Worksheet 4.1. Immigration Research Project Outline.

1. What is the name of your heritage group and country?
2. Why did they come to America?
3. Where did they settle?
4. What language/dialect do they speak?
5. What documentation was required to enter the United States?
6. What were the immigration laws during their arrival to the United States?
7. What are some problems experienced by your group in the United States?

Worksheet 4.2.   Some Factors That Affect Learning English and Maintaining the Heritage Language.

	Helped Development	Did Not Help Development
English		
Heritage Language		

Worksheet 4.3.   School Survey.

Answer the following questions reflecting on your personal school experience:

1. Who do you mostly interact with in school?

2. Tell me about your friends with respect to the following: ethnic background and race.

3. What language is used in your daily social interactions among your peers?

4. Have you experienced or seen anyone experience negative attitudes for speaking in their heritage language? If so, how did it make you feel?

5. How would you describe the school social climate?

6. How does the school address the needs of students who are learning English as a second language?

7. What activities would you like to see organized to promote positive social interaction among the diverse student population?

5

Cultural Context

Culture consists of the values, traditions, social and political relationships, and worldview created, shared, and transformed by a group of people bound together by a common history, geographic location, language, social class and/or religion.

—Nieto (2000, p. 139).

OVERVIEW

The United States is a culturally complex country. Certain values dominate our society, yet different groups hold their own sets of values. These values affect students through the cultural perspectives of the family, the norms imparted by schools, the beliefs and behaviors of their peers, and what they see in the media.

This chapter explores cultural variables as reflected by:

- Families.
- School.
- Peers.
- Media.

Young immigrants often experience conflict as they adjust to a new culture and confront pressures from family, peers, and school personnel. Families and school often pit against each other in relation to the norms that they want to impose on the children. Peers reinforce the values of one or the other or create values of their own and recruit newcomers to join. The language-minority students find themselves torn by these different influences. Study of the cultural context can help students, teachers, and families to understand these conflicting forces that often find the children caught in the middle.

The lesson *Selected Cultural Differences Between U.S. and Heritage-Country Schools* includes several sublessons on:

- Curriculum content and expected background knowledge.
- Philosophy of teaching and learning.
- Communication and discipline.
- Structural differences in schools.
- Parental participation in education.

PART I: CLASSROOM IMPLEMENTATION

The classroom has changed quite a bit since the last visit in late November. Alex had left the class to go to Guatemala for a period of time. When he returned, his parents placed him in the monolingual fifth-grade class. According to the members of the class, they missed him very much and felt that he was having hard time adjusting to the new situation. There were several new students, all recently arrived immigrants, who had joined the class, including: Carmen from El Salvador, Edison from Colombia, and Raúl and Victoria from the Dominican Republic. Today was Edison's first day. There is also a student teacher working with the class.

The lesson objective for the unit *Differences in School Systems* is:

Students will be able to compare and contrast differences between schools in the United States and their heritage country in order to understand how differences between the heritage and U.S. cultures can create difficulties and conflicts.

Day One

It is 8:55 a.m. and Angela greets the class, *"Queremos dar la bienvenida a Edison."* [We want to welcome Edison.] She turns to Edison. *"Por favor, preséntate a la clase."* [Please introduce yourself to the class.]

Edison introduces himself seriously, *"Me llamo Edison. Soy de Colombia."* [My name is Edison. I am from Colombia.]

Angela asks him, *"¿Cuánto tiempo tienes aqui?"* [How long have you been here?]

"Un mes." [One month.]

Angela turns to the class and says, *"Vamos a presentarnos."* [Let's introduce ourselves.]

Raúl begins, *"Me llamo Raúl. Soy de la República Dominicana."* [My name is Raul. I am from the Dominican Republic.]

Angela encourages him to say more, *"¿Cuánto tiempo tienes aqui en este salón?"* [How long have you been here in this classroom?]

"Cuatro meses." [Four months.]

"¿Y como lo has pasado?" [And how have you enjoyed it?] Angela inquires.

"¡Bien!" [Great!] Raúl states emphatically.

"¿Qué es lo que te gusta de esta clase?" [What do you like about this class?] Raúl grins mischievously and points at her.

Angela smiles and says, *"¿La maestra?"* [The teacher?] She laughs. *"¿Y los compañeros?"* [And your classmates?] Raúl nods, still grinning. The students in the class take turns introducing themselves. They say their names and their heritage country. When they finish, Angela says, "Take out your autobiography folders. It's been a while. But we haven't forgotten. Take everything else off your desk." While the students do this, the ESL teacher comes and takes some students. Joanna, Raúl, Carmen, and Victoria all go with her.

Angela says, *"A nuestro amigo Edison, le vamos a ayudar."* [We are going to help our friend Edison.] She addresses Edison, *"Me alegro que hayas venido porque nos puedes ayudar. ¿Qué pensaste anoche cuando sabías que venías a la escuela hoy?"* [I'm glad you came today because you can help us. What did you think last night when you knew that you were coming to school today?]

He thinks for a minute and answers, *"De mis nuevos amigos, como era el colegio, de la profesora."* [I thought about my new friends, how school was going to be, about the teacher.]

"¿Sabías que venías para un salón bilingüe?" [Did you know you were coming to a bilingual class?]

Edison shakes his head no.

Angela continues her questioning, *"¿Pensabas que todos iban a hablar en inglés?"* [Did you think that everyone was going to talk in English?]

"Sí," [Yes.] Edison answers.

"¿Y estabas preocupado?" [And were you worried?]

"Sí." [Yes.]

"This is a lucky day for me. Because I didn't know how to introduce this lesson and who should walk in but Edison!" She grins. "Let's review these critical autobiography lessons. What did we do first?"

Students answer, "Language."

"Then what did we do?"

She writes the students' answers on the board. "Neighborhood, brochures, community ... Wasn't that economics? And the last one was demographic. Right?"

Jenny answers, "Population."

Angela finishes her list and turns back to the class. "Today we are going to tackle something very different and that is culture. What do you identify culture as? *¿Qué es la cultura?"* [What is culture?]

Sandra answers, "Tradition."

William adds, "What people do."

Angela is consciously using Spanish so Edison will understand. *"Deme un ejemplo de lo que representa la cultura."* [Give me an example of what culture represents.]

The students call out ideas and Angela makes a cluster on the board. She writes down their contributions. "Tradition, art, country, foods, dance."

Then she asks, "Do you think language is a part of your culture?"

The students nod. She adds language.

"Culture defines a lot of things in your country right, like what? We are going to investigate. *¿Cuántos nacieron aquí en los Estados Unidos?*" [How many were born in the United States?]

Seven students raise their hands.

"How many of you were born in your countries?" She counts the raised hands. "Five of you." Then Angela asks, "*¿Cuántos estudiaron en su país? ¿Si fueron a la escuela en su país? ¿O han ido a la escuela mientras estaban en su país visitando a sus primos, familiares?*" [How many studied in your country? Did you go to school in your country? Or have you been going to school while you were in your country visiting your cousins and relatives?]

"In second grade I went in March and the school didn't open until June," Sandra explains.

Angela nods and says, "Edison is here. I don't think that he is going to have a lot of problems, but he is going to have adjustments to make. Just like a lot of you did. Just like my experience when I went to Puerto Rico. Boy, was I in for a shock. I'm not going to tell you exactly what happened because I want to see how your experience was. What we are going to do is compare and contrast two countries. I'm going to give you a worksheet. *Vamos a hacer una comparación entre las escuelas en tu país y las escuelas en los Estados Unidos.*" [We are going to compare and contrast schools in the United States and your heritage country.] She asks the student teacher to assist her in passing out the worksheet (see Worksheet 4.1). The students place the sheets on their desks and start thinking about the differences between the educational system in their heritage countries and that in the United States.

José looks down at his paper and then up at Angela. "I don't have any idea," he says.

"Do you know what to do when you don't have an idea?" Angela asks.

"Invent," he says confidently.

"Not invent. What do you do to find out?"

"Ask your parents," Jenny chimes in.

"Ask your parents," Angela affirms.

"Go to the library," Sandra adds.

Angela nods and says, "Look it up in the library. Maybe go to the Internet. What we don't know we find out. What are the categories on the sheet? What does the first category say?"

"Subjects taught," reads Jenny.

"*Lo importante es empezar con lo que saben. Y lo que no saben* you can look up. What's the next category?" [The important part is to begin with what you know. And what you don't know you can look up.]

The students read, "Course requirements for each grade."

"What does that mean? You are being required to do certain things. *Hay unos requisitos cursos y exámenes.*" She turns to Edison, "*¿En Colombia hay unos exámenes? ¿Para pasar de cuarto a quinto grado que tuviste que cumplir?*" [In Colombia are there exams? To pass from fourth to fifth grade what do you have to complete?]

Edison answers without hesitation, *"La disciplina, las tareas."* [Discipline, homework.]

"La disciplina, tareas. ¿Y en cuanto la asistencia? ¿Si no fuiste?" [Discipline, homework. And what about attendance? If you didn't go?]

Edison responds, *"Tenias que llevar una excusa."* [You have to bring an excuse.]

"¿Y si no llevabas excusa?" asks Angela. [And if you didn't bring an excuse?]

"Te ponen 'deficiente.'" responds Edison. [They mark you "deficient."]

"Deficiente. Otra cosa diferente es las notas. ¿Como califican?" inquires Angela. [Deficient. Another different thing is grades. How do they grade?]

Edison gets another opportunity to offer information and knowledge on his first day of school. *"Excelente, aceptable, dificiente."* [Excellent, acceptable, deficiente.]

"Aqui no. ¿Qué se usan? Letras: A, B, C. *Bueno. Vamos al próximo. ¿Qué tienen que saber los niños en quinto grado?"* She looks to the rest of the class for answers. [Here no. What do we use? Letters: A, B, C. Good. Let's go to the next one. What do children have to know in fifth grade?]

"Multiplicación, division," says William.

"Science," adds Christopher.

"Okay," agrees Angela. *"¿Qué quiere decir el curriculo? ¿Uds. tienen que saber los planetas? ¿Qué tienen que saber en tu país?"* [What does the curriculum say? You have to learn the planets? What do you have to know in your country?]

"Geografía, matemática, ortografia," mentions Edison. [Geography, mathematics, handwriting.]

"Todo eso bajo del curriculum," [It's all based on the curriculum.] explains Angela. "Now, 'Promotion Policy.' *Para pasar el grado.* What do you have to do? What you are going to be doing in May?"

"Pass the test," says Sandra.

"Tests. You have to do well on the Stanford."

Angela points back at the worksheet. "Let's go to the next one, Teaching styles, *y la rutina del salón. Es diferente. ¿Cómo se lo imaginan?* [The classroom routine. It's different. How do you imagine it?] Even if you don't know, how can you imagine, knowing what your culture is like?" She pauses. The students are all looking the sheets, reflecting on the different categories. Some have started filling in their ideas. "Okay. So do what you know. *En este lado van a hacer como* bullets—*puntitos. Y si no sabemos, investigamos. Edison, tu pasas para este lado y yo te voy a ayudar."* [On this side we are going to make bullets. And what we don't know, we will investigate. Edison, you come over to this side and I'm going to help you.]

Sandra says to Bernarda, *"Allá,* [over there] they don't let you pass until you know everything."

Hearing this, Angela asks the class, *"¿Tu crees que allá son más estrictos que acá?"* [Do you believe that over there they are more strict than here?] Some students say yes, others no. They start writing and filling in the chart.

Angela continues talking, *"Cuando yo fui* a Puerto Rico back in the 60s I was happy. *Fuimos en julio y la escuela empezó en agosto."* [We went in July and school started in August.] She turns to Edison, *"¿En Colombia cuando tiene vacaciones? ¿Cuándo termina el año?"* [In Colombia when do you have vacations?]

Edison answers, *"En agosto y septiembre tenemos vacaciones."* [In August and September we have vacations.]

It is 9:15; class has been in session for 1 hour and 15 minutes. Angela walks around the room checking work. She points at Edison's paper and asks him, *"¿Uds usan uniforme?"* [Do you use uniforms?]

"Sí," [Yes.] Edison answers.

Sandra says, "In Santo Domingo they had an assistant who went to the house to pick us up."

Angela nods. Raising her voice, she turns to the student teacher, and asks, "Our student teacher taught in Ecuador. *Ella estuvo un semestre enseñando en Ecuador. Cuéntanos."* [She was teaching in Ecuador for one semester. Tell us about it.]

The student teacher starts to share her reflections on the educational system in Ecuador, *"En Ecuador es diferente. Los profesores son bien rígidos. Las niñas y los niños juegan separados y no pueden jugar juntos. Los niños no pueden hablar libremante en la clase. Tienen que levantar la mano o si no, al jefe."* [In Ecuador it is different. The teachers are very strict. The girls and boys play separately and they can't play together. The children can't talk freely in the classroom. They have to raise their hand, or if not, to the principal.]

"Thank you," Angela says. She turns back to the class. *"Otra cosa. ¿Como consideran la profesión de profesora en tu país? ¿Qué valor tiene?* Do you know what I mean? *En Puerto Rico en general, la profesión tiene mucho valor. Mira lo que me dice Raúl, 'Profe.' Aqui en este salón hay una diferencia* in how the teacher is treated. Okay. Get started. I'm not going to talk anymore." [Another thing. How are teachers considered in your country? What value do they have? Do you know what I mean? In Puerto Rico in general, the profession has a lot of value. Look at what Raúl calls me, 'Profe.' Here in this classroom there is a difference in how the teacher is treated.]

The students write. They ask each other questions quietly and share ideas.

Angela has another idea. "What about what is required by the students to bring to school? I know in Puerto Rico, the teachers are required to purchase a lot of materials." Animated, she turns to another student. "The school is to prepare you for the future for getting a job. What are you required to know? And sometimes you learn something a certain way in our country? *¿Se acuerdan como dividen diferente en su país? Y algunos de Uds. nos enseñaron."* [You remember how they do division differently in your country? And some of you taught us.]

William remembers the mathematics lesson to which Angela is referring. She had asked some students to show the rest of the class the way in which they were taught to divide. "You let us do it that way," William recalls.

"A veces cuando aprenden de una manera en su país y despues vienen a este país y es diferente, este hace un conflicto. Por esto, les dejo hacer en su manera. El estilo aqui es diferente," Angela says. *"Otra parte de la cultura es que los niños latinos tiene respeto hacia la profesora. Aqui me respetan porque la profesora es como segunda madre."* [Sometimes you learn one way in your country and later you come to this country, and it's different. This makes a conflict. This is why I let you do it in your way. The style is different. Another part of the culture is that the Latino children have respect for the teacher. Here you respect me because the teacher is like your second mother.]

It is 9:32; the students are filling out the categories on the worksheet. The other classmates return from ESL and sit as one group, working. Mrs. O'Connor (the ESL teacher) enters the room and quickly integrates herself into the lesson. She is walking around helping individual students write down their ideas. Joanna and several students are filling in the compare/contrast worksheet in Spanish.

"Remember in Math we learned: estimation, graphs, multiplication, division, area perimeter. That math curriculum is huge and we are not even finished. Do you think that the math curriculum is bigger or different from in your country? Some of your parents say, 'I'm sorry I can't help you. *A mi no me enseñaron así.*' [That's not the way they taught me.] Right?"

Angela continues to walk around helping. She says, "Back in the 60s they gave me powered milk, rice, and beans for the school lunch."

Angela asks Edison, *"¿En Colombia tenías que llevar comida de la casa?"* [In Colombia did you have to bring food from home?]

Maria calls Angela over and says, "In my country if you don't do your homework they hit you with the ruler."

This sparks Raúl's interest, *"En mi país si hablas te ponen contra la pared."* [In my country if you talk they put you against the wall.]

Sandra says, "At the end of the day they gave you candy."

Raúl, with his mischievous grin, brags to Christopher, *"Cuando yo peleaba, me regañaban."* [When I fought they admonished me.]

Angela is over by a group of students. She asks them, *"¿Cuál es el estilo de la profesora?"* [What is the style of the teacher?]

Victoria answers, *"Mi profesora hacía cosas divertidas."* [My teacher did fun things.]

Sandra says, "If the boys had haircuts that were unacceptable they had to go home. If they cut it too short, they had to go home until it grew again. And the girls couldn't cut it shorter than their shoulders."

The students have been working on their worksheets for half an hour. Edison is filling in all the categories diligently. Students are engaged in the activity and sharing stories about their schools.

Angela says, *"A Edison le pregunté que pensaba que iba a ver hoy en el colegio. Lo que quiero que hagan es completer estas ideas. Algunos de Uds. no fueron al colegio en su país pero si tienen familiares que les pueden contar como son las escuelas. La otra pregunta es: ¿qué encontraron difíciles? ¿Todo el mundo entiende?"* She holds up a Venn diagram (see Appendix B) *"¿Se acuerdan como llenar? Poner en este lado de un país, en el otro lado, lo del otro país y lo que tienen en comun en la mitad."* [I asked Edison what he thought he was going to see today at school. What I want you to do is complete these ideas. Some of you didn't go to school in your country but you have relatives who can help tell you about the schools. The other question is: What did you find difficult? Everyone understand? Do you remember how to fill it out? Put on this side one country and on the other side, everything about the other country and what they have in common in the middle.]

She hands copies of the Venn diagram to José who passes them out. This assignment will be completed for homework.

Day Two

On the second day of the cultural unit, the class starts at the usual time of 8:45. As the class comes to order, Bernarda goes up and shows Angela the work she did. Angela hugs Bernarda and says loudly so that other students may hear, *"Muy bien.* She thinks the teacher doesn't like her. *Pero yo sé que no estabas trabajando a tu potencial.* [But I know that you were not working to your potential.] Let's give her a hand." The students applaud in support of their classmate.

Angela then says, "Let's get in groups and we are going to share for 10 minutes." The students take out their Venn diagrams they did for homework and begin forming groups of two or three. Edison shows Angela his report card. Angela looks very interested and reads the grades aloud, *"Alto, excelente.* Wow, it's interesting. *Tú nos explicas a nosotros ahora. Me alegro que lo hayas compartido con nosotros."* [High, excellent. You can explain it to us now. I'm glad that you have shared this with us.]

The students work with their partners, looking at similarities and differences between the educational systems in their countries of origin. At 8:55 Angela announces, *"Ya ha pasado el tiempo.* It's time to discuss." She has taped a large Venn diagram poster to the chalkboard. She stands in front of the students and asks, "How many went home to ask their parents?" Some raise hands. *"¿Cuando fueron a la casa y les preguntaste cómo era el sistema educativo, cómo reaccionaron?"* [When you went home and you asked how was the educational system, how did they react?]

Sandra speaks up, "My aunt wanted to tell me everything. I was like, 'The paper was full already.'"

Angela looks at the Venn diagram on the board to see how to organize it. "Let's see, we have two sides. We need to put USA on this side. School in heritage country on the right. Heritage means your background."

Sandra says, "I think that in Colombia they put their bookbags in their desks."

William raises his hand, "Free food."

"Come up and put it up. It's not just lunch you get; it's also breakfast. How about the subjects? Do you find them more difficult here or there?"

"Over there," claims Sandra.

"Why is that?"

"Because in third grade they give you like fourth-grade subjects."

Angela writes this comment on the diagram. "Subject matter—courses more difficult." She asks, "Do you think that they expect more? Are they more demanding?"

Edison looks up at what Angela is writing. Maria and Jenny have their hands raised.

José contributes, "Both places have recess and field trips too."

Angela writes in middle section of the diagram, "recess, field trips."

José says that in his country they have school until sixth grade. Angela translates this into Spanish.

Next, Angela takes out Edison's report card and reads aloud the mission statement of Edison's school. She then reads the list of subjects, *"Inglés, ética, tecnología ¿Qué es tecnología?* Computers, right? *educación física, lengua castellana."* Angela turns and writes "phys. ed." in middle of the Venn diagram.

It is 9:25; the class has been engaged in discussion for about 20 minutes. Angela looks at the class and says, "The report cards, why is that important?"

Jenny answers, "To keep a record."

"The teachers wear uniforms over there," adds Sandra. Angela writes this on the diagram.

Christopher says, "Over there they'll be behind you like *una sombra."* [a shadow.]

Raúl clarifies, *"En una escuela de monjas te molestan mucho. En una escuela pública te dejan así."* [In the nun school they bother you a lot. In the public school they let you be.] Angela puts this information to one side of the diagram.

"This is what we are investigating—not whether they are good or bad, but part of the culture," Angela explains. "And sometimes this causes conflict. *Ayer cuando Edison iba a hablar, se paró. Yo tuve que explicarle que no hace falta. A veces hay dificultades en adaptarse. Para ayudar a Victoria, dejamos que se siente al lado de alguien que puede interpretar.* [Yesterday when Edison was going to speak aloud, he stood up. I had to explain to him that it wasn't necessary. Sometimes there are difficulties adapting. To help Victoria, we let her sit beside someone who can translate.] Sometimes teachers don't understand that you don't understand and you have to tell him. Do you see the conflict that creates?"

Sandra raises her hand and says, "In the USA there is transportation to school." Angela adds to this to the diagram. Sandra continues, "Over here you have more possibility of being creative."

Angela nods. "Uh huh. Sandra brought up a very good point. Do you understand this? *Hay más libertad en cuanto lo que el estudiante contribuye.* [There is more liberty with what the student contributes.] So there, it is more teacher centered." She pauses. *"¿Entiendes? Aqui Uds. trabajan en grupos, independientes, hacen proyectos. Allá la profesora esta en control todo el tiempo.* [Do you understand? Here you work in independent groups and do projects.] What about the interaction between boys and girls?"

Sonia says, "They don't play together."

Angela writes this on the diagram. Under *USA* she writes, "boys and girls play." Under *Heritage*, "boys and girls separate." "Some, not all," she emphasizes. "What about promotion policy? Here there is an attendance policy. There too." She writes this in the middle.

She continues, "*¿Qué consejos Uds. le darían a mi amigo Edison quien acaba de llegar? Para evitar conflictos. O que consejo le dan a las escuelas para adaptarse a niños de diferentes culturas.* [What advice would you give to my friend Edison who just arrived? To avoid conflicts. Or what advice do you give to schools to adapt themselves to children of different cultures?] This will be the question to reflect on. *Van a tener dos preguntas. Van a copiar esto.* [You are going to have two questions. You are going to copy this.] We'll do it in English and in Spanish." She writes on board, "Responder:

¿Qué consejos le darían a un estudiante que es nuevo en su clase? ¿Cómo ayudaría a que no tenga conflicto adaptandose al nuevo ambiente?" She writes in English on the chalkboard, "What advice would you give a new student in your class? How would you help so he or she would not have problems or cultural conflicts in the new school environment?" She turns to Edison, *"Edison, tu puedes aconsejar a un alumno que se va a Colombia. Tú lo haces de punto de vista de tu país. Los demás lo dan de aquí."* [Edison, you can advise a new student who is going to Colombia. You can do it from the point of view of your country. Everyone else will do it from here.]

To conclude the lesson, Angela makes ties back to literature that the class had read. She picks up the book *El Chino*, by Allen Say (see Appendix A) and holds it up for the class. She reminds the class about the story they had read last week and briefly summarizes it in Spanish. The main character in the story followed his dream of becoming a bullfighter by moving to Spain. He had to make some adaptations to the Spanish culture to achieve his dream. At the same time he remained true to himself. In this way, Angela draws connections to today's lesson about cultural adaptation.

Day Three

It is 8:45 on the third day of the cultural unit. Angela stands in front of the class, "Okay, what was the question that I posed? *¿Qué fue la pregunta?*"

Bernarda replies, *"¿Qué consejos tienen para un estudiante nuevo en tu clase?"* [What advice do you have for a new student in your class?]

Angela writes on board, *"Consejos para un estudiante nuevo en tu clase.* Advice for new student in your class so that he can adjust to new school environment and routine/culture." She asks the class, *"¿Quién quiere compartir?"* [Who wants to share?]

Joanna raises her hand and reads from her paper, *"Yo le aconsejo que se porte bien con la profesora."* [I advise him to behave with the teacher.]

"So, behavior. *¿Pero como le va a ayudarse adaptar bien? Por ejemplo, tu misma cuando llegaste, para adaptarse.*" [But how are you going to help him adapt well? For example, you yourself, when you arrived, how did you adapt?] Angela addresses the class. "Do you remember when Joanna came into your classroom last year? What did you do to help her? Remember the story, 'Mei Mei'?" Angela pauses before continuing, "For example, what did I do to make the computer teacher aware about Edison? What did he ask me? To assign a partner to help him. What if I didn't introduce him? What would he have felt?"

Soraya answers, "Confusion."

"So I made some accommodations. What happens when family comes to visit? You have to accommodate, you have to give up your bed. Next?" She calls on Victoria.

"Que hagan amigos." [That he should make friends.]

Angela writes her answer on board.

Next, Sandra contributes her advice. "The advice I would give is to ask other students questions. So that way he or she can get to know everybody. Also to do what the teacher says."

Julia translates, *"Debe hacer preguntas y conocer todo el mundo."*

Angela asks Sandra, "What happened to your brother when he first came from Santo Domingo?"

Sandra recalls her brother's difficulties at adapting to school in the United States. "At the beginning he talked back to the teacher and when he got mad he took everything out of his desk and threw it on the floor. He got into fights."

"Did the teacher do anything?" Angela inquires.

"She called my mom."

"Why did he act that way? Did he act that way in Santo Domingo?"

"He was mad because he didn't want to be here," says Christopher.

Angela agrees, *"El estaba protestando. El no quería estar. Tuvo que adaptarse a nuevo sistema."* [He was protesting. He didn't want to be here. He had to adapt to a new system.]

Sandra gives an example of the inconsistencies that her brother experienced. "Over there he put everything in one notebook. Here everything is separate. You put your notes and work in different notebooks for the different subjects."

Angela nods. "He didn't like the system here. Thank you for sharing that."

Julia volunteers her advice, "If I give advice to a new kid I would say, this is a new country and a different school and he or she will get new friends."

"Okay," says Angela. "*¿Quién más?* [Who else?] José, what did you say?"

"My advice to a new student is, 'Don't worry if you are shy. Everybody is shy. There is no right or wrong answer as my teacher says.'"

Angela translates, *"No sea tímido y lo más importante es tratar. No hay respuesta correcta ni incorecta."*

Bernarda continues, "Also, respect your friends. Also always do what the teacher says. If you do your homework she will be happy."

Angela says, "The teacher is happy when do you do your work like you did yesterday with the newspaper assignment. *También el respeto.* [Also the respect.] Edison?"

Edison reads his advice for a student who is trying to adapt to Colombian schools. *"Tener responsabilidad y tratar de adapatarse al nuevo sistema del país."* [To have responsibility and try to adapt to the new system of the country.]

"Bien. El dijo lo mismo que Uds. Pero en otras palabras. 'Responsibilidad.' Ser responsable." [Good. He said the same that you all said but in other words. Responsibility. To be responsible.]

Carmen looks up and says, *"Le ayudaría para que se adaptara un poco."* [I would help him to adapt a little bit.]

Angela tries to clarify, *"¿Quién te ayudo a ti?"* [Who helped you?]

"Doris."

Angela smiles proudly and says, "Doris is the diplomat. She's the welcoming committee. And Julia too. They help out, both of them." Doris and Julia looked pleased at having their role in the classroom recognized.

Angela comments. *"Es difícil adaptarse. La transición de Edison ha sido muy confortable. ¿Cierto?"* [It is difficult to adapt. The transition of Edison has been very comfortable. Is that right?]

Edison replies, *"Sí."* [Yes.]

Other students share their advice.

John says, "I'd ask him, 'How were things in his country?'"

"That is good. If you ask them, *'¿Cómo eran las cosas en Colombia?' ¿Cómo le hace sentir a la persona? Cuando tu le preguntas y le da importancia."* [If you ask them, 'How were things in Colombia?' How is the other person going to feel? When you ask questions, the person will feel important.]

She waits a moment for an answer and then writes on board "valued" *"valorado."* "Your assignment is, write a letter to welcome them, either Edison, Carmen, Raúl, or Sonia. That is your homework." She passes out paper. This initial discussion has lasted about 30 minutes.

The following day José brings in his letter for Raúl, which follows:

Dear Raúl,

Welcome to our class. Here we share stuff and I hope you do too.

Also, don't worry if you're shy, everybody here is shy. Be friends with everybody because nobody likes mean people, and my advice to you is don't get the teacher mad.

Your friend,

José

Lessons Learned

All the phases were achieved in the cultural lesson, from understanding concepts, to finding relationships, to proposing solutions. Coincidentally, a new student arrived from Colombia the day the unit started. Focusing on this student and remembering their own past experiences provided a real example for the students and the teacher to relate to the SC lesson.

The assignment of having the students reflect on the differences between school in their heritage countries and in the United States engaged students on several levels. First, they were able to go home and talk with their family members about the characteristics of education. They were able to draw upon their own experiences and those of family members. Then they were asked to use higher level cognitive skills to compare and contrast these experiences. Using the experience of education as a focus for the unit was inclusive. This was a universal theme that all students had experienced. Even the recently arrived student could participate in the lessons.

Students reflected on the need to adapt to achieve success in the new culture. However, the emphasis on cultural adaptation as problem solving helped the children realize that there are ways to adapt without losing one's identity. The assignment to write a letter of advice to a newly arrived immigrant child reaffirmed the classroom values of community and support. The students were able to use their expertise to help others and be valued members of the classroom.

The unit also provided avenues of information for the teacher about the students' culture. Through the lessons about education, teachers can learn about the past educational experiences of their students. Teachers can become aware of differences that can affect students' attitudes and adjustments as they transition from one culture to another. By comparing different systems in nonjudgmental ways, the lessons serve to inform educators about the lives of their students.

PART II: CULTURAL VARIABLES

Cultural variables are many and change constantly. Because these variables are dominated by context, relevant research is presented as reflected by the various filters that influence students, such as family, school, peers, and media. These filters influence individual students to different degrees. In the case of Edison, the new arrival in Angela's class, analysis of the cultural contrasts between his school experience and the characteristics of U.S. schools facilitated his first encounter with school.

Families

Families nurture cultural values of their own ethnic group and country of origin. Many homes are cross-cultural due to the influences of generations and complexity of ethnic heritage. In the U.S., families of different cultural backgrounds encounter cultural conflicts in their relationships with their children, the schools, and their children's peers. As A. Portes (1995) explained it:

> Growing up in an immigrant family has always been a difficult process of reconciling the language and cultural orientations of foreign-born parents with the demands of assimilation of the host society. In the American experience, the process has traditional been portrayed as a seldom-resolved series of familial and social-psychological tensions which culminate either in a rejection of the parental culture or a retreat from confrontation with outside society. Those children of immigrants who are able to move successfully between the two worlds represent a minority. (p. 248)

Conflict between parents and children are generational as well as cultural. Recent arrivals and fluent bilinguals report little conflict with parents and high levels of family cohesion. On the other hand, embracing cultural norms of the host society and heritage language loss are sources of conflict. Children often are in closer contact to the American culture through school and interaction with peers whereas parents may remain culturally isolated. Parents disapprove of children adopting American cultural norms and children, in turn, feel embarrassed by parents (A. Portes & Rumbaut, 2001; Scheinfeld, 1993).

The one trait of the American culture that many families isolate and encourage their children to pursue is academic success. These families realize the value of education to achieve economic and social mobility. But sometimes parents exercise excessive pressure. One Chinese-American student declared, "They think you're a robot ... that they can set up a program and you will go to school and get good grades. College. Become a doctor. Maybe a lawyer ... this is America, and if they want to be Chinese parents, why come to America?" (Siu, 1992, p. 29).

Many factors play a role in immigrant family life including cultural characteristics of parents, knowledge of American culture by parents, acceptance of cultural traditions by children, and language preferences of children. "It is not acculturation per se but the form that it takes that leads to different degrees of estrangement between immigrants and their children" (A. Portes & Rumbaut, 2001).

Relationships between families and schools are very important for the well-being and academic success of children. Often conflicts catch children in the middle. School communication and relation with families, parent participation in education, and childrearing beliefs can be sources of conflict because both school and families' cultures differ on how these tasks should be carried out.

In addition to language barriers, the form of the contact leads to miscommunication between school and parents. Complicated notices or forms sent by schools often cause problems, making parents feel inadequate. A call from a teacher may be interpreted as a child's misbehavior in school, resulting in severe punishment for that child. Trumbull, Rothstein-Fisch, Greenfield, & Quiroz (2001) reported a mother sending a message to school with an older sibling about the younger child's sickness. The school regarded the message as inappropriate notification, which the parent interpreted as the school's lack of concern. Miscommunication arises when a student is perceived as an individual rather than as a member of a family. Teachers' conversations with students or parents tend to focus only on the student. Parents often prefer to deal with the whole family, making the interactions confusing (Trumbull et al., 2001). A teacher, sensitive to this sense of family as a unit, asked children about the health and well-being of family members as she returned homework (Cazden, Carrasco, Maldonado-Guzman, & Erickson, 1980).

Most parents value their children's education regardless of their socioeconomic background (Nieto, 2000). Immigrant parents often cite better educational opportunities for their children as their primary motivation for immigrating to the United States. Parents of different cultures, however, differ in their school participation. American schools expect parents to do volunteer work and to participate in school governance and other activities. In many cultures, parents are expected to leave the children at the door of the school in the trusted care of their teachers. Parents see their role as supporting and monitoring their children at home by making sure they do their homework and instilling in them a sense of duty to the family to do well in school (Nieto, 2000; Siu, 1992; Trumbull et al., 2001). Often older siblings are responsible for ensuring that homework is done. Even when parents are willing to participate in school, language barriers and the nature of interactions in school activities often inhibit their participation.

Often students feel torn between the pressures of families and peers. Second-generation Haitian students agonize between maintaining their Haitian cultural values and conforming to those of African Americans in the Miami ghetto. Parents understand the social situation of African Americans in the United States and realize that if their children meld into their social milieu they may forgo their "dreams of making it in America" (A. Portes, 1995b, p. 249).

School

Youngsters encounter the main values of society in schools. School culture determines curriculum content, assumptions about background knowledge, learning philosophies, teaching approaches, classroom interactions, and management and school routines. Cultural differences between school and students can cause conflict, affect student performance, and color relations with families. In schools, students are influenced by peers who often reinforce societal and school values, occasionally agree with ethnic family values, and at other times impose their own beliefs, which are counter to those of family and school.

Decisions on school *curriculum content* are based on what society considers necessary and valuable to learn. Mathematics and English literacy presently are top priorities in curricular content. Great emphasis is put on teaching and assessing these two content areas. Science also holds a special high status in schools. However, foreign languages are considered marginal. The perspectives presented reflect the beliefs of the dominant group in society (Cummins, 2000). History lessons often include the United States from the perspective of the 13 colonies, England, Western Europe, and ancient Greece and Rome. Reading fictional literature and developing creative writing occupy a great part of the day in many elementary schools.

Other cultures have different views with respect to what is important to teach. For example:

> Vietnamese parents do not always encourage their children, especially adolescents, to read fiction. They want to maintain some control over the ideological influence of novels, which, for many parents, are considered pervasive with unbridled expressions of passion, vivid and wild imagination against traditions. (Dien, 1998, p. 148)

A fifth-grade teacher of Chinese background taught English literacy through social studies, science, and other content areas. According to her reading fictional literature was a waste of time.

When teachers introduce a topic, they usually make assumptions as to students' *background knowledge* (Igoa, 1995). When students have a very different or limited knowledge on the topic from that expected from American students, curriculum content becomes difficult to comprehend. For example, discussions on the American Civil War often assume knowledge of the tradition of slavery and the social differences between the North and the South.

Ballard and Clanchy (1991) suggested that there are "culturally divergent attitudes to knowledge" (p. 21) that define *teaching and learning philosophies.* Some cultures equate knowledge with wisdom handed down from teachers to students. The duty of the teacher is to impart this knowledge well and that of students is to learn by listening carefully to the teacher without questioning (Trumbull et al., 2001). Such students fail to see the value of working in student groups discussing a topic.

North Americans tend to view students as independent learners, who must learn how to analyze, question, and evaluate material presented in class. While in many Latin America cultures, for example, a teacher introduces a lesson by writing extended text on the board. The students copy it in order to memorize it and later are asked to recite it to prove that they have learned. In the United States, the teacher may write on the board the central topic of the lesson and elicit a discussion among students to discover their knowledge and views on the subject. Later they read books, search the Internet, and work collaboratively to explore the topic and write a synthesis reflecting what they have learned and their own opinion on the subject.

Children are socialized by their parents and communities *to ways of communicating* and relating to others. Cultures differ in their assumptions of proper ways to use language, engage in written discourse, and relate to adults. Ways of interacting and using language, as well as disciplining and motivating students vary from culture to culture (Conklin & Lourie, 1983; Saravia-Shore & Arvizu, 1992). Cultures differ in the verbal and nonverbal behavior of interactions. Of significance in school situations are the rules of communication between adults and children. The ways children are supposed to address an adult differs among cultures. Looking directly at an adult can be interpreted as paying attention or disrespecting, depending on the culture. In some cultures, adults ask many questions of children as a strategy for teaching them, assessing their knowledge, and making them think. In other cultural groups adults ask questions only when they do not know the answer (Conklin & Lourie, 1983). In the typical American classroom, where teachers constantly question students mostly for the purpose of evaluating, children of other cultures may become confused as to the intent of the teacher when asking questions for which she has the answer (Heath, 1983). In nonindividualistic cultures, students may find individual questions embarrassing. Teachers may interpret their lack of response as limited intelligence or knowledge (Jones, 1988).

Different cultures produce contrasting discourse and text structures. In mainstream American culture, speeches are an opportunity to present the speaker's point of view and persuade the audience. Among Native Americans, such a structure would be considered dishonest. Speakers are supposed to present facts in order to allow the audience to reach conclusions (Conklin, 1983). Text organization also differs among cultures. Stories, letters, academic papers, and newspaper editorials follow specific rules of content and organization in different cultures.[1] For example, in Latin America a business letter starts with a salutation of respect whereas in the United States it goes directly to the business at hand.

A teacher's "*classroom management* and instructional practices are tied to her own socialization experiences" (Gutiérrez, Larson, & Freuter, 1995, p. 415). Students often misread the signals given by teachers because strategies for classroom management are very different in other cultures (Ballenger, 1992). American teachers may seem rude to some students while too unpersuasive to others. Unfamiliar disciplinary strategies often defeat the purpose of making students behave. They can affect the relationship between teachers and students. Latin American students find American teachers' commands too direct and rather rude. They interpret them as evidence of personal dislike. This erodes the relationship with the teacher and students' willingness to perform well.

Praising students to raise self-esteem, a typical American teacher strategy, is often misunderstood by parents. They believe that praising one student puts down the others. In parent–teacher conferences some parents get impatient and they want to know the needs of their children (Trumbull et al., 2001). A Chinese teacher once declared that when she praised students she switched to English because did not know such words in Chinese.

School routines such as schedules, organization of the day, and classroom etiquette differ among cultures. Immigrant students find differences in recess, length of days, snack time, informality of the start of the day, and calling the teacher by name rather than title (Clayton, 1993). Igoa (1995) reported on a group of Samoan newcomers. When the students entered the class they expressed their dislike for desks and proceeded to sit on the floor. She brought a rug the following day for their use.

---

[1]See Grabe and Kaplan (1989) for a synthesis on the theory and practical implication of this topic.

In Pakistan, students are required to stand up when responding to a teacher. In an American classroom this would be considered unnecessary and, even disruptive behavior. Edison, on his first day, stood up whenever Angela addressed him. Angela added the behavior in the Venn diagram of school differences they were creating as she explained to him the accepted behavior in an American classroom.

In many countries, especially at the high school levels, students attend same-gender schools. Being with students of the other gender may feel awkward. For example, in one class when Somalian students were directed to work in groups, the girls would not allow a boy in their group unless he was a group member's brother.

Peers

It is in school settings that immigrant youths come most directly in contact with their native peers—as role models or close friends, as distant members of exclusionary cliques, and as sources of discrimination or peer acceptance (A. Portes & Rumbaut, 2001).

New students initially experience culture shock because cultural beliefs, systems of communications, and identities are disrupted when uprooting from native cultures. "Anxiety results from losing all familiar signs and symbols of social intercourse" (Igoa, 1995, p. 39). Peers can play an important role in helping immigrant students adjust to the new environment. As we saw in Angela's class, at the teacher's prompting, students wrote a welcoming letter to a recent arrival with comforting words of advice: "Don't worry if you're shy, everybody here is shy. Be friends with everybody because nobody likes mean people."

Peers can have a positive impact with respect to language, culture, and academic achievement. They can help students develop a positive cultural identity and sense of belonging. Peers' expectations that newcomers can learn English have a strong impact on learning (Fillmore, 1979). Peers can strengthen students' culture by getting them involved in activities that reaffirm their heritage (A. Portes & Rumbaut, 2001). Educational aspirations of peers are a powerful influence on students. Students, in schools that create a culture of getting ahead, often have aspirations for further education.

Fear of discrimination and rejection leads students to succumb to negative peer pressures. Peers often pressure language-minority students to abandon their heritage language and culture. Immigrant students act against their inner wishes to maintain their language and culture in favor of being accepted and feeling that they belong (Fillmore, 1991; Igoa, 1995). In some cases, immigrant students assimilate to minority communities, as is the case with Haitians in Miami. These students adopt the linguistic and cultural norms of the African-American community. Filipinos in the West Coast often abandon Tagalog in favor of Spanish (A. Portes, 1995b).

Show of power is one route taken toward acceptance. Demonstration of power in front of peers can make students, especially teenagers, defiant. Body tattoos, particular attire, hairdos, and other measures are admired by their peers but usually abhorred by adults. A. Portes (1995b) claimed that students who understand mainstream values are capable of changing their appearance when the social context calls for it. They will dress and act to mainstream cultural norms when interviewing for a job or visiting a prospective college. Students whose cultural capital does not include mainstream norms do not understand that behaviors that gave them power around their peers are detrimental in other circumstances. These students can be just as capable of attending the college or performing the job, but they do not know how to act the part.

Minority students can negatively influence each other by devaluing academic achievement, because doing well in school is the "white" thing to do. Rejecting pressures to succeed academically often results in social advancement. Children of immigrants who avoid the pressures of peers and disregard their subsequent rejection manage to succeed in school. By holding on to their ethnic identity they adhere to the strong parental expectations for advancement. They some times even outperform the native White students (A. Portes, 1995b).

In an environment that does not accept cultural diversity, students find themselves needing to choose. "One is either true to oneself and family or one is an American" (Nieto, 2000, p. 335). Students who choose to be bicultural are often pressured or rejected by both groups. For example, a Korean girl was raised in a White neighborhood but her parents insisted she marry a Korean. Her peers called her "Twinkie," yellow on the outside and white on the inside. African Americans considered a Dominican boy not black enough whereas Hispanics saw him as too dark (A. Portes & Rumbaut, 2001).

Peers frighten immigrant students by their behavior and by making them feel unsafe. The presence of gangs, sale of drugs, and fights between racial-ethnic groups create a disruptive school climate that gets in the way of learning (A. Portes & Rumbaut, 2001). School safety is especially important for high school students. When a group of bilingual teachers moved their program from a large urban high school to a community college, the students mentioned feeling safe as the number one improvement of their program (Brisk, 1996).

Peers are a powerful influence on language-minority students in the period of adaptation and in their search for belonging and for defining their cultural identity. Positive or negative influences, to a degree, are fostered by the cultural climate created in the schools.

Media

Media are powerful sources of learning. Students acquire this knowledge directly or through their peers. The media reflect the values and attitudes of the society at large: "Media do influence intergroup, intragroup, and self-perceptions, as well as thinking about other aspects of diversity. Consumers do learn about race, ethnicity, gender, religions, and other dimensions of diversity from both nonfiction and entertainment media" (Cortes, 2000, p. 76).

Educators working with diverse populations need to take the message in the media seriously because "mass media educate more people about issues regarding ethnicity and race than all other sources of education available to U.S. citizens" (Bartolome & Macedo, 1997, p. 223).

Among the most influential forms of media is television. Television influences stereotypes of different groups by the way they are portrayed. For example, in a survey of 30 years of television, Latinos were most likely to be portrayed as lawbreakers and Asians as weak victims. Interracial contact among television characters was more likely to occur in job situations than in social situations. Only some children's television programs discuss race openly (Cortes, 2000).

Advertisements and pictures of models and teen idols greatly influence how teenagers aspire to look and dress. Schools are presently imposing dress codes for girls. Inappropriate dress concerns school authorities and parents.

Media can also alter perceptions of the society. Some books and films attempt to break traditional stereotypes. For example, the movie *Saving Private Ryan* altered views of war, showing the painful and cruel side of it (Cortes, 2000).

Presently, the Internet is another rich source of information. Because of its international reach, cyberspace can provide a more multicultural perspective. Internet communication opens the way to the use of different languages and explorations of a variety of cultures (Cummins & Sayers, 1995).

Suggestions for Additional Reading

- Igoa, C. (1995). *The inner world of the immigrant child.* Mahwah, NJ: Lawrence Erlbaum Associates.
- Trumbull, E., Rothstein-Fisch, C., Greenfield, P. M., & Quiroz, B. (2001). *Bridging cultures between home and school: A guide for teachers.* Mahwah, NJ: Lawrence Erlbaum Associates.

PART III: DOING ANALYSIS
OF THE CULTURAL CONTEXT

There are multiple possibilities for exploring cultural variables and contrasts. Because school is a major encounter with American culture for minority and immigrant students, cultural contrasts as reflected in schooling are helpful to explore. Teachers can use this lesson as a template to study other cultural variables.

Cultural Lesson 1: Selected Cultural Differences
Between U.S. and Heritage Country Schools

Objective: Students will be able to compare and contrast the cultural differences between their heritage country and U.S. schools with respect to:

- Curriculum content and expected background knowledge.
- Philosophy of teaching and learning.
- Communication and discipline.
- Structural differences in schools.
- Parental participation in education.

They need to understand these differences in order to value both their heritage and US cultures. Students will understand how differences between these cultures can create difficulties and conflicts in school.

Rationale: Schools are the major American institution that children of other cultures encounter. Schools reflect mainstream American cultural values, often in sharp contrast to those shared by many students' families. Curriculum content, assumed knowledge, rules of communication, classroom management techniques, daily routines, and expectations of parent participation can be sources of miscommunication and conflict and, even, great embarrassment. Problems arise because students may not be aware of these differences and consequently do not understand the source of conflict. Teachers and peers, representing mainstream America, may also believe that their values are the norm. They consider the behavior of children from other cultures deviant. This lack of awareness impairs relationships between students of other cultures and teachers and peers. It can also affect student performance. Some students may rebel, exacerbating already poor communication.

Understanding the new culture as something different, not necessarily better, helps students learn how to function in the American society. It is important to address these cultural differences, even if students have done all their schooling in the United States. Family values will reflect the heritage culture and can contribute to cultural conflicts with schools. These students need to involve their families as informants of the heritage country experience to understand the cultural differences.

Time: Four to 5 days (60–90 minutes per day)

Materials:

- Books that address cultural differences: (a) *El Chino* by Allan Say (available in English and Spanish) will assist in generating a general discussion on cultural difference, conflict, and communication; (b) *My Name Is Maria Isabel* by Alma Flor Ada (available in English and Spanish) provides a meaningful way of examining several cultural differences in school communication and discipline; and (c) see annotated bibliography (Appendix A) for additional literature.
- Additional books for primary: *Baseball Saved Us, The Always Prayer Shawl, El Chino, Tea and Milk, Tree of Cranes, How My Parents Learn to Eat,*

Dumpling Soup, An Ellis Island Christmas, American Too, Faraway Home, The Folks in the Valley; A Pennsylvania Dutch ABC, The Bracelet, Friends From the Other Side, Gold Dust, How My Family Lives in America, I Hate English, I Speak English for My Mom, Journey Home, Molly's Pilgrim, So Far From the Sea, Watch the Stars Come Out, Where Did Your Family Come From?, I Was Dreaming to Come to America: Memories From the Ellis Island Oral History Project.

- Additional books for secondary: *Autobiography of a Chinese Woman, Buwei Yang Chao, Becoming a Citizen: Adopting a New Home, Inside Separate Worlds: Life Stories of Young Black, Jews and Latinos, Rain of Gold, Sadako and the Thousand Cranes, Samurai and Silk: A Japanese and American Heritage, The Far East Comes Near: Autobiographical Accounts of Southeast Asian Students in America, The Joy Luck Club, The Woman Who Outshone the Sun, Taida Umeko and Women's Education in Japan, Turning Japanese: Memoirs of a Sansei, When I Was Puerto Rican.*
- Student journals.
- U.S./Heritage Country Venn Diagram (Appendix B).
- Comparing/Contrasting Schools in United States and Heritage Country (Worksheet 5.1).
- Parental Participation Survey (Worksheet 5.2).
- Textbook Survey (Worksheet 5.3).
- School Discipline Survey (Worksheet 5.4).
- Chart paper.

Overview of Activities

- Definition of culture.
- Cultural differences and conflict: Discussion of the book *El Chino.*
- Discussion of the book *My Name Is Maria Isabel.*
- Schools in the United States and the heritage country.
- Similarities and differences between the U.S. and heritage country's schools.
- Advice for newcomers.
- Summary and reflection.

Definition of Culture

1. Create a semantic map for the concept of culture. Write on chart paper the word *culture* and ask students to define what it means. Write students' responses and categorize them.
2. Discuss the results and probe students for additional ideas.

3. Keep the map in view during this whole lesson to add new things that emerge from the lesson.

Cultural Differences and Conflict: Discussion of the Book El Chino

1. Write the title of the book *El Chino* (or your own selection) and the author on chart paper. Show the book cover to the class, and ask students to predict what the story will be about. Write the students' responses on chart paper. For example, students may infer that the main character is a Chinese man who is dressed in a silk matador outfit.
2. Read the story aloud. Consider pausing at certain instances in the story to probe students' understanding and relation to their own experiences. At the conclusion of the read-aloud, ask students to share their reactions to the story. It is important to mention adjustment to cultural differences, self-empowerment and determination, and valuing and embracing two cultures.
3. Ask students to respond in their journals to the following prompts:
   • What difficulties did the main character experience in fulfilling his dream to become a bullfighter?
   • How was he able to overcome these obstacles and gain acceptance?
   • What lesson did you learn about valuing our own culture while adapting to the new culture?
   Suggest that the students describe their reactions to the story using examples from the book. They should explain how the story relates to their experiences or to those of someone they know.
4. Share responses to *El Chino*. Have students read aloud their journal responses to the class. Ask the class for their reactions after each individual reads. Compare essays to the content of the book. This activity takes time because each student gets a turn. The discussion is essential for examining the issues relevant to the objective of this lesson.
   Alternative: If the class is very large, select a group of students to share with the whole class. Choose students who cover different important topics related to cultural differences and coping with cultural conflict.

Discussion of the Book My Name Is Maria Isabel

1. Prior to reading the book aloud, write the title of the book and the author on chart paper. Show the book cover to the class and ask the students to predict what the story will be about. Write students' responses on chart paper. For example, students may infer that the main character is a Spanish girl in school and that the teacher is watching her from behind.

2. Read the story aloud. Pause occasionally to probe students' understanding. Encourage them to relate the story to their own experiences. At the conclusion of the read aloud ask students to share their reactions to the story. Some of the points that are important to raise are: differences between U.S. and heritage country's school systems, communication between teacher and students, and classroom participation.

3. Ask students to respond in their journals to the following prompts:
   • Maria Isabel had difficulties adjusting to being called Mary Lopez. Why do you think the teacher was not aware of the effect the name change was having on Maria Isabel?
   • Why do you think Maria Isabel wrote a composition to communicate her desire to recover her real name?
   • What lesson did the teacher and Maria Isabel's classmates learn about the value of cultural pride?

   Suggest that the students describe their reactions to the story using examples from the book. They should explain how the story relates to their experiences or to those of someone they know.

4. Share responses to *My Name Is Maria Isabel.* Have students read aloud their journal responses to the class. Ask the class for their reactions after each individual reads. Compare essays to the content of the book. This activity takes time because each student gets a turn. The discussion is essential for teasing out the issues relevant to the objective of this lesson.

   Alternative: If the class is very large, select a group of students to share with the whole class. Choose students who cover different important topics related to cultural differences and to coping with cultural conflict.

Schools in the United States and the Heritage Country

1. Survey the students by asking how many were born in the United States or in their heritage country. Write their responses on chart paper.
2. Display a large compare/contrast chart on blackboard (see Worksheet 5.1).
3. Provide students with the worksheet titled *Comparing/Contrasting Schools in United States and Heritage Country* (Worksheet 5.1) and review the following categories:
   • Subjects taught.
   • Course requirements for each grade.
   • Promotion policy.
   • Teacher teaching styles.
   • School and classroom routines.
   • Discipline codes.
   Note: If students raise additional issues, add categories to the compare/contrast chart and worksheets.

4. Initiate a whole-group discussion using some of the following questions:
   - What are some of the course requirements for each grade?
   - What are students expected to know?
   - Which subjects are difficult/easier?
   - What is the promotion policy?
   - How does the teacher teach?
   - What does the teacher do when students misbehave or do not bring their homework?
   - What are some of the classroom routines?
5. Have students complete the information for each of the categories by comparing and contrasting with the schools in the United States and in their heritage country.
6. For homework, have students complete the compare/contrast worksheets. Encourage those students who have not attended school in their heritage country to ask their parents for assistance.

Similarities and Differences Between the U.S. and Heritage Country's Schools

1. Display a large Venn diagram on the board.
2. Pair students and ask them to share their completed *Compare/Contrast Worksheets* from the previous homework assignment.
3. Initiate a discussion by having students write information on the large Venn diagram, comparing and contrasting school systems.
4. Review with students the completed diagram and reflect on what they learned. Some important issues that may be pointed out are:
   - Difficulties in adapting to school routines and teaching styles.
   - Student expectations and acceptance in a new setting.
   - Difficulties in subject content.
   - Difficulties with student social interaction.
   - Difficulties with code of discipline.

Advice for Newcomers

1. Have students reflect, in writing, to the following prompts (this could also be assigned as homework):
   - What advice would you give new students in your school?
   - How would you assist them in avoiding difficulties or conflicts in the new school environment?
2. Ask students to share their reflective writing on the advice they would give new students in their class. Write on chart paper students' responses to facilitate further discussion. For example, recommendations may include some of the following:

- Rely on peer assistance.
- Get to know everyone in class.
- Be responsible and try to do your best to adapt to new environment.
- Share your heritage country with class.
- Value, respect, and embrace diverse cultures.
- Observe how others behave, and which behaviors are rewarded or punished.
3. Have students write a friendly letter welcoming a new student to their class. Have new students write to their peers. (These could be homework assignments.)

Summary and Reflection

Have students reflect, in writing, on to the following prompt: Have the school differences between the United States and your heritage country caused you embarrassment or problems?

Possible Additional Activities

Note: Many of the differences between U.S. and heritage country schools can emerge from the discussion around the preceding activities. If some of the objectives have not been included or you want to go into more detail, the following activities are suggested:
- Survey on parental participation in school.
- Survey on topics in textbooks in the United States and heritage country.
- Survey on school discipline across cultures.

Survey on Parental Participation in School

1. Ask students to conduct a survey to help the school find ways to improve parental participation.
2. Have students design a parental participation survey form by generating a list of questions (see Worksheet 5.2). The following questions may be included:
   - How often do you visit the school?
   - Do you attend school meetings?
   - Do you attend teacher/parent open houses? If you are not able to attend, does the teacher provide alternative meeting times or call the home?
   - Do you assist your children with their homework?
   - What school activities have you participated in?
   - Does your child's school have parent centers?
   - What types of special programs should the parent centers offer?
   - How does the school keep you informed of school events?
   - Are notices sent home in English and the heritage language?
   - Are you satisfied with the manner in which the school engages parents? If not, what recommendations would you make to the school?

3. Distribute the *Parental Participation Survey.*
4. Have students conduct the survey, tabulate the results, and write a summary of their findings.
5. Discuss the survey results. The following guided questions are suggested:
   - How do parents view their participation in school?
   - What factors affect parents' lack of participation?
   - What suggestions were made for improving parental participation?
   - Do parents feel comfortable with the manner in which schools organize parental participation?
   - Do you think parent participation in school is important? Why?
6. Have students provide results of the survey to the school principal and parent council.

Survey on Topics in Textbooks in the United States and Heritage Country

1. Select books in various content areas from the United States and heritage countries. Secure assistance from librarians, parents, community agencies, and/or local consulates to obtain books from the heritage country.
2. Tell students that they will be conducting an investigation to find out what topics are covered in textbooks in the United States. These will be contrasted with those from the heritage country.
3. Design a textbook survey form by generating a list of the following questions:
   - What is the subject of the textbook?
   - How is the book organized?
   - What topics are covered in each unit?
   - How are the topics similar and different?
4. Distribute the *Textbook Survey* (Worksheet 5.3).
5. Have students work in teams. Each team could work with books in a different content area.
6. Have students discuss the survey results. The following guided questions are suggested:
   - What topics were included?
   - What topics were similar or different?
7. Have students reflect in writing to the following prompt: What were the major differences between the topics covered in textbooks in the United States and in your heritage country? What topics were new or difficult to you?

Survey on School Discipline Across Cultures

1. Ask students to conduct a survey in their school and/or home on the subject of school discipline.
2. Have students design a school discipline survey form by generating a list of questions. The following questions may be included:

- What is the code of discipline for your school?
- How do teachers structure their classroom discipline?
- How are the rules established in the classroom?
- What are the major classroom rules?
- What happens if a student does not follow the rules?
- Which style of disciplining is stricter or more lenient? Why?
- Are there any differences between discipline policies in the United States and in the heritage country? Why or why not?
- How does students' behavior affect the relationship between the teacher and the students?

3. Distribute the *School Discipline Survey* (Worksheet 5.4).
4. Have students work on the survey either individually or in teams by interviewing teachers and their families. Students conduct the survey, tabulate the results, and write a summary of their findings.
5. Have students discuss the survey results and reasons given by those polled. The following guided questions are suggested:
   - What were the major differences between classroom discipline in United States and in the heritage country.
   - What were the major differences between teachers' styles of discipline?
   - Were there any surprises in the results?
6. Have students reflect in writing responding to the following prompt: Have you or somebody you know ever been confused or embarrassed when disciplined? Tell us about it.

Outcomes

These activities are geared to achieve the outcomes listed in fig. 5.1. The teacher will keep a record for each student using the rubric in Fig. 5.1 as a guideline.

	1	2	3	4
Concepts Students understand (check the level for each concept): • What are considered important things to know in a particular culture. • What is considered good teaching and learning. • How students and teachers communicate in a classroom. • How teachers and families discipline children. • How school structure the day and activities. • How parents relate to the school.				
Relationships: Students understand the relationship between culture and adjustment to school, the perceptions people of different cultures have of each other, and how people of different cultures get along.				
Connection to self: • How cultural differences affect their performance in school.				

Key (for further explanation, see Appendix C)
Each concept, relationship, and connection to self covered in the lessons can be graded with respect to the following levels of understanding:
1. Misguided notion or no recognition.
2. Passive understanding.
3. Expresses some understanding of concept or relationship.
4. Expresses full understanding of concept or relationship.

Proposing a Solution	1	2	3

Key
Solutions proposed can be noted with respect to whether student:
1. Does not propose a solution.
2. Engages in a solution proposed by the teacher.
3. Proposes a solution.

FIG. 5.1   Cultural context rubric, Lesson 1.

Worksheet 5.1. Comparing/Contrasting Schools in the United Sates and Heritage Country.

List the similarities and differences between schooling in the United States and your country of origin.

School in U.S.   **Schools in My Country**

Subjects Taught

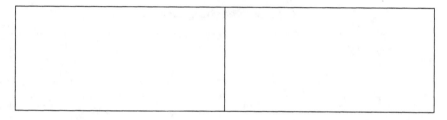

Course Requirements for Each Grade

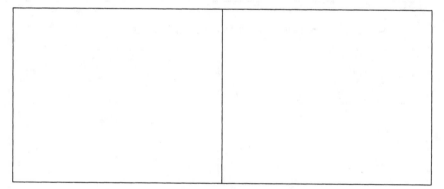

The Contnets of Math, Science, Social Studies

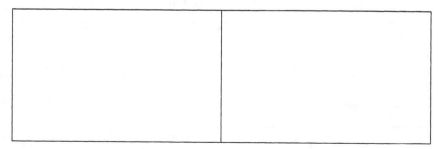

Promotion Policy

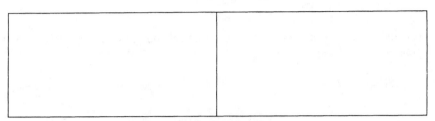

Teacher Teaching Styles

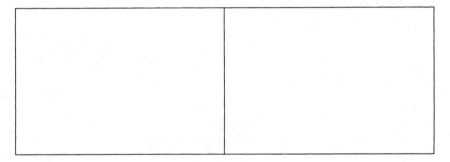

School and Classroom Routines

Codes of Discipline

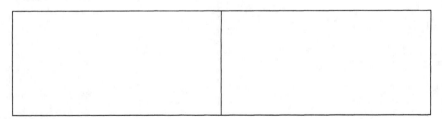

Worksheet 5.2. *Sample Parental Participation in School Survey*

- How often do you visit the school?

- Do you attend school meetings?

- Do you attend teacher/parent open houses? If you are not able to attend, does the teacher provide an alternative meeting time or call the home?

- Do you assist your child with their homework?

- What school activities have you participated in?

- Does your child's school have parent centers?

- What types of special programs should the parent centers offer?

- How does the school keep you informed of school events?

- Are notices sent home in English and the heritage language?

- Are you satisfied with the manner in which the school engages parental involvement? If not, what recommendations would you make to the school?

Worksheet 5.3. *Sample Textbook Survey*

- What is the subject of the textbook? _____

United States Textbook   **Heritage Country Textbook**

- How is the book organized?

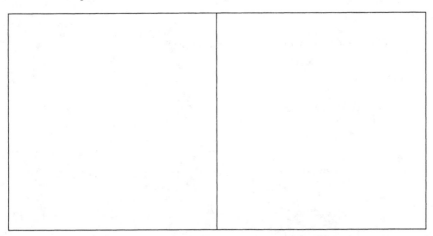

- What topics are covered in each chapter unit?

- How are the topics similar and different?

Worksheet 5.4. *School Discipline Survey*

United States   **Heritage Country**

- What is the code of discipline for the school?

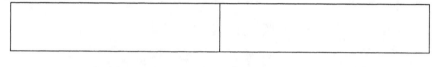

- How do teachers structure their classroom discipline?

- How are the rules established in the classroom?

- What are the major classroom rules?

- What happens if a student does not follow the rules?

- Are there any differences between students' behavior in the United States and in the heritage country? Why or why not?

- Which style of disciplining is stricter or more lenient? Why?

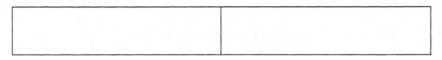

- How does students' behavior affect the relationship between the teacher and the students?

6

Political Context

OVERVIEW

Language policy in the United States has been one of *laissez faire*. Consequently, use of languages in education is vulnerable to political swings. Since the founding of this nation the choice of languages for education has changed due to different political, economic, and social pressures. Language policies are influenced by political relations between the United States and countries that represent those languages, by views toward immigration and the rights of language-minority populations, and by beliefs about the relationship between the language of the people and national unity.

Angela's students struggled through the political unit. Children's literature and connections with personal experiences engaged the students in exploring political factors.

This chapter explores the following political variables:

- Language use in education.
- Incorporation of cultural perspectives in the curriculum.
- Accountability.
- Government policies toward immigrants and language-minority groups.
- Language and political unity.

Political factors greatly affect the adults surrounding students. Families' welfare often depends on government's treatment of immigrants. Government policies color societal attitudes toward specific ethnic groups. Educational policies sometimes support what research says are best practices for bilingual learners. Often these policies directly oppose such research evidence. Bilingual students may misinterpret these ideological battles as personally directed at them. These students feel disenfranchised from the educational system. Careful investigation of the historical and political roots of attitudes and ideology helps students understand their depersonalized nature. Two lesson plans outlined in the last section of this chapter can help students explore some of the political variables, such as:

151

- Language diversity and political unity.
- Government policies toward immigrant and language minorities.

PART I: CLASSROOM IMPLEMENTATION

Angela implemented one more unit before the end of the year. The objective of the political unit on *Foreign Relations and Treatment of Immigrant* is as follows:

> Students will be able to explain the political relationships between the United States and their places of origin (or of their families' origin) and how those relationships affect the treatment of people coming from those countries to the United States.

It is the end of the school year and the students have developed academically. Yet, the political unit is complex and deals with abstract concepts. It is a challenge for Angela to explain the topics of the lessons in comprehensible language for the students. She wants to address the issues surrounding foreign policy, negotiating, treaties, and political alliances with the students. While planning the unit, she is unsure how to introduce the topic of foreign policy until she realizes that the daily newspaper is a good place to start.

Day One

It is 9:00 a.m. on a morning in mid-May; Angela puts a political world map up on the chalkboard. Veronica helps her. Christopher and José bring in stacks of *The Boston Herald.*
   "*Saquen su libro de estudios sociales.* Take out your social studies book. We need to find a political map. Go to page okay, *vayan* a 526." She says to the class, "Look on the map for your family's country of origin. Bernarda, can you point to yours?" Bernarda points to the Dominican Republic. "How many people from the Dominican Republic are represented in this classroom." She counts the raised hands. "Six people. Who is from Puerto Rico? *Tú también? Cuatro de Puerto Rico.* Who can come up and point to this?"
   Jaime comes up to the political map on the board and points to Puerto Rico. While he does this, Angela draws a table on the board. In one column she writes "country" and in the other "number of students represented".
   "*¿Qué otros paises están representados en el salón? Edison y Joanna son de Colombia. Vengan a mostrarnos.*" [What other countries are represented in this classroom? Edison and Joanna are from Colombia. Come and show us.] Edison walks up to the map and points out Colombia. Angela asks, "*¿De Guatemala son dos?*" [From Guatemala are two?] Next to Dominican Republic, she writes 6. Next to Puerto Rico 5, and Colombia 2. Jenny goes to board and points to Guatemala.
   Angela ensures that she includes all the students, "*Carmen enséñanos de donde eres.*" [Carmen, show us where you are from.] Carmen walks up and points to El

Salvador. *"¿Y José? Honduras."* He also points out his country on the map. "Did we cover everybody?" Angela continues, "You are probably asking yourselves why are we doing this?"

To make students understand about relations between countries, she starts with personal reactions. "You as kids have a special relationship with each other. You are friends. What are some of the things that you share as friends?"

José says, "Trust. Secrets."

"Yes. What else? It is like a policy. What is your policy about being friends? What would you accept? What wouldn't you accept? As friends, what is your policy about friendship?"

William contributes, "If one of us gets in trouble the rest of us help him. We protect each other."

"Good." She writes on board. "If classmates get in trouble- protect each other." Turning to the class she asks, "What does 'foreign policy' mean?"

Sandra says, "From other countries."

"What does foreign mean? From other places. Last week we studied about the three branches of government. Who is in charge of the executive?" The room is quiet as the students try to remember.

"The president," Sandra answers.

The president. Remember last week, we talked about the problem with China. What about the relationship between the U.S. and other countries? What about the U.S. and England, are they friends?" The students nod their heads. "Yeah... The U.S. and Honduras?" The students look quizzical and don't answer. "The U.S. and Cuba?" The students shake their heads. Angela continues, "Right now what is the relationship between the U.S. and Japan? Do you know?"

The students are unsure and answer, "No."

"With China are they on good terms right now?" Angela asks. She turns to make a chart on the board. She lists the names of some countries and asks the students about their status with the United States. If the country is regarded as "on good terms" she puts a "Y" next to it. If the two countries are not on good terms, she puts an "N."

Angela turns back to face the class. She reminds them of an international incident that had just taken place. The United States had just bombed the Chinese embassy in Belgrade. "Last week we talked about why China is upset with the U.S. President Clinton has apologized five times for this error. The people of China refuse e to accept this because they cannot understand this atrocity. The embassy was bombed and people were killed. There is also tension between the U.S. and China over civil rights. Some people think that the Chinese do not protect the civil rights and we know how important those are. What are some of them?"

The students call out, "Speech, voting."

"Right. Foreign policy has to do with the agreements we make with other countries. These agreements we make have to do with trade and also with how people are treated. Why is trade important? It helps the economy of countries. When people start hearing about what happens in other countries, we get involved. What did you write about what you thought about whether China should accept the apology? What did the CIA say about the error?"

José answers, "That they used an old map."

"Will you accept that excuse?" asks Angela.

Christopher shakes his head and says, "They should know more."

"The people who are organizing the bombing should have new maps. Take out what you had written about this. Julia, do you want to read what you wrote?"

Julia reads from her journal, "I think China should forgive them. Because they made a mistake and everybody makes mistakes. The leaders should talk about it privately. China has also made mistakes."

Doris raises her hand to read, "I think that the soldiers who did the bombing should go in jail for one year. Then China will forgive them."

Angela says, "So you think some action should be taken. How else could they make it up to China? What else could they do?"

William says, "Give them money."

"That is interesting that you brought that up, William."

Angela continues, "What about Chinese people who live in the U.S.? How do they feel? Let's look at this article in the newspaper." She picks up *The Herald* and reads aloud. "Many demonstrated at the U.S. and British embassies in Beijing. China has harshly condemned NATO's campaign since it began." That is one example.

"Do any of you know of anything that happened in your country that was kept quiet by the United States?"

No one answers.

"Look at page 6 and 7 in the paper. Look at the picture there a woman holding a sign. These people are protesting here in the U.S. What is happening in other countries is affecting them. What is this telling you? What are these protesters doing? Do they think the U.S. is doing enough? They are saying that still more needs to be done. Why do you think it is important to talk about this? Because it affects how you are being treated here. If your country is in good relations with the U.S. it may affect your life."

She pauses. "What we are going to do now is I want you to choose one country to investigate. I have a worksheet to give you. You need to find out what is the relationship between that country and the U.S. What type of support is given? Does it involve trading? We'll hand these out later." This initial lesson has introduced to the student the importance of foreign policy.

Day Two

It is the second day of the political unit. Angela addresses the class, *"Busquen en los periódicos a ver si encuentran algo sobre* foreign policy. Look on page 6 at the top. National and International. *Estas son noticias nacionales y internacionales. ¿Qué esta pasando?"* [Look in the newspapers to see if you find something about foreign policy. Look on page 6 at the top. National and International. These are the national and international news. What is happening?]

Sandra says, "The UK."

"United Kingdom." Angela tapes a piece of poster paper on board and writes the names of countries as students list them. *"¿Cuáles son los paises y cuidades? Yugoslavia-Kosovo-Belgrade."* [What are the countries and cities? Yugoslavia, Kosovo, Belgrade.]

José says, "Israel."

William says, "Tokyo."

"¿Y dónde está Tokyo?" [Where is Tokyo?] Angela asks.

José answers, "China."

"Japan," Angela says. She writes. "What are the headlines? *¿Qué esta pasando?"* [What is happening?]

Victoria says, *"Los niños tienen hambre."* [The children are hungry.]

"Muchos de estos niños tienen la edad de Uds. ¿Qué está alrededor de ellos en la foto? Imaginanse Uds. no tienen nada que comer. ¿Donde están? Levantan la mano. En un refugio. Campamento. Están durmiendo en unas casitas en el campo." [Many of these children are the same age as you. What is around them in the photo? Imagine they have nothing to eat. Where are they? Raise your hand. They are in a refugee camp.] She writes next to Yugoslavia- "battling for food." "The headline is 'Belgrade ready to 'cut deal.' *¿Qué pasa cuando un país tiene todos los paises en contra? ¿Qué están destruyendo? Las fábricas, los puentes, estaciones militares. Es importante que Uds. entiendan que está pasando en el mundo y como les afecta a Uds."* [What happens when a country has many countries against them? What are they destroying? The factories, the bridges, the military stations. It is important that you understand what is happening in the world and how it affects you.]

The students are listening to Angela talk as they skim through the articles in *The Boston Herald* looking for news about other countries.

"Okay, lo que vamos a hacer es buscar en encyclopedia. ¿Qué país van a investigar?" [Okay, what we are going to do is look in the encyclopedias.] She calls on students and repeats the names of the countries they have chosen to research. *"Colombia? Canada? Grecia?* [Colombia, Canada. Greece.] Very good. We are going to do that for the rest of the time. Then we are going to use the internet too." She hands out a worksheet (see Worksheet 5.6) to help them organize their findings.

At this point, some of the students get up and move to the back of the room to use the computers to do a Web search. Angela gives another group the list of countries and instructs them to go downstairs to the library to search for books on those countries. The students quickly go to the section of books on different countries and find the appropriate books. They also take the corresponding encyclopedias in both Spanish and English. The books are outdated, and because they are geared toward elementary readers, they do not include much information on foreign policy. The encyclopedias are current and some articles have fairly detailed information on some of the foreign policies of the 1980s and early 1990s. The students go back upstairs with their information. The group at the computers is busy printing out information from Web sites. Angela allows them about 40 minutes to conduct individual research. Some students elect to work in pairs.

Intervening Week

Students worked individually or in pairs, during a whole week, researching their countries. They made posters with the information they found. Angela felt that they still did not understand that the status of relationships with other countries can affect their citizens or descendants living in the United States. To help the students she turned to children's literature.

On Monday Angela decided to introduce the story *The Bracelet* by Yoshiko Uchida, which relates to the Japanese-American experience during World War II. The book illustrates the feelings of a young girl, Emi, who is forced to leave her home because the government is sending Japanese-Americans to prison camps. Her best friend has given her a bracelet to remember her by. Emi soon realized that she didn't need objects to hold onto precious memories.

These fifth-grade students had little background knowledge about World War II. To provide more context for the story, Angela asked the students to look up World War II in the social studies textbook. There they saw an actual photograph of Japanese-American internment camps. This additional information made the connection between the historical fiction and real events. For homework the students read the textbook selection and answered comprehension questions.

Throughout the unit, Angela tied the concept of foreign policy to other literature the class had read. Students discussed the book *Mayfield Crossing* by Vaunda Micheaux Nelson, about African-American children in the 1960s. The story addresses the difficulties the children face when they need to change schools and illustrates the discrimination that members of ethnic- minority groups have faced throughout U.S. history. One student in Angela's class recommended the book *El Béisbol Me Salvó*, (*Baseball Saved Us*, by Ken Mochizuki), another story of survival in the Japanese-American internment camps. The class read and discussed the book, then compared it to *The Bracelet* (see Worksheet 5.5). Students began to understand how ethnic populations may be affected by governmental policies.

Angela assigned the following question for homework: Do you think that what happened to the Japanese-Americans during the internment was an injustice? Support your point of view with information either from the stories or from the social studies textbook.

Sandra's reflection indicates that she understood how foreign relations can affect residents of the United States:

Era una injusticia por parte de los Estados Unidos poner a los japaneses en campos de prision durante la segunda guerra mundial. No porque Japan haya bombadeado a

Pearl Harbor significana que todos los Japaneses que vivían en los estados unidos eran espías. Por ejemplo, en el cuento "El Brasalete" la historia es de una familia que fue separada. El papá fue llevado a Montana y el resto de la familia en California y iban a ser traslados a Utah. Yo creo que la familia no debe ser separada porque sospechan que eran espías sin tener pruebas. Tampoco es just o que los ninos tengan que ir a los campamentos porque ellos no tieren la culpa de nada si son niños. Y Estados Unidos es un pais libre y si no les da la libertad a todos los innocentes entonces ese dicho no es verdad. Por eso es que yo creo que los Estados Unidos hizo una gran injust icia que ojalá no se vuelva a repetir ni con los japoneses o cual quier otro grupo de imigrantes en este pais.

It was unjust on the part of the United States to put the Japanese in prison camps during the Second World War. Just because Japan had bombed Pearl Harbor doesn't mean that all the Japanese that lived in the United States were spies. For example, in the story, *The Bracelet,* the story is about a family that was separated. The father was brought to Montana and the rest of the family in California and they were going to be moved to Utah. I believe that the family shouldn't be separated because they suspected that they were spies without having proof. I also don't think it is fair that the children would have to go to the camps because they weren't guilty of anything since they were children. And the United States is a free country and if they don't give liberty to all the innocents then this saying is not true. This is why I believe that the United States made a great injustice that I hope will not be repeated; not against the Japanese nor any other immigrant group in this country.]

Sandra eloquently wrote about the injustices perpetrated in World War II against the Japanese-Americans. Sandra recognized the incongruity between the ideal of "The United States as Land of the Free" and the actions of the government. In the final sentence of her response, she stated her hope that this type of injustice would not occur against any ethnic group within the United States.

Students spent the rest of the week researching on their chosen countries. Angela assisted them as needed and created mini lessons on related themes that emerged. After a week of hard work, Angela was ready to resume the lesson.

Day Three (One Week Later)

On this day, Angela starts the class at 8:45. "We are all excited this morning because everyone is going to be presenting their posters." She gives the students a moment to take the posters out and get organized.

Angela has three blank poster papers on the board with three titles: "Countries/*Paises*, Foreign Policy, Describe present relationship with U.S., How does this affect the manner in which people are treated in the U.S.?"

Angela addresses the class, *"Quiero que todo el mundo escuche bien por si tienen preguntas."* [I want you all to listen well in case you have questions.]

Joanna begins, *"Mi país es Colombia."* [My country is Colombia.]

When she finishes, Angela asks her, *"¿Cómo se lleva Colombia con los EEUU? ¿Como afecta la relacion entre Uds?"* [How do Colombia and the United States get along? How does this affect the relationship between you?] Joanna thinks about this but isn't sure of an answer. Jenny presents next and tells U.S. about China. Her topics are: Languages spoken, Relationship between China and the USA, and China's enemies.

When she finishes Angela says to the class, "We talked about spying. *¿Se acuerdan en el periódico que dijo que China estaba espiando? ¿Qué está pasando con los estudiantes chinos en Estados Unidos? La gente piensa que son espias. Eso no es verdad.* [Remember in the newspaper that said that China was spying? What is happening with Chinese students in the U.S.? The people think that they are spies, but that is not true.] So that's important. How does that affect the Chinese living here?"

"They are treated like suspects?" asks Sandra, tentatively.

"Unfortunately, sometimes people think they are suspicious . Right." She turns back to Jenny. "Good job Jenny!" The students clap. Angela turns to Christopher and José. "Christopher and José, are you going to go next? They picked Yugoslavia. Show your poster and why you have two maps there."

José says, "It was a whole country and they separated. As you can see, the map of Yugoslavia is completely separated." In their presentation they also note that, "Two basketball players on the same team were from Yugoslavia but since they separated they hate each other."

Angela says, "That shows how quickly relationships change. Just like friendships, one day they are friends and the next they are not. How does that affect people who live here in the U.S.?"

No one answers

Next, Bernarda steps up the chalkboard and writes her country's name on the poster, "Canada." She reads from her poster, "Canada has relationships with Colombia. They used to have disputes with Alaska and Quebec."

"What is their relationship with them?" Angela asks.

"Good."

"How do you know?"

"Because it is right next to it." She continues speaking of Canada's flag.

"How does this affect Canadians who live here in the U.S.?" She pauses.

Some students say, "They are happy." "They are treated well."

Students take turns presenting their countries. Angela asks every time about the treatment of people from those countries in the United States and relates it to the U.S. relationship with those countries.

The projects on individual countries were of varying levels of sophistication. Angela was pleased with the outcome:

I wanted to validate what everyone had done, even those students who mainly talked about superficial aspects such as the flag and the money. Unfortunately, the resources available to investigate foreign policy were a hindrance. But it is still evident that the level of sophistication and maturity has increased greatly during the year.

Lessons Learned

This unit on politics was intellectually demanding. These fifth graders were able to engage in political topics presented in age-appropriate literature. They were also able to investigate in depth the political histories of specific countries. With this knowledge, they had a better understanding of how countries and ethnic groups within countries relate.

The teacher has an important role in actively instructing the students in this unit. The teacher needs to present literature and provide opportunities for reading response at all levels. The teacher also plays an active role in guiding the students through the research process step-by-step. Current resources are essential to provide perspective on the continually changing relationships between countries. In this unit, the teacher learns with the students as they investigate the political ties that bind the world.

The political unit was very complex for this age group. The teacher had to break it down into several concepts including countries in the world, human relationships, policy, and foreign policy. There were three relationships: those between countries, those between foreign policy and groups in the United States, and treatment of groups in the United States. The first four concepts were defined through lengthy classroom discussions in which the teacher asked students for examples. Students did research on chosen countries or discussed current issues that illustrated relationships between the United States and other countries. As two students researched Japan they came across World War II events. Their curiosity led the teacher to bring in books on the war. Pictures of the internment camps reminded one of the students of a story he had read the previous year about Japanese children in these camps. The teacher found an additional story, which she also read to the students. Through the reading of these books students got to the heart of this objective. Written reflections on these stories revealed that some students made the connection between foreign policy and treatment of ethnic groups in the United States.

The teacher recognized the difficulty students had in understanding the factors. It was particularly hard for them "to start thinking beyond the superficial and actually finding that connection with their own lives."[1] She felt that the lessons allowed for flexibility. Although students reached different levels of understanding, they all benefited from the experience. They found "that they are not alone in their struggle"; they became confident that "whatever they shared with the group was validated and supported at all times"; and they realized "how

---

[1]Angela's exit interview at the end of piloting the lessons.

much they've accomplished" in their struggle to adjust to a difficult social situation at such young age.

PART II: POLITICAL VARIABLES

Politics fuels the debate around a number of educational policies. Particularly vulnerable are those policies where the government intervenes on behalf of special populations with limited political power. Legislation supports women's sports (Title IX), special education, bilingual education, Head Start, and school desegregation. Fiscal support for those programs wavers along opposing political ideologies. Changes in policy make programs unstable, impacting quality. More specific concerns such as decisions on choice of language or languages of instruction, incorporation of cultural perspectives in the curriculum, and the trend for accountability and high-stakes testing affect bilingual students' education as well.

General policies toward immigrants and views on the role of language in achieving national unity impact bilingual children and their families. Differential policies for specific groups contribute to variation in support families receive and attitudes toward groups. The role of language in achieving political unity has been used as banner for attacking uses of languages in education and public life.

Language Use in Education

The United States was founded as a multilingual nation, where a variety of languages were used for daily life, government, and education. Toward the end of the 19th century, several states in the union enacted legislation requiring knowledge of English to vote, cementing the political power of English speakers. Unassimilated groups, including Native Americans and Hispanics, whose ancestors preceded English speakers in North America were effectively disenfranchised. Neither their linguistic and cultural rights, nor those of the immigrants that followed have ever been clearly established or respected.

The second half of the 20th century witnessed the passing of legislation that encouraged the use of various languages in schools with increasing numbers of language-diverse populations. Toward the turn of the century these policies are being once more reverted to.

During the initial colonization of the United States, European settlers Used the languages of their countries of origin. They established schools that educated their children in their own languages, especially French, German, Spanish, and Swedish, while teaching English as a second language. Schools that Used English as the medium of instruction taught one of the other European languages as a second language .

As immigrants settled during the 19th century, parochial and private schools Used the community language for instruction. When public schools were first established in the 1820s, they often Used the language of the population in the area to attract students. Once public schools became more popular than parochial schools, there was less concern for catering to the different linguistic groups. Even schools run by Native Americans used their own languages. Their efforts were squelched when the Bureau of Indian Affairs established schools with the purpose of isolating "the Indian children from their families in order to instruct them in western culture and the English language" .

During the first half of the 20th century, English was imposed as the language of instruction in most states. Indeed, many as 34 states enacted laws mandating English as the language of instruction. Other languages were forbidden and teachers could be fined or jailed if found using them. Imposition of English often retarded the academic progress of immigrant children in the public schools. Students were often retained and only a small percentage completed high school .

Despite the lack of public support for bilingual education, there were bilingual programs—mostly dual-language programs—in private or parochial schools. These schools extended the required curriculum to include instruction in the cultural, linguistic, and religious heritages of the particular ethnic group. A great number of them were bilingual.

The massive school failure of students in the public schools who were Native American and Spanish-speaking background attested to failure of "sink or swim" strategies (U.S. Commission on Civil Rights, 1971). In isolated communities in Arizona, California, Florida, New Mexico, Texas, and New Jersey, educators and parents created bilingual education programs to improve the education of their children. Programs such as those in the Coral Way school in Miami (W. F. Mackey & Beebe, 1977). Rock Point in Arizona, Nye school in Texas, and Calexico, California (Anderson & Boyer, 1978), and P.S. 25 in New York City (Von Maltitz, 1975) were initiated in the early 1960s. These programs used English and the native language of the students in all grades for language and content area instruction. In most cases these programs included English speakers. These programs were hailed as examples of educational excellence. Several of them still exist.

National interest in bilingual education spread when Title VII, the Bilingual Education Act (an amendment to the Elementary and Secondary Education Act), was enacted in 1968. This federal legislation provided funds to create bilingual programs in poor school districts . Following on this, a number of states reversed the laws that permitted only English as the language of instruction by passing bilingual education legislation. These programs differed from those that had began to emerge in the early 1960s in that the native language of the students was only used as a bridge until they knew enough English to be transferred to the mainstream. Bilingual education, then, became an educational strategy to address the English-language needs of the students rather than a full program of instruction in which native language and English have equal status.

Court cases, some related to desegregation, helped defend the rights of bilingual students to education in their native languages (Teitelbaum & Hiller, 1977). Parents entered desegregation suits as secondary parties or sued school districts to force them to provide for bilingual students. *Lau v. Nichols* had the widest impact because it was decided in favor of bilingual education by the Supreme Court in 1974 (*Lau v. Nichols,* 1974). Such a favorable decision gave impetus to the spreading of bilingual education programs throughout the country. Several major studies documented the benefits of such programs (Green, 1997; Ramirez, 1992; Willig, 1985).

In the 1980s opposition toward the use of languages other than English in education and other services for language-minority students swept the country. Criticism extended even to transitional programs that use the native language temporarily and only for the purpose of developing English. This xenophobic intolerance to other languages was partly a reaction to mounting immigration, especially from Latin America and Asia, facilitated by the passing of the National Immigration Act of 1965.

A national organization, U.S. English, was founded in 1983 to defend the perceived threats on the English language. U.S. English led the national effort at the federal and state level to pass legislation making English the official language. Although it did not succeed in amending the federal Constitution, 23 states passed such legislation (Crawford, 2000b).[2] During the last two decades of the 20th century, federal legislation and court cases reflected the erosion of support for bilingual education (Brisk, 1998).

Paradoxically, opponents of bilingual education for language-minority students do not oppose programs for English-speakers. Bilingual education programs that include English speakers proliferated throughout the country, many supported by Title VII funds (Christian, Montone, Lindholm, & Carranza, 1997). Arizona, New York, North Carolina, and Massachusetts enacted laws mandating foreign-language education programs or proficiency in a foreign language as a requirement for graduation.

Policies promoting bilingual education for majority students and rejection of bilingual education for minority students have accelerated their pace in the 21st century. To prepare their citizens to participate in global affairs, schools support bilingual programs to develop high levels of proficiency in foreign languages. The number of foreign language programs at the elementary schools and bilingual two-way programs in general continues to grow. Moreover, schools are encouraged to promote language teaching based on the fact, that following September 11, 2001, the public realized that knowledge of languages is necessary for protection against the country's enemies. "The F.B.I. acknowledges that before the World Trade Center bombing in 1993 it had tapes, notebooks and phone taps that might have provided warning signs—but it hadn't been able to decipher them because they were in Arabic" (Baron, 2001 p. 19). Therefore, Baron claimed, "the first step in addressing our language deficiencies is a national recognition that they exist" (p. 19).

Census results in 2000 made headlines when it was reported that Spanish background population had increased to 35.3 million (U. S. Census Bureau, 2000). Increasing immigration often produces xenophobic responses, including rejection of

---

[2]For frequent updates check Crawford, 2000b.

bilingual instruction for those who are not native speakers of the national language. Bilingualism and maintenance of the heritage language is considered subversive and unpatriotic whereas proficiency in the national language is imperative.

In 1998 California passed by referendum Proposition 227 requiring replacement of bilingual education by 1 year of English immersion followed by immediate integration into mainstream classrooms. Parents can petition for a waiver in order to maintain bilingual education programs. The movement against bilingual education succeeded in passing Proposition 203 in Arizona and Question 2 in Massachusetts, similar but more restrictive legislation with respect to parental choice (Crawford, 2000a). Opponents of bilingual education continue their efforts in other states. At the federal level, the *No Child Left Behind* Act of 2001 supports bilingual programs for non-English-speaking students (Title III) but it sets as the priority the acquisition of English. Title III of the No Child Left Behind Act of 2001 states as its purpose "to help ensure that children who are limited English proficient, including immigrant children and youth, attain English proficiency, develop high levels of academic attainment in English" (National Clearinghouse for Bilingual Education, 2001). This legislation will evaluate the success of bilingual programs based on the number of students reclassified as fluent in English. Notably the term *bilingual education* has been eradicated from the language of the legislation and offices supporting its implementation. The new term, *English language acquisition*, reflects the sentiment toward promotion of English only.

Incorporation of Cultural Perspectives in the Curriculum.

Curriculum content reflects societal values. Some believe that schools should concentrate in teaching the canon that reflects the European tradition of this country (Hirsch, 1987), that language brings unity to a country. Many of these same people contend that Americans should be schooled to a narrow set of values based on a mostly British tradition.[3] Such a view ignores that what defines American identity is the coexistence of different ethnic groups constantly reshaped by immigration.

Others feel that, for the curriculum to be relevant to the culturally diverse school population, it should contain themes and literature of the various traditions in the school including African American, Latin American, Asian, and others (Nieto, 2000):

> The use of materials reflecting the culture of the students' allows students' experience to be expressed and shared within the classroom context. This expression and sharing of experiences makes possible the affirmation of students' identity. By contrast, banking approaches usually employ textbooks that reflect only the values and priorities of the dominant group, thereby effectively suppressing the experience of culturally diverse students. (Cummins, 2000, pp. 257–258)

---

[3]This view is often described as Eurocentric. This is inaccurate because it does not reflect traditions of Spain, Italy, and various other European countries.

Accountability

Although there is no disagreement as to the need to promote *academic achieve-ment,* educators and policymakers often disagree on how to measure it. Many edu-cators believe that academic achievement should be demonstrated in a variety of ways, including performance in long term projects that reflect skills required in real-life situations. (T. R. Sizer, 1992; T. Sizer, 1995).

The accountability movement currently sweeping the United States narrows the definition of academic success to passing standardized tests usually in Eng-lish. The high-stakes nature of some of these tests creates barriers for lan-guage-minority students in their progress through school. Often these students are retained, placed in special education classes, or drop out of school (Haney, 2002). In the United States, to cope with this predicament, schools have experi-mented with accommodations or have exempted bilingual learners from tests. Policies of accommodations (such as extended length of time, breaking up the tests, assessing in the native language or in both, providing dictionaries, reading items aloud, and others) are promoted by some but opposed by others (August & Hakuta, 1997; Rivera, Stansfield, Scialdone, & Sharker, 2000). Of greater con-cern is the practice of exempting students. Although it sounds fair, the motivation is not to help students but to help raise the districts' total scores (C. Suárez-Orozco, & M. M. Suárez-Orozco, 2002). Failing to monitor such stu-dents' performance can, in the long run, jeopardize their academic development.

Government Policies Toward Immigrants and Language-Minority Groups

Government policy is presently quite inconsistent toward various immigrant groups. It is receptive, indifferent, or hostile depending on the group (Portes & Zhou, 1993). For example, the U.S. government in the 1980s and 90s welcomed and assisted Vietnamese refugees escaping the communist regime, is indifferent to most legal immigrants from Latin America, and is hostile to Haitian boat people. This policy can change at different points in history. Economic, political, and de-mographic reasons influence the government stance.

In the present economy's driven by the needs of the technology industry, the gov-ernment is pressured to relax immigration restrictions to highly qualified foreigners capable of working in the software industry. At the turn of the 20th century, manual laborers who could fill manufacturing jobs were more attractive immigrants.

The types of political regime that refugees escape and the political relations with the country of origin influence the treatment of refugees and immigrants. For exam-ple, Russian Jews were welcomed in the 1980s because they were escaping the communist regime of the former Soviet Union. On the other hand, Salvadorans, es-caping a U.S. supported rightist regime were considered illegal immigrants and even those who applied for asylum were ignored by most government programs.

Attitudes toward Japanese immigrants have changed dramatically. Where at one time they were perceived as mortal enemies, they are now considered economic partners. Reading and discussing *Baseball Saved Them* helped the students in Angela's class understand these connections between foreign policies and the treatment of particular ethnic groups.

The present increasingly negative attitude toward immigrants and giving special rights to language minorities (such as use of their language in education) is closely tied to the perceived threat of increasing immigration. The events of September 11, 2001, exacerbated such feelings. For the last 20 years legislators have unsuccessfully put forth bills in Congress promoting English and restricting other languages in government agencies and public schools. Immigrant phobia led California's government to pass Proposition 187, denying services to illegal immigrants, and Proposition 227 curtailing the use of native languages for instruction (Crawford, 2000a, 2000b).

Language and Political Unity

A common argument against support of languages and cultural diversity is the belief that diversity brings divisiveness. But, "unity and diversity are not necessarily incompatible. Tolerance and cooperation between groups may be as possible *with* linguistic diversity as they would be *unlikely* when such linguistic diversity is repressed." (Baker, 1993, p. 253).

The concept that a single language in a country ensures unity is a myth. Switzerland, a country with four official languages, is a model of unity, whereas Spain launched into a fierce civil war at a time when Spanish was the country's sole official language. Even our own history proves the contrary. Linguistically diverse European settlers rebelled against the British crown to form the *United* States of America. Their desire to be freed from British rule, not language, united them. Political, social, religious, and economic factors caus e division far more than differences in language.

The quest for language unity pressures schools to impose English only. Opponents of bilingual education view even temporary use of home languages as inciting separatism. What is problematic is that "such unitary linguistic philosophy is taken as the most natural state of affairs" rather than as a more recent historical development. The rise in power of middle classes, industrialization, and the development of the European nation-state established the importance of local national languages. The move to universal education further encouraged imposition of the language of those in power upon the masses. Those who argue against bilingual education based on the need to support political unity do not seem to be aware that there is no evidence that a "uniformist language policy does safeguard the integrity of a linguistically diverse state" (Lewis, 1977, p. 25).

Imposition of English and White middle-class American culture often backfires. Students from multiethnic backgrounds sometimes feel schools want to destroy their identity and ties with their home and community. They reject American White values, including success in school, and may drop out of school. Concerned families redouble their efforts to impose the ethnic language and culture as the only avenue to save their children from gangs, drugs, sex, crime, and other features of the American society they greatly fear .

Those who believe that a single language brings unity naturally support policies to assimilate immigrants to English and mainstream American culture. Yet the imposition of English and prejudice toward cultural groups is a sure recipe for formation of ethnic enclaves, which is exactly the opposite of what is sought. Child (1943), in his study of Italian-American second-generation immigrants, found that whereas some of the Italian-Americans assimilated, others formed self-sufficient "in-groups." They rejected everything American, associated only with the Italian community, and felt that all their needs were taken care of by this community. A. Portes and Zhou observed that well-established ethnic communities remain within themselves, because they can enjoy social and economic mobility ("the American dream") without having to face intense prejudice. Crawford , studying the effects of U.S. English's efforts to impose English, concluded that it heightened divisions in communities whose ethnically diverse groups had previously managed to get along with each other.

On the other hand, when the native languages of students have been accepted, relations between English speakers and language minorities blossom. For example, in two-way bilingual programs the language of bilingual students is welcomed and learned by English speakers. These programs have fostered cooperative relationships between English-speaking and language-minority parents as well as friendships between their children .

Suggestions for Additional Reading

- Corson, D. (1999). *Language policy in schools*. Mahwah, NJ: Lawrence Erlbaum Associates.
- Crawford, J. (2000b). *English-only vs. English-only: A tale of two initiatives*. Retrieved 1/22/03 from http://ourworld.compuserve.com/homepages/JWCRAWFORD/203-207.htm
- Crawford, J. (2000a). *At war with diversity: U.S. language policy in an age of anxiety*. Clevedon, England: Multilingual Matters.

Part III: Doing Analysis of the Political Context

Political lessons are recommended for upper-elementary and secondary students. The concepts and relationships are difficult for students to understand. Teachers can use some of the children's literature suggested in the lessons to elicit issues related to their immigration experience.

The first lesson on language and political unity can help students practice developing opposite sides of an argument. It is an important skill to teach students different points of view. The second lesson contains topics that are very close to the students' experiences. This lesson is multifaceted. Angela chose to implement only one aspect of it because she felt she needed a lot of time to introduce the concepts. This was time well spent because the students explored a number of historical, geographical, and political concepts included in their social studies curriculum.

POLITICAL LESSON 1: LANGUAGE DIVERSITY AND POLITICAL UNITY

Objective: Students will identify and understand the differences between opposing views with respect to language diversity and political unity.

Rationale: A common argument against support of languages and cultural diversity is the belief that diversity brings divisiveness. The concept that a single language in a country ensures unity is a myth. There is unity in multilingual countries and deep divisions among people who speak the same language. Political, social, religious, and economic factors cause division far more than differences in language. Students need to understand that loyalty to the country does not have to go along with denial of their ethnic and linguistic heritage. There is a lot more to being a good American citizen than just knowledge of English.

Time: *Four to 5 days (60–90 minutes per day)*

Materials:

- The book *Citizenship: Adopting a New Home Land.*
- Additional books for primary or middle school: *Becoming a Citizen: Adopting a New Home, American Too, Don't Forget, The Folks in the Valley: A Pennsylvania Dutch ABC, Grandfather's Journey, My Grandmother's Journey, Heroes, I Hate English, So Far From the Sea.*
- Additional books for middle school or high school: *Alicia: My Story, Autobiography of Chinese Woman: Buweig Yang Chao, Child or War: Woman of Peace, Don't Be Afraid, Gringo, So Far From the Bamboo Grove, Testimony: Contemporary Writers Make the Holocaust Personal, Tsuada Umeko and Women's Education in Japan, Women in Exile: German-Jewish Autobiographies Since 1933.*
- Friendship Conflict Survey (Worksheet 6.1).
- World Nations In the News (Worksheet 6.2).
- Causes of Wars Within Nations (Worksheet 6.3).
- Social studies textbooks and other reference books.
- Encyclopedia.
- Student journals.
- Possible Internet addresses:
  http://www.yahooligans.com>
  http://www.worldbook.com>
- Chart paper.

Overview of Activities

- Survey on conflict factors in friendship.
- Definition of nation.
- Countries in the news.
- Causes of wars within nations.
- Reading and discussion of the book *Citizenship: Adopting a New Home Land.*
- Summary and reflection.

Survey on Conflict Factors in Friendship

1. Tell students that they will be conducting an investigation to find out what factors cause disagreements or fights with their friends.
2. Design with your class a conflict survey form by generating a list of possible questions to include in the survey? The following questions are suggested:
   - Have you ever had a disagreement or fight with a friend?
   - What was the fight about?
   - Was your language an issue of conflict?
   - How did the conflict affect your friendship?
   - How was the conflict resolved?
   - Are you still friends with the person you had the conflict with? Why or why not?
   - Do you think the factors leading to the conflict are worth ending your friendship over? Why or why not?
3. Distribute the *Friendship Conflict Survey* (See Worksheet 5.1).
4. Have students conduct the survey, tabulate the results and write a summary of their findings.
5. Discuss the results. The following guided questions are suggested:
   - What factors were major causes of conflict among friends?
   - Was language an issue of conflict?
   - What effects did the conflict have on the friendship?
6. Have students keep a journal for a month in which they will write detailed accounts of the conflicts with friends or school peers.
7. At the end of the month, have students share the factors involved in their conflicts.

Definition of Nation

1. Create a semantic map for the concept of nation. Write on chart paper the word *nation* and ask students to define it. Write students' responses on chart paper.
2. Discuss the results and probe students for additional ideas.

3. Keep the semantic map in view during this lesson to add new points.

Countries in the News

1. Display the world map and ask students to identify nations of the world and languages spoken. Write students' responses on chart paper titled "Nations of the World" and "Official Languages."
2. Distribute the "international" section of the newspaper and ask students to identify nations in the news. Provide students with the worksheet entitled: *Nations in the News* (see Worksheet 6.2) and have them complete it by providing information from the article they read.
3. Have students share their findings with the class.
4. Initiate a class discussion using some of the following questions:
   • What nations are in the news?
   • Is the conflict between its own people or does it involve other countries?
   • Has the conflict caused dissension among its people?
   • What is the primary issue affecting the country or nation? For example, is it political, economic, social, linguistic, or religious?

Causes of War Within Nations

1. Tell students they will conduct research investigation on the causes of wars within nations.
2. Initiate a discussion with the whole class listing wars they are familiar with throughout history. For example, the list may include some of the following: Revolutionary War, the Civil War, and so on.
3. Brainstorm with the whole class causes for wars. Write students' responses on chart paper.
4. Discuss the results and probe students for additional ideas.
5. Keep the chart in view during this lesson to add new things that emerge from the lesson.
6. Distribute and review with the students the worksheet titled, *Causes of Wars Within Nations* (see Worksheet 6.3).
7. Organize students in groups of four. Using the worksheet *Causes of Wars Within Nations*, the students will search information using the Internet, books, encyclopedias, and other sources.
   The following Internet address are helpful:
   http://www.yahooligans.com
   http://www.worldbook.com
8. Have students write a summary of their research and present their findings.

9. Initiate a whole-class discussion about the factors leading to dissension within countries. The following questions are suggested:
   - What were the major causes of wars?
   - What groups of people were affected within the particular country?
   - How did this affect the unity of the country?
   - Was language policy a factor?
   - What changes have taken place in these countries over time?

Reading and Discussion of the Book *Citizenship: Adopting a New Home Land*

1. Initiate a whole-class discussion about what they think are the rights and privileges of citizenship in the United States. Write students' responses on chart paper.
2. Write the title of the book *Citizenship: Adopting a New Home Land* and the author's name on chart paper, show the book cover to the class, and ask students what the story will be about. Write the students' responses on chart paper. For example, students may infer that people pictured on the cover represent people from various ethnic backgrounds being sworn in as citizens of the United States.
3. Read aloud chapter 1 entitled "Citizenship." Consider pausing at certain instances in the chapter to probe students' understanding. Help them relate the content to their own experience. Some of the points that are important to raise are rights of citizenship in the United States and in other nations, loyalty to heritage, and political unity.
4. Lead a whole-class discussion about the rights of citizens. The following questions are suggested:
   - How important do you think rights of citizens are and how does they affect political unity?
   - How does this affect their feelings and allegiance to their heritage country and language?

Summary and Reflection

Have students reflect in writing responding to the following prompts:

- What are your feelings toward being a loyal citizen of the United States?
- What is your allegiance to your heritage country and language? Is it important? Why or why not?

Outcomes

	1	2	3	4
Concepts (check the level for each concept) • What is a nation. • Nations of the world. • Languages of nations. • Official language of a nation. • How nations have changed over time. • Wars within nations.				
Relationships: (check the level for each relationship) • Different linguistic groups in a nation. • Factors and dissension among groups. • Factors and wars within a nation. • Language(s) of a nation and political unity.				
Connection to self: Their feelings about being citizens of this country and allegiance toward their heritage country. Their own feelings about knowing English and their heritage language and their loyalty toward the United States.				

Key (for further explanation, see Appendix C)
Each concept, relationship, and connection to self covered in the lessons can be graded with respect to the following levels of understanding:
1. Misguided notion or no recognition.
2. Passive understanding.
3. Expresses some understanding of concept or relationship.
4. Expresses full understanding of concept or relationship.

Proposing a Solution	1	2	3

Key
Solutions proposed can be noted with respect to whether student:
1. Does not propose a solution.
2. Engages in a solution proposed by the teacher.
3. Proposes a solution.

FIG. 6.1. Cultural context rubric, Lesson 1.

POLITICAL LESSON 2: GOVERNMENT POLICIES TOWARD IMMIGRANTS AND LANGUAGE MINORITIES

Objective: Students will be able to explain government policies toward immigrants and language minorities due to (a) economic, (b) political, and/or (c) demographic reasons. Students will understand that such policies affect the treatment of people of diverse linguistic backgrounds. They will also understand that these policies are related to time and place and not to a specific language or group of people.

Note: You may choose to implement a lesson concentrating on one of the factors—economic, political, or demographic—to show how government policies affect immigrants and language minorities.

Rationale: Government policies toward different linguistic groups have varied throughout our history depending on economic, political, and demographic factors. These policies also vary at the federal and state levels. Demand for different types of laborers favors different kinds of immigrants. Presently European and Asian immigrants with strong technology backgrounds are welcomed whereas blue-collar workers are seen as a threat to shrinking manufacturing jobs.

Foreign policy influences how immigrants or refugees from different countries are received. Because this policy changes over time, so does how these groups are viewed. For example, Japanese-Americans were interned during World War II yet they are welcomed currently because the foreign relations between Japan and the United States are strong and amicable.

Legislation or proposed legislation against immigration usually coincides with the presence of a large number of immigrants. Legislation that curtails the rights of immigrants and language minorities is prevalent in states where there is a large number of such groups. Government policies affect the treatment of immigrants in the society and in school and influences school policies with respect to immigrants' rights, and the use of their language for instruction.

Time: Four to 5 days (60-90 minutes per day)

Materials:

- A large political world map.
- The book *Becoming a Citizen: Adopting a New Home.*
- *Waves of Immigration: Changes in Labor Demands* (Worksheet 6.4).
- Various international newspaper articles.
- The Books *The Bracelet, Baseball Saved Us*, and *Sadako and the Thousand Paper Cranes.*

- Venn diagram (Worksheet 6.5).
- Haiku poems.
- Encyclopedia and other reference books.
- Large construction paper.
- Glue.
- Journals.
- *Country Research* (Worksheet 6.6).
- Additional books for primary or middle school: *Who Belongs Here?: An American Story, Abuela, American Too, Coming to America: The Story of Immigrants, Don't Forget, The Folks in the Valley: A Pennsylvania Dutch ABC, How My Family Lives in America, I Was Dreaming to Come to America, Memories From the Ellis Island Oral History Project.*
- Additional books for middle school or high school: *Forced to Move, I, Rigoberta Menchu: An Indian Woman in Guatemala, The Far East Comes Near: Autobiographical Accounts of Southeast Asian Students in America, The Fourteen Sisters of Emilio Montez O'Brien, If Your Name Was Changed at Ellis Island.*
- Chart paper.
- Possible Internet address: http:www.yahooligans.com

Overview of Activities

- Investigating changes in labor demands and government policy.
- Defining branches of government and "foreign policy."
- Examining international current events through newspapers.
- Reading and discussion of the books *The Bracelet, Baseball Saved us ,* and *Sadako and the Thousand Cranes.*
- Sharing responses to the books: *The Bracelet, Baseball Saved U.S.* and *Sadako and the Thousand Cranes.*
- Comparing and contrasting the books *The Bracelet* and *Baseball Saved us .*
- Haiku poems.
- Investigating heritage country foreign policy with the United States'.
- Poster class presentation.
- Summary and reflection.

Investigating Changes in Labor Demands and Government Policy

1. Display a large political world map on the blackboard and have students locate their heritage countries.
2. On chart paper draw a two-column table with the following headings: "Country and "Number of Students represented." Write the name of the country identified and the total number of students from that country in your class.

3. Initiate a class discussion by asking students what were the major reasons for immigrating to the United States. (If students have not been taught this topic, you may wish to do so at this time.) Write on chart paper the heading "Reasons for Immigration" and list students' responses. Some possible responses may include some of the following: political freedom, economic opportunities, better life, and religious freedom.

4. Inform students that the United States had four major waves of immigration. Display a chart entitled *Waves of Immigration* (Worksheet 6.4) listing the following: 1600–1776, 1820–1870, 1880–1964, and 1965–present.

5. Inform students they will be investigating the changes in labor demands and which groups were favored or not favored due to immigration government policies over time.

6. Distribute copies of the book *Becoming a Citizen: Adopting a New Home* and provide the *Waves of Immigration: Changes in Labor Demands* worksheet (Worksheet 6.4) and review the following categories:
   - Waves of immigration.
   - Countries of origin.
   - Economic opportunities/labor demands.
   - Immigration policy.

7. Have students read independently or with a partner chapter 2, "Early Immigration to the United States" and chapter 3, "Later Immigration, "from the book *Becoming a Citizen: Adopting a New Home.*

8. Have students complete the information for each of the categories on their worksheets.

9. Initiate a whole-group discussion using some of the following questions:
   - What were the types of laborer needed during each wave of immigration?
   - What are the present laborer needs?
   - Which groups of immigrants were welcomed and why?
   - Which groups of immigrants were not welcomed and why?
   - What caused the government to lift its ban of Chinese immigration?
   - How have the immigration laws changed over time?
   - What groups of immigrants were given preference during the last wave of immigration?
   - Which groups' status changed overtime and why?

10. Have students reflect in writing to the following prompt (this could also be assigned as homework): What lesson did you learn about changes in labor demands over time and how immigration government policy affected the treatment of particular groups in the United States?

Defining Branches of Government and Foreign Policy

1. Using the theme of friendship, lead a class discussion on the special relationships students have with their peers. To facilitate the discussion use some of the following questions:

- What are some things you share as friends?
- What is your policy on friendship?
- What are some conditions you consider in your friendships?
- How do you handle disagreements or conflicts?

Possible responses may include some of the following:

- Secrets and interest.
- Trust.
- Assist one another when in trouble.
- Protect each other, be supportive and respectful.
- Compromise by talking things over in a calm manner.

2. Write the term "foreign policy" on chart paper and ask students what they think it means? Write students' responses.

3. Initiate a whole-group discussion by asking students what are the branches of government? (If students have not been taught this yet, you may want to teach it at this time.) On chart paper write the heading: "Branches of Government" and list the following: Legislative- Congress, Executive- President and Judicial- Supreme Court.

4. Ask students to imagine themselves as presidents of their heritage countries. How would they establish relationships with the United States and other nations? Responses may include some of the following: trading goods, peace talks, support one another in times of crisis, civil rights, freedom, and end of conflicts.

5. Explain to students that foreign policy is the action chosen in order to guide people in making decisions for their country. Write a list of countries on chart paper and survey students' prior knowledge of the United States' current relationships with other countries by having them respond *yes* or *no* to whether they think each country enjoys good relations with the United States.

Name of the Country	Relationship With the U.S.

6. Review the list of predictions and ask students to explain how the decisions and agreements on these issues support human world relationships and why each is important? Responses may include some of the following:

- Trade- helps country's economy.
- Peace-no wars.
- Freedom-people liberties.
- Protect civil rights-freedom of speech, voting.
- Political asylum-assist those wanting freedom.
- Alliance-Support overtaking by another country.

Examining International Current Events
Through Newspapers

1. Distribute the international news section of the newspaper. Explain to students that this section informs the reader about news around the world. Ask students to review this section and name countries and headlines in the news. Write students' responses on chart paper.
2. Choose one of the articles. Initiate a whole-group discussion Using the following questions:
   - What is the headline?
   - What country is involved?
   - What is the problem?
   - How does this affect people from that country living in the United States?
   - Why do you think its is important to know about what is occurring in the world?
   - How does this affect those living in the United States?

Reading and Discussion of the Books: *The Bracelet,*
Baseball Saved U.S., and *Sadako and the Thous*
and Paper Cranes

1. Prior to reading each of the books aloud write the title of the book and author's on chart paper. Show the book cover to the class and ask the students to predict what the story will be about. Write students' response on chart paper.
2. Read the story aloud. Pause at certain instances in the story to probe students' understanding and how it relates to their own experience. At the conclusion of the read aloud, discuss with students the history behind this story by reading information provided in the book's back cover about internment camps for Japanese-Americans and about the effects of radiation from the atomic bomb. Ask students to share their reactions to the story. Some important points: how the relationships between the United States and Japan affected the treatment of Japanese-Americans living in the United States.
   Ask students to respond in their journals to the following prompts:
   - What were the Americans and Japanese-Americans thinking during this uprooting and how are the two groups related to one another?
   - What do you think the bracelet, the baseball, and the paper crane symbolize for each of the main characters in the stories?
   - How does the power of memory sustain you during a difficult situation?
   - Have you ever been mistreated because of your heritage?
   - Why did Sadako wish the bell tolled on Peace Day?
   - What caused Sadako's leukemia?
   - What keeps Sadako's hopes alive throughout her illness?
   - How is Sadako's death commemorated and why?

- What lessons did you learn from reading these books?
3. For homework, have students reflect in writing to include in their Critical Autobiography, responding to the following prompt:

    Do you think that what happened to the Japanese-American being sent to internment camps by the United States government was an injustice? Why or why not? Explain your answer using supportive details from each book.

    Suggest that the students describe their reactions to the story using examples from the book. They should explain how the story relates to their experiences or to those of someone they know.
4. The teacher should respond briefly in writing to journal entries.

Sharing Responses to the Books *The Bracelet, Baseball Saved Us*, and *Sadako and the Thousand Paper Cranes*

Students will read aloud their journal responses to the class. Ask the class for their reaction after each individual reads. Ask questions by comparing with the contents of the books. This activity takes time because all students get a turn. The discussion is essential for teasing out the issues.

Alternative: If the class is very large, you can have a selected group of students share with the whole class and others share afterward in small groups. For a whole-class presentation, choose those students who cover different topics related to the treatment of people coming from other countries who live in the United States.

Comparing and Contrasting *The Bracelet* and *Baseball Saved Us*

1. Provide students with a Venn diagram (Worksheet 6.5) and ask them to compare/contrast the books *The Bracelet* and *Baseball Saved Us*. Students may work in pairs during this activity.
2. On chart paper draw a large Venn diagram and have individual students volunteer to write similarities and differences they have found. Review the completed Venn diagram with students.

Haiku Poems

1. Introduce Haiku poetry to students. Inform students that Haiku poetry is a style that originated in Japan. The format has 17 syllables consisting of three lines. Write the model format on chart paper with an example, such as follows:

    Line 1: Five syllables She did not know why
    Line 2: Seven syllables Her mother said we must go
    Line 3: Five syllables A gift from a friend
2. Have students choose one of the main characters from the books *The Bracelet, Baseball Saved Us,* or *Sadako and the Thousand Paper Cranes.* Follow-

ing the aforementioned format, have students write a Haiku poem about their character. Ask students to share their completed poems with the class.

Investigating Our Heritage Country Foreign Policy With the United States

1. Distribute and review with students the *Country Research* worksheet (Worksheet 6.6). Inform students that they will investigate the foreign policy for their heritage country or country of their choice as it compares with that of the United States.
2. Have students write on their worksheet the name of the country chosen for their research. They can work individually or in groups.
3. On chart paper write the list of countries students chose as they to refer to their *Country Research* worksheet.
4. Discuss and review with students the worksheet. Inform students that they will conduct an investigation by researching information with regard to the foreign policy relationship between their country and that of the United States. Provide students with access to various reference materials such as encyclopedias, news periodicals, other resource materials, and the Internet to begin their investigations. * If you have access to the Internet, you may choose to bookmark Web sites for students to use. (http://www.yahooligans.com).
4. Tell students that they will create a poster with the information they gather and present it to the class. Their posters should include the following areas of information:
   - Type of government.
   - Resources.
   - Current foreign policy.
   - Alliances with other countries.
   - Relations with the United States.
   - Flag.
   - Map.
5. Have students begin their investigation using the various reference materials. You may want schedule use of the school library at this time to assist them in selecting materials for their research project.
   Note: The gathering of information should take about a week. You may wish to set aside 1 hour each day for students to work on their projects. For homework, encourage students to visit the public libraries and interview relatives and neighbors to assist in their research.
6. Have students work on their poster research projects. Suggest that students design a rough-draft sketch of what their poster will look like for the presentation.
   Note: During this time you may wish to meet with individual students or groups and review their work. Students will be at different stages in their research projects. You may want to have a checklist displayed in the classroom where students can check off the tasks completed.

Homework: Students complete their poster for whole-class presentation

Poster Class Presentation

1. Organize the class poster presentations by listing the names of the countries on the blackboard. As each country is announced, have students present their poster to the class.
2. Ask probing questions to elicit further discussion of the students' presentation with some of the following questions:
   * What is the current foreign policy toward your heritage country (or country chosen)?
   * What is the relationship of your country with the United States?
   * What other countries are in alliance with your country?
   * What are the present concerns for your country?
   * How does the relationship with the United States affect those living in the United States?
   * Are there presently any conflicts between your country and other nations?
   * What type of government does your country have?
   * Are there any trade agreements between your country and the United States?
   * What valuable lesson did you learn in doing this project?
3. Arrange a bulletin board display of students' posters in school.

Summary and Reflection

Have students reflect in writing, responding to the following prompt: What is the importance of the political relationship between the United States and your heritage country and how do those relationships bear on the treatment of people coming from that country to the United States?

Outcomes

	1	2	3	4
Concepts (check the level for each concept) • Labor demands at different times in history. • Reasons for immigration. • Branches of government. • Foreign relations. • International current events. • Situation of different immigrant groups at different times in history.				
Relationships: (check the level for each relationship) • Labor demands and treatment of particular immigrants. • Reasons for immigration and treatment of immigrants. • Foreign relations and treatment of immigrants.				
Connection to self: Treatment of their particular group. Reasons for that treatment.				

Key (for further explanation, see Appendix C)
Each concept, relationship, and connection to self covered in the lessons can be graded with respect to the following levels of understanding:
1. Misguided notion or no recognition.
2. Passive understanding.
3. Expresses some understanding of concept or relationship.
4. Expresses full understanding of concept or relationship.

Proposing a Solution	1	2	3

Key
Solutions proposed can be noted with respect to whether student:
1. Does not propose a solution.
2. Engages in a solution proposed by the teacher.
3. Proposes a solution.

FIG. 6.2.   Political context rubric (Lesson 2).

Worksheet 6.1.　Friendship Conflict Survey.

- Have you ever had a disagreement or fight with your friend?

- What was the fight about?

- Was your language an issue of conflict?

- How did the conflict affect your friendship?

- How was the conflict resolved?

- Are you still friends with the person you had the conflict with? Why or why not?

- Do you think the factors leading to the conflict are worth ending your friend-ship over? Why or why not?

Worksheet 6.2.   World Nations in the News.

- What world nations/countries are involved?

- Is the conflict within its own nation or does it involve others?

- Has the conflict caused dissension among its people?

- What is the primary issue affecting the country or nation? For example, is it political, economic, social, language related, or religious?

Worksheet 6.3.   Causes of Wars Within Nations.

- What year did the war take place?

- What were the major causes of wars?

- What groups of people were affected within the particular country?

- How did this affect the unity of the country?

- Was language policy a factor?

- What resolutions were made in ending the war?

Worksheet 6.4. Waves of Immigration: Changes in Labor Demands

First Wave: 1600–1776

Countries of Origin

Economic Opportunities/Labor Demands

Immigration Government Policy

Second Wave: 1820–1870

Countries of Origin

Economic Opportunities/Labor Demands

Immigration Goverment Policy

Third Wave: 1870–1964

Countries of Origin

Economic Opportunities/Labor Demands

Immigration Government Policy

Fourth Wave 1965–Present

Countries of Origin

Economic Opportunities/Labor Demands

Immigration Goverment Policy

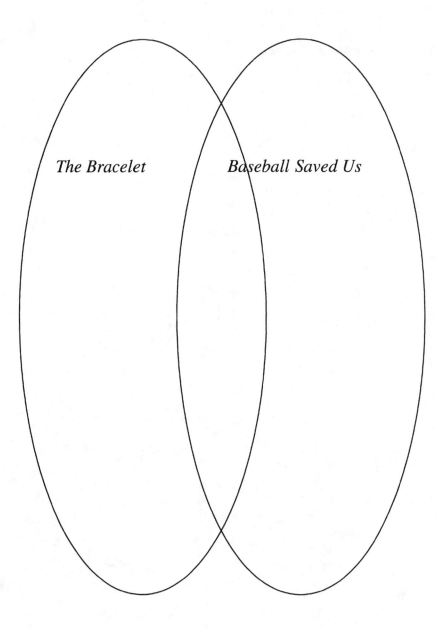

The Bracelet

Baseball Saved Us

Worksheet 6.6.   Country Research.

Identify the political relationship of the heritage country with the United States. Describe one country that is a major foreign policy concern for the United States.

Country _____

- Type of Government _____

Flag	Map

- Resources

  _____

  _____

- Alliances with other countries

  _____

  _____

- Relationship with the United States

  _____

  _____

In what ways does relationship between the United States and the heritage country affect the manner in which immigrants from that country are treated in the United States?

_____

_____

_____

_____

_____

_____

Appendix A

Annotated Bibliography

The selections included in this annotated bibliography contain topics related to the linguistic, social, economic, cultural, and political factors. They can be helpful in promoting discussions and understanding of the many topics included in the content objectives. These books help students recognize experiences similar to their own. When students are provided with literature that portrays factors directly related to them, their interest and understandings may be piqued. In addition, teachers should look in the local newspapers for articles that relate to the discussion topics of the lessons.

In the following selections the language, context, and illustrations reflect the aspects of many cultures. The selected books are listed in alphabetical order by title with all relevant information following (author, illustrator, copyright, awards received, summary, appropriate grade level, and content objectives). Teachers may use the resources as a guide. The list is not exclusive and welcomes personal additions as teachers implement the curriculum and continually explore ways to make the content objectives accessible to their students.

The grade level is indicated as follows: P = Primary Grades (K-3) ; M = Middle Grades (4-8); and U = Upper Grades (9-12). These levels are not fixed. Teachers can use a higher level book by reading it aloud or a lower level book for students to read to each other or to younger children.

Bibliography: Primary and Middle Grades

Title:	*A Day's Work* (P/M)
Author:	Eve Bunting
Illustrator:	Ronald Himler
Copyright:	Houghton Mifflin (1994)
Summary:	Francisco and his *abuelo* (grandfather) are looking for work to make money for food and living expenses. The grandfather speaks no English so Francisco speaks for him. He tells a lie that his grandfather is an experienced gardener. When the two finish a hard

day of work gardening in the hot sun, their supervisor Ben is very angry because they ripped out all the good plants and left the weeds. Francisco feels horrible, and he and his grandfather will return the next day to complete the job properly. The grandfather refuses pay until the job is done right and Ben decides to keep him as a permanent employee.

Title: *A Piece of Home* (P/M)
Author: Sonia Levitin
Illustrator: Juan Wijngaard
Copyright: Dial Books for Young Readers (1996)
Summary: Gregor is leaving Russia to move to America. He fears losing his friends, school, teacher, and all the places he calls home. The family is immigrating to America by plane. Each member chooses one item they wish to bring with them to America. Gregor chose to bring a blanket from his childhood. When the family is happily reunited with their relatives, Gregor discovers a new feeling of comfort. His cousin Elie is the owner of the other half of the blanket.

Title: *Abuela* (P/M)
Author: Arthur Dorros
Illustrator: Elisa Kleven
Copyright: Dutton Children's Books (1991)
Summary: The story portrays lovely communication between a grandmother and her granddaughter using both English and Spanish. Rosalba and her grandmother (Abuela) soar all over New York City by flying in the sky. They visit many places: where the ships are docked, the park, the building where Rosalba's father works, the clouds, Elisa's store, and even the Statue of Liberty.

Title: *The Always Prayer Shawl* (P)
Author: Sheldon Oberman
Illustrator: Ted Lewin
Copyright: Puffin Books (1994)
Awarded: National Jewish Book Award and Sydney Taylor Award
Summary: This story illustrates Adam's adjustment to life in America through the comfort of a prayer shawl his grandfather gave him before leaving Russia. Adam's grandfather, also named Adam, remained in Russia because of his elderly age. The prayer shawl had previously belonged to his own grandfather and is representative of the importance of continuity between generations, traditions, and cultural heritage. Through all the adjustments Adam and his family are forced to make, one thing always stays the same: the always prayer

shawl. The illustrations also add to the overall immigrant experience and resounding characteristics of both cultures.

Title: *American Too* (P/M)
Author: Elisa Bartone
Illustrator: Ted Lewin
Copyright: Lothrop, Lee & Shepard Books (1996)
Summary: Rosina, a young Italian immigrant, is living in New York City just after World War I. Her only wish is to become "modern" and "really American." It is her belief that to do so she must ignore the "Italian" aspects in her life while she tries to enhance her "American side." Rosina names her doll an American name, doesn't want to wear the color red or her necklace from Italy, won't eat eggplant for her lunch at school, and even wants to be called "Rosie" not Rosina. In order to prove her loyalty to her new country, she decides to lead the traditional Italian celebration dressed as the Statue of Liberty.

Title: *Angel Child Dragon Child* (P/M)
Author: Michele Marie Surat
Illustrator: Vo-Dinh Mai
Copyright: Scholastic Inc. (1983)
Summary: Story about a Vietnamese girl who has just come to the United States with her father and older sister and has difficulty in her new American school. The children all make fun of her when she speaks in Vietnamese and one boy especially, named Raymond, constantly picks on her every day. Her given name is Nguyen Hoa, but her family call her Ut. Ut has a fight with Raymond, which causes the principal to place them in a room to complete written assignment. Raymond is to listen to Ut's life story and write a composition. Raymond begins to cry for his mother and Ut tries to console him. He asked her what does she keep in her little match box. She reveals that it's a picture of her mother, who is still in Vietnam because they did not have enough money to pay for her ticket.
              After his composition is read to the school, they decided to have a Vietnamese festival and raise money for Ut's mother's trip to America. Then, one day Ut and Raymond come home from school and Ut and her mother are reunited.
              This story develops understanding between Vietnamese children and American peers. It facilitates the appreciation for sensitivity to those who are newcomers and bridges the gap between negative attitudes and social understanding.

Title: *A Visit With Great-Grandma* (**P/M**)
Author: Sharon Hart Addy
Illustrator: Lydia Halerson
Copyright: Albert Whitman & Company (1989)
Summary: Barbara loves visiting her great-grandmother. Together they bake strawberry kolach, a traditional Czechoslovakian dessert. She enjoys looking at all the old pictures, reading the storybook, and playing with the Czechoslovakian dolls. Great-grandmother speaks little English and sometimes uses hand motions to try to get her thoughts across accurately. The book truly portrays the special relationship and culture Barbara and her great-grandmother share. The book concludes as the two enjoy not only each other, but the finished strawberry kolach with powdered sugar.

Title: *Baseball Saved Us* (P/M)
Author: Ken Mochizuki
Illustrator: Dom Lee
Copyright: Lee & Low Books (1993)
Summary: This story is about a Japanese-American boy who is sent along with his family to an interment camp. The time is World War II, and the boy explains that Americans didn't trust those of Japanese ancestry at this time because they didn't know who was loyal to Japan. The individuals at the camp are miserable and uncomfortable due to heat, cold, lack of private sanitary facilities, boredom, and homesickness. The boy's father organizes a group to build a baseball field at the camp. The people play organized games to pass the time by and the young boy practices hard to improve his skills. He even ends up saving the championship game by hitting a home run hit. When the family returns home, the boy has no friends left at school and nobody talks to him. He feels the same way on his baseball team. The people call him "Shorty" and yell comments that the "jap" is an easy out. Once again, the young boy hits a grand slam. The book closes with an uplifting illustration of the team surrounding and embracing the boy with smiles and hugs.

Title: *The Bracelet* (All)
Author: Yoshiko Uchida
Illustrator: Joanna Yardley
Copyright: Philomel Books (1993)
Summary: This story is about a 7-year-old Japanese-American girl, Emi, whose life is getting torn apart. The time is during World War II, and the government is sending Japanese-Americans to prison camps. The situation is very hard for Emi to understand. Emi's father has

also been separately sent to a prison camp because he worked for a Japanese company. Before Emi is leaving for the train station, her best friend Laurie gives her a bracelet to remember her by. The train brings Emi, Reiko (Emi's sister), and their mother to a racetrack where they will be housed in a stall. Emi soon discovers she has lost the bracelet, and is very upset. She later realizes she doesn't need objects to remember people; wherever she is sent to she will always remember Papa and Laurie.

Title:	*Coming to America: The Story of Immigration* **(P/M)**
Author:	Betsy Maestro
Illustrator:	Susannah Ryan
Copyright:	Scholastic Inc. (1996)
Summary:	The text illustrates the history of the many immigrants who have come to the United States in both the past and present. The makeup of early civilizations in America are noted, as we are introduced to the immigration of the nomads, Native Americans, and westward expansion. When settling in America there was even competition for land and food between the Europeans and the Indians. The book points out that though many people came to America in search of a better life, and to escape religious freedom, many others were forced here. Beginning in 1619, many African Americans were brought to the states, against their will, and forced into slavery. The voyage to America was miserable for many people. Ships were crowded and food was scarce. Horrible weather conditions often added to the immense fears of those locked inside the ships' holds. Upon arrival, immigrants had to experience harsh inspections and wait in long lines. Individuals had to answer several questions, and when communicating with Ellis Island inspectors, troubles often resulted because of language barriers. The book concludes with a special note made of the wonderful contributions the many cultural and ethnic groups have uniquely made to this country.

Title:	*Dream Freedom* (P/M)
Author:	Sonia Levitin
Copyright:	Silver Whistle (2000)
Summary:	Based on contemporary events, this eye-opening novel focuses on Sudanese slaves, and the efforts of an American fifth-grade class to free them. The heart-wrenching, often brutal experiences of the Dinka and Nuba tribes are portrayed through multiple viewpoints of characters who learn the grim realities of oppression: the enslaved, the abandoned, the freedom fighters, and an American inner-city youth who learns of the situation in class and is inspired to act.

Levitin's introduction states that her aim is to "touch the conscience and stimulate action," and she succeeds, describing experiences both harsh (rapes, beatings) and poignant, unappologetically tugging heartstrings and individualizing a group tragedy. Evocative language and details convey characters' diverse daily lives, cultures, and backgrounds, heightening realism and impact. By juxtaposing the lives of American and Sudanese youth, Levitin offers perspective on what really matters: compassion, freedom, and how individuals can make a difference. Included are a brief description of Sudan's history of conflict, an afterward by the founder of the student abolitionist campaign, and an extensive bibliography.

Title:	*Don't Forget* (P/M)
Author:	Patricia Lakin
Illustrator:	Ted Rand
Copyright:	Tambourine Books (1994)
Summary:	Sarah, the main character in the story, sets off to get the ingredients necessary to bake her first cake, a surprise for her mother's birthday. Sarah goes to each shopkeeper to buy exactly what she needs, each of them giving her a special secret to bake an outstanding cake. However, Sarah must go to the Singers' store to buy baking powder, sugar, and eggs. Sarah feared going there because she hated seeing the numbers tattooed on Mr. and Mrs. Singer's arms. The Nazis put these blue numbers on their arms when they were put into concentration camps during the war. Sarah always thought she was not to see these numbers, that they were supposed to be a secret. Mrs. Singer points out to her that the numbers should never be a secret. People must see them so that bad things won't happen all over again. Sarah enjoys the afternoon she spends with Mrs. Singer and no longer fears going to their store.

Title:	*Dumpling Soup* (P/M)
Author:	Jama Kim Rattigan
Illustrator:	Lillian Hsu-Flanders
Copyright:	Little, Brown and Company (1993)
Awarded:	New Voices, New World Winner
Summary:	Marisa, a young girl from Oahu, Hawaii, shares with readers her experience preparing for a traditional family New Year's celebration. Her family comes from a variety of cultures, Japanese, Chinese, Hawaiian, and Korean. Marisa explains the preparation for the holiday, and the diverse cultural contributions different family members add to the feast. Marisa herself is quite concerned with learning to make the perfect dumplings for the soup, a tradition she values in her fam-

ily. The Hawaiian New Year's Eve is portrayed as a celebration of family, food, and fireworks. The book lends for a great discussion and investigation on cultural tradition in terms of family, food, and the celebration of holidays. A glossary is located in the beginning of the text to provide readers with accurate definitions, and pronunciations of the various English, Hawaiian, Japanese, and Korean words used throughout the text.

Title and level: *El chino* (P/M) *(Available in Spanish)*
Author/   Allen Say
Illustrator:
Copyright: Boston, Houghton Mifflin Co. (1990)
Summary: A biography of Bill Wong, a Chinese-American who became a famous bullfighter in Spain.

Title: *An Ellis Island Christmas* (P/M)
Author: Maxinne Rhea Leighton
Illustrator: Dennis Nolan
Copyright: Puffin Books (1992)
Summary: Krysia Petrowski and her family are leaving Poland where the streets are currently filled with soldiers and guns. They immigrate to America where Papa is visiting. The boat ride is long and the journey is hard. The Petrowskis endure horrible meals, unpleasant sleeping conditions, and bad weather to finally reach Ellis Island on Christmas Eve. Krysia is very nervous. She must have a medical examination, have her papers signed, and locate Papa. The family is happily reunited with Papa, and they say goodbye to Ellis Island, "To New York. We are going home" (p. 31). An author's note at the end of the book discusses the immigration journeys many endured during the years of 1892-1924.

Title and level: *F Is for Fabuloso* (P/M)
Author: Marie G. Lee
Copyright: Avon Books (1999).
Summary: Seventh grader Jin-Ha (Korean) finds her adjustment to life in America complicated by her mother's difficulty in learning to speak English.

Title and level: *Faraway Home* (P/M)
Author: Jane Kurtz
Illustrator: E. B. Lewis
Copyright: Harcourt (2000)

Summary: Desta's father, who needs to return briefly to his Ethiopian homeland, to see his mother who is ill, describes what it was like for him to grow up there. Desta at first didn't want her father to go but after hearing her father's stories she understands how much her grandmother must miss her father and how much her father wants to go back to Ethiopia.

Title: *Felita* (P/M)
Author: Nicholasa Mohr
Illustrator: Ray Cruz
Copyright: Bantam Books Inc. (1990)
Summary: Felita Maldonado's parents inform her that the family will be moving to a better neighborhood. Felita doesn't want to leave her friends and the close-knit Puerto Rican community that has been her home for a long time. The move to the new neighborhood does not offer the family "a better future" as they had thought it would. Instead the family is confronted with racial discrimination and violence from their White neighbors. When they are forced to move back to the old neighborhood, Felita is elated. She discovers, however, that things are not the same upon her return, including herself.

Title: *The Folks in the Valley: A Pennsylvania Dutch ABC* (P/M)
Author: Jim Aylesworth
Illustrator: Stefano Vitale
Copyright: Harper Collins Publishers (1992)
Summary: This book takes our ABC's to capture a rural part of our country where folks enjoy farming, baking, building, crafting, and quilting. An author's note following the story explains that the individuals who arrived in American and settled in the valleys of Pennsylvania were seeking political and religious freedom. Making up the "Pennsylvania Dutch" are the Amish, Mennonites, Moravians, and others.

Title: *Friends From the Other Side* (P/M)
Author: Gloria Anzaldua
Illustrator: Consuelo Mendez
Copyright: Children's Book Press (1993)
Summary: Prietita, a young Mexican-American girl, becomes friends with Joaquin, a Mexican boy who would cross the river to find work. One day, when the two are playing a Mexican card game, they hear that the border patrol is coming. Joaquin and Prietita run and get Joaquin's mother and they hide under the herb woman's bed. They are safe here, and the herb woman shows Prietita how to use herbs to heal the horrible sores on Joaquin's arms.

Title and level: *Gold Dust* (P/M)
Author: Chris Lynch
Copyright: HarperCollins (2000)
Summary: In 1975, 12-year-old Richard befriends Napolean, a Caribbean newcomer to his Catholic school, hoping that Napolean will learn to love baseball and the Red Sox, and will win acceptance in the racially polarized Boston school.

Title: *Grandfather's Journey* (P/M)
Author/
Illustrator: Allen Say
Copyright: Houghton Mifflin Company
Awarded: Caldecott Medal (1994)
Summary: This story bridges two cultures together as Say tells a story about his grandfather's moves between the United States and Japan. While adapting to two different cultures and lands, he experiences a confusion that is hard to understand. When he is in Japan, he is homesick for the United States, and when he is in the United States he is homesick for Japan. While in Japan, Say's mother marries and his grandfather longs to return to the States. However, the war going on ruins these plans. At the end of the story, readers find out that the author's feelings of acculturation parallel those of his grandfather.

Title: *My Grandmother's Journey* (P/M)
Author: John Cech
Illustrator: Sharon McGinley-Nally
Copyright: Bradbury Press (1991)
Summary: The book begins as a young child requests a bedtime story from her grandmother. The child wishes to hear, "Your story, Gramma," referring to the immigration tale of her grandmother. The grandmother's story begins in Russia on a cold December day. A group of gypsies are welcomed into her home and heal the grandmother's sickness. Ten years later, a group of gypsies predicted the family will soon have to endure great hardship. Following comes the Russian Revolution and World War II. The family is forced to run from soldiers wandering through many lands. It is then that the grandmother gives birth to the child's mother, the family's only symbol of peace and hope. After surviving German slave camps, the grandmother and her family find a new, safe life in America. The story is based on the life of a "remarkable grandmother," Feodosia Ivanovna Belevtsov.

Title: *Heroes* (P/M)
Author: Ken Mochizuki
Illustrator: Dom Lee
Copyright: Lee & Low Books (1995)
Summary: The story is about a boy named Donnie who is struggling with acceptance both inside and outside of school. Donnie is an Asian American and the children at school view him as being the "enemy." When the children play war, they always make Donnie be the enemy because "he looks like them." He tries to explain that his dad and his uncle were both in the army and they fought in Italy and France. The children can't understand how people looking like they do could be "on our side." One day, Donnie's dad and his uncle pick him up from school. They both wear their veteran's caps, uniforms, and have medals and ribbons to show. The children see this and Donnie receives a new acceptance. As he plays with the children in the school yard that day, for once they follow him and do not chase him.

Title: *Home Is Where Your Family Is* (P/M)
Author: Katie Kavanagh
Illustrations: Gregg Fitzhugh
Copyright: Steck-Vaughn Company (1994)
Summary: Maria is leaving Poland with her family in search of a better life in America. The story takes place on the ship, where the passengers endure a long journey to the new land. Maria vividly shares her thoughts and fears as she longs for Poland, and fights the constant uneasy feeling in her stomach. Panic, hunger, unpleasant weather, homesickness, uncertainty, death, and tears are the many hardships Maria and her family are faced with. Maria is comforted by her brother, Doniske, who explains to her, "Home is where your family is," which will soon be America.

Title: *How Many Days to America? A Thanksgiving Story* (P)
Author: Eve Bunting
Illustrator: Beth Peck
Copyright: Clarion Books (1988)
Summary: The setting is the Caribbean, from which a refugee family leaves and travels by boat with the hopes to soon reach America. The family takes with them only money and a change of clothes. "How many days to America?" the little sister asks. The father tells her not many, and not to be afraid. The people on the boat overcome many hardships—engine failure, robbery, low supply of food and water—be-

fore reaching American land. Many days later, the boat finally reaches America and the family is thankful for many reasons.

Title: *How My Family Lives in America* (P/M)
Author and
Photographer: Susan Kuklin
Book Design: Jo Anne Metsch
Copyright: Simon & Schuster books for Young Readers (1992)
Summary: The voices of the three children tell the story of how their families live happily in America, while holding on to culture and customs. Readers will be exposed to the lively photographs and story of an African-American, Chinese-American, and Puerto Rican-American family. As stated in the beginning of the text, the story shows an "importance of choice and adaptation in forging a cultural identity."

Title: *How My Parents Learned to Eat* (P)
Author: Ina R. Friedman
Illustrator: Allen Say
Copyright: Houghton Mifflin Company (1984)
Summary: The book is narrated by the daughter of the main characters. She tells the story about why in her house on some days they eat with knives and forks, and on others they eat with chopsticks. She is the daughter of an American man and a Japanese woman. Before her parents were married, they valued the other's culture.

Title: *I Hate English* (P/M)
Author: Ellen Levine
Illustrator: Steve Bjorkman
Copyright: Scholastic Inc. (1989)
Summary: Mei, a Chinese girl, moves with her family to New York. Here, she is very unhappy in school because everything is in English. Mei Mei won't work or speak in English in school. She goes to a learning center in Chinatown and still does everything in Chinese. Mei Mei likes math because numbers are just numbers. Mei Mei doesn't want English to take Chinese away from her and she doesn't want to know English words that she doesn't know in Chinese. An influential teacher, Nancy, slowly instills a desire in Mei Mei to learn and speak English. Mei Mei realizes both languages can belong to her, and she can talk in Chinese and/or English whenever she wants.

Title: *Isla* (P/M)
Author: Arthur Dorros
Illustrator: Elisa Kleven
Copyright: Dutton Children's Books (1995)
Summary: Rosabella and her grandmother are enjoying each other's company once again (see *Abuela*). Abuela brings her granddaughter back to the island where she grew up by telling her a vivid story full of people to see and places to go. They visit relatives, the house Rosabella's mother grew up in, the rain forest, the market, and the harbor. Soaring through the sky once again they return to where they presently live, magical New York City. A glossary is provided for Spanish words used throughout the text.

Title: *I Speak English for My Mom* (P/M)
Author: Muriel Stanek (1989)
Illustrator: Judith Friedman
Copyright: Albert Whitman & Company (1989)
Summary: Lupe, a Mexican-American girl, and her mother live happily together. Lupe can speak both English and Spanish. Her mother only Spanish. In school Lupe speaks English, at home Lupe speaks Spanish, and outside of the home Lupe must speak for her mother. Lupe's mother soon realizes the importance of learning to speak English, especially because it may improve her credentials to a better job. With the encouragement and support of her daughter, Rosa enrolls in English classes on Tuesday and Thursday evenings. Lupe even helps her mother with her homework, and they joyfully begin speaking both languages at home together.

Title: *I Was Dreaming to Come to America: Memories From the Ellis Island Oral History Project* (All)
Selected and
Illustrated by: Veronica Lawlor
Foreword: Rudoph W. Giuliani, Mayor, New York City
Copyright: Puffin Books (1995)
Summary: This book is a collection of quotes made by inspectors, interpreters, and immigrants, all of whom have vivid pictures of arriving on Ellis Island. The truly realistic voices add to the comprehension of the varied experiences immigrants around the world feared and endured. Adults and children alike describe the traveling conditions on the crowded ships, and the fears of reaching an island "haven" that was more like a "heaven." An introduction to the book outlines the impor-

tance of our lady Liberty. Concluding the book is a collection of detailed bibliographies of each person quoted throughout the story

Title and level: *Journey Home* (P/M)
Author: Lawrence, McKay
Illustrator: Dom & Keunhee Lee
Copyright: Lee & Low Books (1998)
Summary: Mai returns to Vietnam with her mother to try to find her mother's lost past. Mai's mother was born in Vietnam and adopted by Americans. when she was still a baby. As they go through this journey, Mai discovers both a new country and something about herself.

Title: *Maranthe's Story: Painted Words/Spoken Memories* (P)
Author: Aliki
Copyright: Greenwillow (1998)
Summary: One picture book tells two stories and two aspects of the immigrant experience from the perspective of a child. The first story, ``Painted Words,'' follows Marianthe, new to the United States, and her mother on the dreaded first day of school. Her mother tries to reassure the girl, but the classroom experience is all but overwhelming. Knowing no English, Marianthe draws pictures about herself during the art period, communicating in the only way she can. A patient teacher, some not-always-nice classmates, and success in English ("Slowly, like clouds lifting, things became clearer. Sticks and chicken feet became letters. Sputters and coughs became words. And the words had meanings") give Marianthe the courage to take part in Life-Story Time, in the "Spoken Memories" section of the book. She tells the class about the baby brother who died before she was born, the village where she lived, and the closeness of friends and neighbors who rejoiced with the family when twin sons were born. Softly colored pencil and crayon drawings show the loving, supportive family, and the anxious and finally triumphant Marianthe, who finds a place in a new country.

Title: *Molly's Pilgrim* (P)
Author: Barbara Cohen
Illustrator: Michael J. Deraney
Copyright: Lothrop, Lee, & Shepard Books (1983)
Summary: Molly is an immigrant girl from Russia. She moved to New York and then to a small town. She is now having a hard time adjusting to a new life in the small town. She misses both Russia and New York where she felt more comfortable. Molly's most significant struggle

is in school where the children tease her about her English and unfamiliarity with the American culture and traditions. At Thanksgiving, Molly's teacher asks the class to make pilgrim dolls. Molly's mother, who doesn't speak much English, offers to make the doll for her. The pilgrim doll was made resembling Molly's mother, a modern-day Pilgrim. She too had come to this new land in search of religious freedom. At first, Molly is embarrassed by her doll, and the students think she is dumb. Miss Sickley teaches the class the influence of the Jewish festival, Sukkoth, on the first Thanksgiving. Both Molly and her classmates realize "it takes all kinds of Pilgrims to make a Thanksgiving."

Title:	*My Name Is Maria Isabel* (P/M) *(Available in Spanish)*
Author:	Alma Flor Ada
Illustrator:	K. Dyble Thompson
Copyright:	Aladdin Paperbacks (1993)
Summary:	Maria Isabel Salazar Lopez was born in Puerto Rico. Recently she and her family have moved to the United States. Maria wants nothing more then to fit in at school with the other children. When Maria arrives at school her teacher decides it would be best to call her Mary Lopez because they already have two Maria's in the class. Maria cannot respond to this name, and wants her teacher to see that she has taken away the most important part of her. The teacher has deprived Maria of an essential part of her Latino culture. Maria is proud of her name, which has come from her father's mother and her Puerto Rican grandmother. Finally, Maria finds the courage to share her deeply hidden feeling in an essay assignment titled, "My Greatest Wish." School becomes a more pleasant and accepting place. Text is available in both Spanish and English.

Title:	*A Picnic in October* (P)
Author:	Eve Bunting
Illustrator:	Nancy Carpenter
Copyright:	Harcourt (1999)
Summary:	Every October, on Lady Liberty's birthday, Tony and his extended family have a picnic on Liberty Island. The family rendezvous at Battery Park to take the ferry out to the island. Waiting in line, Tony, who thinks the picnic is pretty corny, is approached by a woman, obviously a new immigrant. She gestures her alarm when the ferry departs without her; she is soothed when Tony motions that the ferry will return. Once on the island, Tony's family has the picnic before toasting the statue and blowing kisses to her. Later, Tony spies the woman he had helped earlier, and the way they look

up at the statue, "so still, so respectful, so, ... so peaceful, makes me choke up."

Title: *The Silence in the Mountains* (P)
Author: Liz Rosenberg
Illustrator: Chris K. Soentpiet
Copyright: Orchard Books (1999)
Summary: Iskander and his family flee their unnamed war-torn homeland for America, but even in the rolling farmland they settle in, he longs for his homeland's prewar rural tranquility. This immigrant story is original and satisfying, although young Iskander's adult like preoccupation with silence mildly strains the plausibility.

Tithe: *So Far From the Sea* (P/M)
Author: Eve Bunting
Illustrator: Chris K. Soentpiet
Copyright: Jacket Illustrations (1998)
Summary: This story takes place in 1972. The Iwasakis are American citizens of Japanese ancestry. The family goes back to the Manzanar internment camp in California. Their father was held there for 3 1/2 by the American government during World War II. The family is moving from California to Massachusetts. The grandfather passed away in 1943 while being held at the camp and is buried on the grounds. The family brings the grandfather silk flowers to put by his grave which lies on the campgrounds. The father explains to his daughter, Laura, and son, Thomas, how unjust their treatment was at this time. Black-and-white pictures illustrate the father's thoughts as he recalls characteristics of the camp at that time. The story is narrated by the 8-year-old girl, who tries to explain her fears as she attempt to identify with this dark moment of history. Laura brings her grandfather her father's Cub Scout neckerchief, which symbolizes that they were both true Americans.

Title: *Talking Walls* (All) *(Available in Spanish)*
Author: Mary Burns Knight
Illustrator: Anne O'Brien
Copyright: Tilbury House Publishers (1992)
Summary: This book illustrates and explains the significance of many fascinating walls around the world: the Great Wall of China, the Aborigines' Rock Wall in Australia, the Walls of a Lascaux Cave in the French woods, the ancient Western Wall in Jerusalem, the Cliffs near India's Bay of Bengal, outside walls of Egyptian homes, the ancient gray-green granite walls of Great Zimbabwe in southeast Africa,

the walls of the Incas in Cuzco, Peru, the residents of Taos pueblo and their surrounding walls, the walls in Diego Rivera (Mexico), the limestone walls of the Canadian Museum of Civilization in Hull.

Linguistic: Illustrates various writing systems.

Title: *Tea With Milk* (P/M)
Author/
Illustrator: Allen Say
Copyright: Houghton Mifflin Company (1999)
Summary: May's parents move back to Japan and May is very homesick for America. In America, everyone called her May, not Masako, which everyone calls her in Japan. She misses her friends, the food she ate, and the clothes she wore. Her mother sets her up with a matchmaker to help her find a husband. May states that she would rather have a turtle than a husband. She breaks away from her unhappiness and goes to the big city Osaka. Here, she will live and work. Her first position is operating the elevator. She soon gets bored with this and is promoted to being the store's guide for foreign businessmen. While doing this she meets Joseph. Joseph grew up in an English school because his parents were English and he works for Hong Kong and Shanghai Bank. When he finds out that he will soon be transferred to Yokohama, hey decide to go home together.

Title: *Tree of Cranes* (P/M)
Author/
Illustrator: Allen Say
Copyright: Houghton Mifflin Company
Summary: This story is about a boy's recollection of his first Japanese-American Christmas.

Title: *Watch the Stars Come Out* (P/M)
Author: Riki Levinson
Illustrator: Diane Goode
Copyright: Dutton Children's Books (1985)
Summary: The story is about a brother and sister who join their family. The young girl doesn't like that when she goes to sleep at night she can't see the stars come out in the sky. The children are happily reunited with their parents and sister, and the girl can watch the stars come out in her new home.

Title: *Where Did Your Family Come From?* (P)
Author: Melvin and Gilda Berger
Illustrator: Robert Quackenbush

Copyright: Ideal's Publishing Company (1993)

Summary: The book begins by introducing important facts about immigration in context for a young reader. It describes the definition of an "immigrant," why people choose to leave their homelands, how people became immigrants, and the important skills and talents many immigrants bring to the United States. The author then introduces the experiences of four immigrant children who have recently come to the United States. Borris is from Moscow (Russia), Rosa is from Taxco (Mexico), Maria is from Rome (Italy), and Chang is from Sinpo (Korea). Readers will find out why and how they came to the United States, how they are getting along, and what their hopes and dreams are for the future.

BIBLIOGRAPHY: MIDDLE
AND HIGH SCHOOL STUDENTS

Title: *Alicia: My Story*

Author: A. Appleman-Jurman

Copyright: NY: Bantam. Jewish (1988)

Summary: This is an autobiographical account of Alicia Appleman-Jurman, a Jewish woman whose family suffered deaths as a result of the Holocaust. She was from Poland. She tells about the journeys she made throughout Europe and the experiences living under different governments in the late 1930s and 1940s.

Title: *All God's Children Need Traveling Shoes*

Author: Maya Angelou

Copyright: Random House (1986)

Summary: This story tells what it means to be an African American on the mother continent (Ghana), where color no longer matters but where American-ness keeps asserting itself in ways both puzzling and heartbreaking. Angelou's journey into Africa is a journey into herself, into that part of every African-American's soul that is still wedded to Africa, which still yearns for a home.

Title: *Autobiography of a Chinese Woman, Buwei Yang Chao*

Author: Chao P. Y.

Copyright: Greenwood Press (1947)

Summary: This is an autobiography of a Chinese woman growing up in the 20th century. It explains cultural traditions in China, where the author grew up, and the political changes she witnessed since the early 1900s. The author's move to the United States is explained and maps of China, a glossary, and a genealogical tree are all included.

Title: *Becoming a Citizen: Adopting a New Home* (M)
Author: Fred Bratman
Illustrator: photo research by Grace How
Copyright: SteckVaughn Company (1993)
Summary: This book is part of the "Good Citizenship Library," which is a se-
               ries of books about the branches of the federal government and the
               individual's role in the political process. *Becoming a Citizen* pro-
               vides the readers with a brief history of immigration in the United
               States and what it means to be a citizen. It explains the reasons that
               people from other countries have to come to the United States and
               what it means to them to be an immigrant in this country. The book
               gives an accurate review of all the procedures and requirements that
               the immigrants have to go through to get a visa or a green card, and
               how this affects their lives.

Title: *Bill Peet*
Author: B. Peet
Copyright: Houghton Mifflin (1989)
Summary: What a success story Bill Peet's life has been! From early boyhood
               in Indiana, his love for drawing was much more than a hobby; every
               day he drew secretly in his school books during classes. After art
               school Peet went on to win prizes for his paintings. Then he went to
               work for Disney studios, where he gained Walt Disney's respect and
               friendship and progressed to top writer illustrator on such
               well-loved films as *Dumbo* and *Peter Pan*. While still at Disney,
               Peet began writing children's stores, and his popularity soared. Now
               his picture books—more than 30 of them—are read by kids the
               world over. In this autobiography, Bill Peet tells in words and pic-
               tures the fascinating tale of his life.

Title: *Bloodlines*
Author: J. C. Hale
Copyright: NY: Random House (1993)
Summary: Hale is the Daughter of a Coeur d'Alene Indian father and a
               Kootenay-Chippewa-Irish mother. The book is an autobiography in
               fiction. It tells the story of her family and the legal and social diffi-
               culties growing up in the 20th century as a Native American.

Title: *Child of War: Woman of Peace*
Author: L. L. Hayslip
Copyright: Doubleday (1993)
Summary: Le Ly Hayslip's extraordinary memoir of growing up in a
               war-ravaged Vietnam garnered high praise for the "passion and

suspense" of its searing and human account of Vietnam's destruction. Now, Ms. Hayslip continues her remarkable autobiography, arriving in the United States as a young bride wise in the ways of war, yet charmingly naive about the habits of "giant round-eyed Americans."

Told in exquisite detail, *Child of War, Woman of Peace* is, in many ways, a timeless immigrant's tale. Ms. Hayslip recounts with humor and goodwill her apprenticeship as a U.S. housewife in a land where kitchen sinks "swallow food," and neighborhood church ladies strive to save her "heathen Buddhist soul." Her uncanny ability to attract colorful characters—from con artists to despondent suitors—only muddles her search for the true peace she hoped America would grant her. Yet beneath Le Ly's amusing view of America, her emotions are torn between the promise of her adopted country and the land—full of pain, but also the pleasures of an ancient and beguiling way of life —she left behind. "Home" is more than a place, she discovers: it is a state of grace.

Title: *Don't Be Afraid, Gringo: A Honduran Woman Speaks from the Heart: the Story of Elvia*
Author: E. Alvarado
Copyright: Harper & Row (1989)
Summary: Elvia Alvarado speaks as a woman, a mother, and a peasant organizer. Her story tells of the courageous efforts of peasant communities to obtain such basic needs as land, food, education, and health care. It is an important contribution to the firsthand accounts that communicate the everyday effects of political and social forces. It is autobiographical and includes a map of Honduras and appendixes of Honduran chronology (1524–1987), campesino organizations, political parties, and U.S. economic and military aid.

Title and level: *Esperanza Rising* (M)
Author: Pam Muñoz Ryan
Copyright: Scholastic Press (2000)
Summary: Esperanza and her mother are forced to leave their life of wealth and privilege in Mexico to go work in the labor camps of Southern California, where they must adapt to the harsh circumstances facing Mexican farm workers on the eve of the Great Depression.

Title: *Forced to Move*
Author: R. Camarda
Copyright: Solidarity Publications (1995)

Summary: Presents the case of the Salvadorian peasant refugees in Honduras
             who fled in the 1980's to escape a harsh military-civilian regime that
             systematically killed thousands of peasants and displaced hundreds
             of thousands more to the United States, Mexico, and other Central
             American countries. This book transmits Salvadorian peasant refu-
             gees' appeal to the international community for help in preventing
             their forced transfer deeper into Honduras. It includes autobio-
             graphical accounts of refugee experiences—why they fled, their life
             inside Honduras, the fears of relocation. It also adds information on
             Salvadorian refugees throughout the Americas, organized by coun-
             try and provides photographs.

Title: *I Know Why the Caged Bird Sings*
Author: Maya Angelou
Copyright: Bantam Books (1971)
Summary: This story quietly and gracefully portrays and pays tribute to the
             courage, dignity, and endurance of the small, rural community in
             which Angelou spent most of her early years in the 1930s. This is an
             autobiographical narrative about an African-American girl growing
             up in Stamps, Arkansas, with her grandmother and uncle.

Title: *I, Rigoberta Menchu: An Indian Woman in Guatemala*
Author: R. Menchu
Copyright: Verso (1984)
Summary: This is the story of a Guatemalan Indian woman who fought for
             Indian and workers' rights in Guatemala and the consequences
             she and her family and friends suffered because of a harsh mili-
             tary regime that discriminated against Guatemalan Indians. In
             this narrative, Menchú discusses the culture (spiritual, ceremo-
             nial, and family) of her people, how she decided to learn Spanish
             and become politically active, and finally about her exile.
             Menchú was awarded the Nobel Peace Prize in the early 1990s
             for her heroic efforts.

Title: *If Your Name Was Changed at Ellis Island* (M)
Author: E. Levine
Illustrator: Wayne Parmenter
Copyright: Scholastic Inc. (1993)
Summary: The immigration journey and the hopes, difficulties, and adventures
             are shared in this account. The book covers the details of those who
             immigrated, mainly during the period 1880–1914. Eighty pages of
             informational text answer common questions in great detail about

the immigration process and procedure. From the journey of traveling to America, to what happened when one reached Ellis Island, students will have a heightened awareness of the experiences of more than 12 million people. The book also discussed that many individuals changed their names when they first met with the Ellis Island inspectors. Due to concerns and the misunderstanding of one's spoken language, many immigrants entered America with a new name, and a new beginning of life.

Title:	*Inside Separate Worlds: Life Stories of Young Blacks, Jews and Latinos*
Author:	D. Schoem
Copyright:	University of Michigan Press (1991)
Summary:	Fourteen young people from Black, Jewish, and Latino backgrounds have contributed their voices to this unique and powerful collection of contemporary ethnic autobiographical essays. They speak of their lives marked by a complex interplay of race, class, and gender and by the inconsistencies that they encounter "just growing up" as minorities in the United States. They speak of joys and difficulties: from the support, confidence, and pride of being an identified member of an ethnic group to the powerful hurts inflicted by racism; from the enormous attention given by society to shades of skin color to the overwhelming effort needed to hold onto one's heritage—often in the face of great personal ambivalence. Their stories represent what have remained secret worlds for those from other groups, and much of what they relate is often unspoken even among their peers.

Title:	*Narratives by Twentieth Century American Women Writers*
Copyright:	Harper Perennial
Summary:	Ranges in works from Jane Addams (1860–1935) to Natalie Kusz (1962-present). Includes such authors as Jamaica Kincaid, Sandra Cisneros, and Maya Angelou.

Title:	*Night*
Author:	E. Wiesel
Copyright:	Bantam Books (1982)
Summary:	Wiesel's personal Holocaust memoir. He had seen his mother, little sister, and all his family except his father disappear into an oven fed with living creatures. As for his father, the child was forced to be a spectator day after day to his martyrdom, his agony, and his death. The fate of the Jews from the little town called Sighet, their blindness in the face of a destiny from which they would still have had time to flee; the incon-

ceivable passivity with which they gave themselves up to it, deaf to the warnings and pleas of a witness who had himself escaped the massacre, and who brought them news of what he had seen with his own eyes; their refusal to believe him, taking him for a madman.

Title:	*Rain of Gold*
Author:	V. Villaseñor
Copyright:	Arte Publico Press (1991)
Summary:	This is the story of a Mexican-American man who grew up in California. He tells the stories of his heritage through interviews with family members, and of his Indian European culture as handed down to him by his parents, aunts, uncles, and godparents. He provides family trees and photographs.

Title:	*Sadako and the Thousand Paper Cranes* (M) *(Available in Spanish)*
Author:	E. Coerr
Illustrator:	Ronald Himler
Copyright:	Scholastic (1977)
Summary:	This story is based on the life of a real little Japanese girl who lived from 1943 to 1955. She lived in Hiroshima when the United States air force dropped the atomic bomb and some years later she died from a cancer that originated from the bomb's radiation.
	Sadako, the little girl, was very athletic; her mother always told her that she was born to be a runner. Suddenly she got severely ill. Sadako approaches her illness as she participated in the running team at school, with a lot of courage and an irrepressible spirit. Recalling a Japanese legend that says if a sick person folds 1000 paper cranes, the gods will make her healthy again, Sadako starts folding cranes.

Title:	*Samurai and Silk: A Japanese and American Heritage*
Author:	H. M. Reischauer
Copyright:	Belknap Press of Harvard University Press (1986)
Summary:	This is the story of author's search for his heritage in Japan and America. It consists of biographies of his grandfathers and shorter accounts of some of their descendants and relatives. It is a personalized view of modern Japanese history and Japanese-American relations.

Title:	*So Far From the Bamboo Grove*
Author:	Watkins, Y. K.
Copyright:	NY: Lothrop, Lee, & Shepard (1986)
Summary:	For most of World War II, Yoko Kawashima lived peacefully with her family in north eastern Korea. Korea was not at war, and Yoko

was not a Korean. She was a Japanese girl who longed to visit her grandparents in Japan, a homeland she had never seen. But in 1945 the threat of war disrupted her village. While Yoko's father and brother, Hideyo, were away, the Kawashimas were warned of a possible communist attack. All at once Yoko, her mother, and older sister, Ko, were leaving home, fleeing to Seoul, where they expected to make connections to Japan. Their life as refugees had begun. Yoko Kawashima Watkins tells vividly what happened in the months that followed; her memories are intense and personal. Yet, in this gripping and inspirational account, the particular circumstances of one family's flight from Korea blend into a larger historic context, revealing what it is to be a refugee and illuminating events in Asia during and after the war.

Title:	*Testimony: Contemporary Writers Make the Holocaust Personal*
Author:	D. Rosenberg
Copyright:	Times Book (1989)
Summary:	This is a compilation of 27 essays written by Jews whose lives or families have been altered because of the Holocaust. Each tells his or her experience as a Jew living and growing up during the Holocaust. The stories range from United States to Europe.

Title:	*The Far East Comes Near: Autobiographical Accounts of Southeast Asian Students in America*
Author:	L. H. Nguyen
Copyright:	University of Massachusetts Press (1989)
Summary:	This book contains 25 autobiographical essays and 1 poem by Vietnamese, Khmer, and Lao refugee students. They describe life in the home countries, escape by land or by sea, life in refugee camps, and adaptation to life in America. It is a forceful testimony of hardship and suffering, harrowing escape, and the renewal of hope, and is an important contribution to the emerging literature on Cambodians, Laotians, and Vietnamese in America. Important as an account of how young Asian American view their experiences as refugees, as new immigrants, and as the new generation in touch with two distinct, and often incompatible, cultures. All of these students were barely beyond adolescence when they fled their countries, and regardless of how adaptable and successful they have become, this book reminds us that they will always have the horrors of extreme human destructiveness deeply embedded in their psyches.

Title: *The Big Sea*
Author: L. Hughes
Copyright: Thunder's Mouth Press (1963)
Summary: "Literature is a big sea full of many fish. I let down my nets and
               pulled. What I caught was amazing." So ends this autobiographi-
               cal narrative of a fine poet, novelist, and playwright. But life is a
               big sea, too. And what Hughes has pulled out of it is also amaz-
               ing. He has lived warmly, adventurously, sometimes danger-
               ously, and he has lived among interesting and often famous
               people. Langston Hughes came of age early in the 1920s. He
               lived through fabulous years in the two great playgrounds of the
               decade—Paris and Harlem. In Paris he was a cook and waiter in
               nightclubs, and he witnessed the seemingly endless carnival in
               which men and women of all races and colors took part. He knew
               the musicians and dancers, the queer people, the drunks and dope
               fiends. In Harlem he was a rising poet in the center of the "Black
               Renaissance" when Black art and entertainment were the fads.
               He went to the parties, the clubs, and dives, acquired friends and
               patrons. He did other things, too, to earn a living. He was a sea-
               man on freighters to Europe and Africa, he taught English in
               Mexico, he was a busboy in a Washington hotel. He published
               two volumes of poems.

Title: *The Fourteen Sisters of Emilio Montez O'Brien*
Author: O. Hijuelos
Copyright: Farrar Straus Giroux (1993)
Summary: A novel about a family growing up in Pennsylvania with a father
               who immigrated to the United States from Ireland at the turn of the
               20th century and a Cuban mother.

Title: *The Joy Luck Club*
Author: A. Tan
Copyright: Putnam (1989)
Summary: In *The Joy Luck Club*, vignettes alternate back and forth between
               the lives of four Chinese women in pre-1949 China and the lives
               of their American-born daughter in California. Each story is fas-
               cinating and together they weave the reader through a world
               where the Moon Lady can grant any wish, where a child, prom-
               ised in marriage at 2 and delivered at 12, can, with cunning free
               herself, where a rich man's concubine secures her daughter's fu-
               ture by killing herself, and where a woman can live on, knowing
               she has lost her entire life.

Title: *The Temple of My Familiar*
Author: A. Walker
Copyright: Pocket Books (1989)
Summary: This book tells the stories of the lives of several people who are all connected in some way (family relations, friendships, and affairs). The stories range from the United States, to England, Africa and South America. They tell of lives lived from the late 19th century to the 1980s.

Title: *The Woman Who Outshone the Sun* (M)
              This text is a *bilingual edition* with wonderful illustrations. The text is provided in both *Spanish and English*.
Author: Alejandro Cruz Martinez
Illustrator: Fernando Olivera
Copyright: Children's Book Press (1991)
Summary: Lucia Zenteno arrives in a village and her beauty astonishes the people. Some, however, were afraid of her and her powers. Some people treated her meanly, and drove her from the village. The river in the village especially loved Lucia, and every time she bathed in it, all the water, fish, and otters would gather in her long black hair. When she went to the river to say goodbye, the river would not leave her hair, so she left with it. The village suffered tremendously from drought, and the people had to go beg Lucia for her forgiveness. She returns, and the river is back in the village, and Lucia continues to guide and protect them.

Title: *The Woman Warrior: Memoirs of a Girlhood Among Ghosts*
Author: M. H. Kingston
Copyright: Knopf (1976)
Summary: With stunning force, Maxine Hong Kingston evokes the China that lives for the child with a bizarre vigor in the endlessly fascinating cycle of her mother's "talk-story." Her aunt, her father's sister, willed by the village to kill herself and her bastard child, her punishment continuing even after death... her mother, Brave Orchid, learning (in a time and place that considered it "better to raise geese than girls") to be a doctor and a "capable exorcist," and, above all, the fabled "woman warrior." So fascinating to the little San Francisco girl that she "became" Mu Lan, seeing herself led away to the mountains to be magically trained in the arts of war, returning to right the rwrongs done to the villagers ("their grievances carried into my back with knives"), leading avenging troops against the Emperor... And here, all the while, is the peculiar, impinging America where things never shut down...where laundry is

fearfully hot on summer days —the parents working deep into the night, sorting clothes, while the little ones sleep on shelves... where there are bitter silences ("we have so many secrets to hold in") ... where Maxine, entering her teens (and her parents, saying nothing, begin to look for a husband for her), wears shoes with the tongues flapping and talks in her "dried-duck voice" to scare the chosen suitors away.

Title:	*Tsuda Umeko and Women's Education in Japan*
Author:	B. Rose
Copyright:	Yale University Press (1992)
Summary:	Examines the intersection of two cultures: post-restoration Japan of the Meiji and Taisho eras (1868 -1926), and the United States of the late 19th and early 20th centuries. More specifically, the values that underlay one of the contentious debates of the period—women's higher education—are represented in Tsuda's life, work, and person. Tsuda was sent by the government of her newly created nation to study the essentials of the "woman's sphere" in another recently formed nation. She returned to Japan over a decade later thoroughly steeped in the standards of the Western domestic ideal, standards that she regarded as the elements of civilization. This biography focuses on how these ideas were received in Japan, which was just then articulating its ideal of domesticity, and how Tsuda appealed to both the American and the Japanese versions of the domestic ideal to establish herself as an authority on female education.

Title:	*Turning Japanese: Memoirs of a Sansei*
Author:	D. Mura
Copyright:	Atlantic Monthly Press (1991)
Summary:	This is a story of a third generation Japanese-American man who writes poetry and travels to Japan. He struggles with the familiarity and foreignness of the United States upon his return.

Title:	*When I Was Puerto Rican*
Author:	E. Santiago
Copyright:	Vintage (1993)
Summary:	This book is bittersweet story of a young girl trapped between two cultures. It is filled with coming-of-age anecdotes and sweet memories of family. Brothers, sisters, neighbors, aunts, and uncles are delightfully woven into the fabric of the book.

Title: *When Heaven and Earth Changed Places: A Vietnamese Woman's Journey from War to Peace*
Author: L. L Hayslip
Copyright: Doubleday (1993)

Title: *Who Belongs Here?: An American Story* (M) *(Available in Spanish)*
Author: Margy Burns Knight
Illustrator: Anne Sibley
Copyright: Tilbury House (1993)
Summary: This book describes the new life of Nary, a Cambodian refugee, in America, as well as his encounters with prejudice. It includes some general history of U.S. immigration.

Title: *Widows of Hiroshima: The Life Stories of Nineteen Peasant Wives*
Author: M. Kanda
Copyright: St. Martin's Press (1989)
Summary: This book comprises 19 autobiographical accounts of the lives of women from the Hiroshima area who lost their husbands in the nuclear attack on Hiroshima. Their accounts are vivid portrayals of the hardships of women's lives among the Japanese peasantry and expressions of lament and anger over the killing of their husbands. It includes map and photographs.

Title: *Wild Swans: Three Daughters of China*
Author: J. Chang
Copyright: Simon & Schuster (1991)
Summary: This is an autobiographical and biographical account of the author's life and family starting with her maternal grandparents. Her grandmother, who was a concubine of the leader General Xue during the 1920s, moves to Jinzhou with the author's mother when the general dies. Later, the author's parents join the Communist Party in the 1930s and 1940s and later meet and get married. They continue a life of political activism, sometimes being imprisoned. The author herself joins the Red Guard and later leaves and is exiled to Ningman. Later she works as a "barefoot doctor," a steelworker, and an electrician before becoming an English language student. She goes on to become an assistant lecturer at Sichuan University. In 1978, she left China for Britain and went on to be the first person from the People's Republic of China to earn a PhD (linguistics) in England. The book includes a family tree and political chronology (1870–1978).

Title: *Working Cotton* (M)
Author: Sherley Anne Williams
Illustrator: Carole Byard
Copyright: Voyager Books (1992)
Awarded: Caldecott Honor Book (1991), Coretta Scott King Award
Summary: The book explains the typical day of an African-American girl and her family working hard in the cotton fields. In this family of migrant workers, the children are required to help, and miss playing with other children. The story is narrated by Shelan, who admires the hard work and large amounts of cotton her father picks each day. When sun sets a bus comes to pick up the tired workers, who will most likely be moved to a different field the following day.

Title: *Women of Exile: German-Jewish Autobiographies Since 1933*
Author: A. Lixl-Purcell
Copyright: Greenwood Press (1988)
Summary: This is a compilation of 26 essays written by German-Jewish women. It is divided into three distinct parts: I, Persecution and Displacement; II, Exile and War; III, Exile in Hindsight. These are autobiographical accounts of Jewish women who survived the Holocaust. They talk about growing up as Jewish women in Europe at the time of the Holocaust and their experiences as a result of the Nazi regime.

Appendix B

Instructional Approaches

Various instructional approaches were recommended throughout the lessons to introduce and discuss a topic and to introduce and discuss books. There are many occasions for writing, especially reflective pieces. These do not need to go through the revision and editing process unless they will become public. The process approach to writing can be applied to pieces or collections of writings that will become public. The Cross-Age Approach is helpful for working across grade levels.

APPROACHES FOR INTRODUCING TOPICS

Graphic organizers such as semantic maps, Venn diagrams, K-W-L, and compare/contrast graphs are employed during brainstorming and discussing.

Semantic Maps

1. Brainstorm a topic with the students. Write the topic on the board/paper and have students write it on their paper as well.
2. Brainstorm other words related to topic. These become the secondary categories written around the central theme or topic. Connect them with lines to the topic. The students write them on their papers.
3. Be creative: Use words, pictures, phrases, geometric shapes, colors, and so on to portray the map. Once the students have the idea, they can create maps in a variety of ways.
4. Discuss the ideas generated on the map.
5. Group the words into categories; the groups can be labeled (Brisk & Harrington, 2000).

Venn diagrams (see, e. g., example chap. 3)

1. Venn Diagrams are appropriate to use when comparing two or even three things. One circle is drawn for each. The circles overlap.

2. Write each item to be compared on the top of each circle. For example, when comparing places where English and the Heritage language are used, one circle will be labeled English, the other heritage language.
3. Start the discussion. For example, ask students: Where do you use English? Where do you use your heritage language?
4. Write the answers that are the same for both languages in the section where the circles overlap. Write the answers that are different within the circle for each language but outside from where the circles overlap.

K-W-L

1. Establish the topic for reading or writing.
2. Make three columns on the blackboard.
3. Put the following titles above each column: I know, I want to learn, I learned.

I KNOW	*I WANT TO LEARN*	*I LEARNED*

4. Discuss with your students what they know about the topic and list it in the first column.
5. Ask them what they would like to learn and list it under the second column (it can be done in the form of questions).
6. Have the students read a passage in that particular content area.
7. Have them discuss what they learned and list it in the third column.
8. Have them write about it (Brisk & Harrington, 2000).

Compare/Contrast

This a good strategy when comparing two things across a set of factors; for example, comparing school systems with respect to subjects taught, schedule, forms of discipline, and so on.

1. Draw a matrix with three columns and as many rows as there are factors to compare.
2. Write the factors in the left-hand column. Write the two objects of comparison on the top of the second and third column.
3. Discuss the factors with respect to the two objects of discussion.
4. Write responses under the corresponding column.

5. Students should use the graph as a guide to write about the two objects of comparison.

	Schools in the U.S.	Schools in Heritage Country
Subjects		
Schedule		
Etc. etc.		

APPROACHES FOR INTRODUCING AND DISCUSSING BOOKS

Books can be introduced in different ways depending on the age and reading ability of the students. For young students, the teacher reads the books aloud. The students follow with their own copies or, if there is only one copy available, the teacher can use a large version that can be seen by all students. Before reading the book the teacher should elicit background knowledge and check on essential vocabulary. To elicit background knowledge, the teacher reads the title, asks the students what they think the book will be about, shows pictures, and asks the students what they think is going to happen.

An approach that helps students develop comprehension skills is called Reader Generated Questions. This approach takes time but it builds good reading habits. Vocabulary Connections is a good approach to check on vocabulary as well as background knowledge.

Reader-Generated Questions

1. *Stimuli.* Introduce the topic of reading through: (a) pictures, graphs, maps, time lines;(b) semantic map; (c) real objects; (d) title of the reading (and initial sentence); or (e) statement of the general theme. During this step explore the students' background knowledge on the topic, relate it to their own experiences, and clarify any misconceptions.
2. *Generation of Questions.* Ask the students to generate from 1 to 10 questions (depending on ability) about this topic. This can be done in several different ways: (a) Write questions on the board or chart paper as students suggest them. (Put the name of the author by the question); or (b) Let students generate and write down questions in small groups; or (c) Let students write questions individually.
3. *Responding to Questions.* Have students guess responses to the questions. Depending on the size and level of the class, do it as a whole class or small-group activity. Different groups can work on different questions.

4. *Presentation of the Text.* Depending on the age and level of students and text difficulty, present the text by: (a) telling the story or content of the text to the students. (b) reading aloud the text, or (c) letting the students read the text individually or in groups, either in class or as homework.
5. *Checking Out Responses.* Ask the students to check the accuracy of their responses.
6. *Final Activity.* Have the students write a summary, prepare a graph, outline the content, draw a picture, or some other activity that will help synthesize the content gained on the subject (Brisk & Harrington, 2000).

Vocabulary Connection

1. Choose a reading selection.
2. Choose 5 to 10 words crucial to understanding the selection, preferably in no more than one or two semantic fields.
3. Ask the students to look up the definition of the words in the dictionary. (This can be done as homework.)
4. Have students discuss the definitions as well as give examples in their own lives of the selected words and their meanings. Clarify added meanings the words may have in the cultural context of the author.
5. Have students read the selection.
6. Have students retell or write a summary of the selection. Encourage them to use their new vocabulary.

Response to Literature Journals

After students have read the text, teachers are encouraged to use Response to Literature Journals to stimulate reflection and reveal the students' understanding of the text and the connections they make with the topic of the text and their own lives. Traditionally, Response Journals allow students to write about anything that comes to mind in relation to the text. Throughout the lessons in this book there are prompts suggested for the Response Journals to specifically elicit thinking in relation to the content objective of the lessons. Teachers can experiment using or not using these prompts:

1. Introduce the approach by modeling your own responses to a book the students have just read. Brainstorm with the students the kinds of things they could have written about. Use questions to help. For example: How had they wished the story had ended?, What did they think of the characters?, What did they like and why, and so forth.
2. Give students a notebook.
3. Ask them to write their reactions to the book or chapters assigned. Use the prompt suggested in the lesson. Tell the students not to write a summary of

what they read, but to write their personal reactions to the readings (i.e., feelings, ideas, or questions). They can justify their responses with details from the text.

4. Respond to the students' writings. Focus on what they are saying and on their questions (Brisk & Harrington, 2000).

The Process Approach to writing can be used for writing assignments that will become published pieces.

PROCESS WRITING

Allow flexibility of language use between English and the students' heritage language in the planning and drafting stages of the process. For the final published version, the students may have a choice or a particular language may be required.

1. *Planning.* Critical Autobiography lessons include a number of activities—such as brainstorming, graphic organizers, and interviews—that prepare your students to write a particular piece.
2. *Drafting.* Drafting and planning are recursive. As students start drafting, they may decide they need to reorganize or read and/or research more about the subject. Students write by themselves and consult each other. Walk around the room interacting with students.
3. *Revising.* Revisions can be done in pairs, groups, or as a whole class. Students work on one person, draft. The author reads aloud his/her piece and entertains comments and questions of the other students. Often at this point the author notices things s/he wants to change. Model how to direct comments to the content and organization. The audience is there to offer suggestions and comment positively on the author's writing. Revision focuses on content and organization. Is the content accurate and complete? Does it make sense? Is it appropriate for the audience? Does it follow the organization that the particular genre requires? Demands on revision increase as the students become more experienced writers.
4. *Editing.* Editing follows the same procedure as revision, but focuses on grammar, punctuation, and spelling. Many of these errors, however, get corrected while revising for meaning. Use students' errors as the source for needed lessons.
5. *Publishing.* Students continue to work to produce a final draft for publication. Each student should decide when the final draft is ready. (Brisk & Harrington, 2000).

CROSS-AGE APPROACH

The Cross-Age Approach can be used with older students implementing the lessons with younger students. This approach is particularly helpful for older students.

Much learning occurs in trying to teach others. Older students should be well prepared before they meet their younger charges.

1. Choose two classes, one with students older than the other.
2. Explain to both classes what the project is all about. Introduce the classes to each other through an activity.
3. Start working with the older students by doing the following: (a) model the chosen method or approach; (b) train, explain, and discuss the method with students; and (c) let them rehearse with each other and do any preparation needed.
4. At all times the older learners should keep a journal in which they reflect, first about the training, later about the actual experience as teachers.
5. Read and respond to the journals. Steps 1–5 should take a minimum of 2 to 3 weeks to ensure that the older students are ready.
6. When the "teachers" (older students) are ready, start implementation.

Pair the older with the younger students. If the classes are uneven, some groups may be larger than two. Divide the two classes into two groups. Each group stays with one of the two teachers involved.

Appendix C

Scoring Rubrics
for Content Objectives

Lessons included in chapters 2–5 contain rubrics to evaluate the students' understanding of the SC lessons. Each concept, relationship, and connection to self covered in the lessons can be graded with respect to the following levels of understanding:

1. Misguided notion or no recognition.
2. Passive understanding.
3. Expresses some understanding of concept or relationship.
4. Expresses full understanding of concept or relationship.
5. Expresses full understanding of concept or relationship and proposes a solution.

Level 1 means that the student does not express anything with respect to that concept or expresses something very different from the concept. Level 2 is evidenced when the teacher asks a leading question and students respond affirmatively. It is also the case when one student says something that shows she or he knows that particular concept or relationship and other students react with similar comments. Level 3 is reached when students on their own say or write something that shows some understanding of the concept. Level 4 is achieved when students discuss or express complex thoughts that reveal a more complete understanding.

Proposing a Solution. Level 5 includes the ultimate achievement which is to propose a solution. Some students do not propose a solution, others do when prompted by the teachers, yet others do it on their own. These levels are developmental. As students get older they initiate their own solutions more readily.

Appendix D

Contrastive Study
of Situational Context

This project can be given to pre- and in-service teachers participating in a Social Context of Education course or related professional development.

Course Project: Understanding the Situational Context

The course project will have three components due at different times. Each section will be between 1,500 and 2,000 words, *double-spaced,* 12p font.

A. Self Study of Situational Context. Write about your own experiences as a student from preschool through Grade 12. Include all the topics outlined in the framework for situational context of education (see Fig. 1.1). This can be written in first person.

B. Social Context of Another Person. Write about the experiences of a person, from a different linguistic and cultural background from yourself, as a student from preschool through Grade 12 or less if the person is still in school. Include all the topics outlined in the framework for situational context of education. Preserve the anonymity of your subject. Use a pseudonym: you can even ask you subject to give you a name to use. Don't identify schools she or he attends by name.

C. Comparison, Conclusions, and Implications. Using the framework for social context of education, compare of both experiences, discuss how they influenced both subjects' ability to achieve. Apply the literature covered in this course to explain your findings in this study. Conclude on how can you apply what you learned as an educator.

The focus of the first two sections is the subjects. The focus of the comparison section is the Situational Context. Therefore, you need to write in this section about the variables and how they affected the education of these two people.

Elements That Should Be Included in the Paper. (This can help create evaluation rubrics.)

- The paper is about the social context of education as learned from the experience of two learners.
- The paper shows an understanding of major factors impacting the social context of education.
- The paper shows an understanding of the complexities of how factors combine in different ways to impact the educational outcomes of individuals.
- The paper includes implications for educators and in particular for the author.
- The paper shows connection with the literature.
- The paper shows connections with course content.
- The paper shows evidence that the author thought about the data and made inferences from it.
- The paper is reader friendly (i.e., well organized, clear, uses graphs or other devices to highlight the message).
- The paper taught something new.

References

American Association of University Women. (1992). *How schools shortchange girls: A study of* American Council on the Teaching of Foreign Languages. (2002). *Foreign language enrollments in U.S. public high schools, 1890–1994.* Retrieved February 13, 2002, from http://www.actfl.org/public/articles/details.cfm?id=139 *Major findings on girls and education.* Wellesley, MA: College Center for Research on Women.

Alali, A. O. (Ed.). (1991). *Mass media sex and adolescent values: An annotated bibliography and directory of organizations.* Jefferson, NC: McFarland.

Ali, R., & Jerald, C. D. (2001). *Dispelling the myth in California: Preliminary findings from a state and nationwide analysis of "High–Flying" schools.* Oakland, CA: The Education Trust West.

Alva, S. A. (1991). Academic invulnerability among Mexican–American students: The importance of protective resources and appraisals. *Hispanic Journal of Behavioral Sciences, 13,* 18–34.

Anderson, T., & Boyer, M. (1978). *Bilingual schooling in the United States* (2nd ed.). Austin, TX: National Educational Laboratory.

August, D., & Hakuta, K. (1997). *Improving schooling for language minority children: A research agenda.* Washington, DC: National Academy Press.

Baker, C. (1993). *Foundation of bilingual education and bilingualism.* Philadelphia: Multilingual Matters.

Ballard, B., & Clanchy, J. (1991). Assessment by misconception: Cultural influences and intellectual traditions. In L. Hamp–Lyons (Ed.), *Assessing second language writing in academic contexts.* (pp. 19–36). Norwood, NJ: Ablex.

Ballenger, C. (1992). Because you like us: The language of control. Making school reform work. *Harvard Educational Review, 62,* 199–208.

Banks, J. A. (1991). Teaching multi cultural literacy to teachers. *Teaching Education, 4,* 135–144.

Baron, D. (2001, October 27). America doesn't know what the world is saying. *The New York Times,* (p. 19.)

Bartolome, L. I. (1993). Effective transitioning strategies: Are we asking the right questions. In J. V. Tinajero & A. F. Ada (Eds.), *The power of two languages: Literacy and biliteracy for Spanish–speaking students.* (pp. 209–219). New York: Macmillan/McGraw–Hill.

Bartolome, L. I., & Macedo, D. P. (1997). Dancing with bigotry: The poisoning of racial and ethnic identities. *Harvard Educational Review, 67*(2), 222–246.

Ben–Zeev, S. (1977). Mechanisms by which childhood bilingualsim affects understanding of language and cognitive structures. In P. A. Hornby (Ed.), *Bilingualism: Psychological, social, and educational implications* (pp. 29–55). New York: Academic Press.

Benesch, S. (1993). ESL authors: Reading and writing critical autobiographies. In J. G. Carson & I. Leki (Eds.), *Reading in the composition classroom* (pp. 247–257). Boston: Heinle & Heinle.

Bialystok, E., & Hakuta, K. (1994). *In other words: The science and psychology of second-language acquisition.* New York: Basic Books.

Brisk, M. E. (1981). Language policies in American education. *Journal of Education, 163*(1), 3–15.

Brisk, M. E. (1996). *The Multi cultural Middle College High School: An attempt at creating an innovative bilingual high school.* Providence, R. I: Educational Alliance, Brown University.

Brisk, M. E. (1998). *Bilingual Education: From compensatory to quality schooling.* Mahwah, NJ: Lawrence Erlbaum Associates.

Brisk, M. E. (1999). *The transforming power of critical autobiographies,* [ERIC Document Reproduction Service No. ED 424 739].

Brisk, M. E., & Harrington, M.M. (2000). *Literacy and Bilingualism, A Handbook for ALL teachers.* Mahwah, New Jersey: Lawrence Erlbaum Associates.

Brisk, M. E., & Zandman, D. (1995). A Journey Through Immigration: Writing a critical autobiography. *Chelkat Lashon,* 19–20, 87–117.

Cahnmann, M. (1998). Over thirty years of language–in–education policy and planning: Potter Thomas bilingual school in Philadelphia. *Bilingual Research Journal, 22*(1), 1–17.

California Commission on Teacher Credentialing. (2001). *Serving English Learners. Leaflet Number CL–622.* Retrieved March 9, 2001, 2001, from http://www.ctc.ca.gov

Central Intelligence Agency. (2000). *The world fact book.* Retrieved July 23, 2001, from http://www.cia.gov/cia/publications/factbook/index.html

Canda, E. R., & Phaobtong, T. (1992). Buddhism as a support system for Southeast Asian refugees. *Social Work, 37*(1), 61–67.

Cazabon, M., Lambert, W. E., & Hall, G. (1993). *Two–way bilingual education: A progress report on the amigos program.* Santa Cruz, CA: National Center for Research on Cultural Diversity and Second Language Learning.

Cazabon, M. T., Nicoladis, E., & Lambert, W. E. (1998). *Becoming bilingual in the Amigos two–way immersion program.* Washington DC:

Cazden, C. B. (1990). Differential treatment in New Zealand: Reflections on research in minority education. *Teaching & Teacher Education, 6*(4), 291–303.

Cazden, C. B., Carrasco, R., Maldonado–Guzman, A. A., & Erickson, F. (1980). The contribution of ethnographic research to bilingual bicultural education. In J. Alastis (Ed.), *Current issues in bilingual education. Georgetown University Round Table on Languages and Linguistics* (pp. 64–80). Washington, DC: Georgetown University.

Center for Applied Linguistics. (2002). *Directory of Two–Way bilingual immersion programs in the U. S.* Retrieved May 15, 2002, from: http://www.cal.org/twi/directory

Chamot, A. U., & O'Malley, J. M. (1994). *The CALLA Handbook: Implementing the Cognitive Academic Language Learning Approach.* Rowley, MA: Addison–Wesley.

Child, I. L. (1943). *Italian or American? The second generation in conflict.* New Haven, CT: Yale University Press.

Chiswick, B. R. (1978). The effect of Americanizations on the earnings of foreign–born men. *Journal of Political Economy, 86,* 897–921.

Christian, D., Montone, C., Lindholm, K., & Carranza, I. (1997). *Profiles in two–way immersion education*. McHenry, IL: Center of Applied Linguistics and Delta Systems.

Clayton, J. B. (1993). *Your land my land: The process of acculturation for four international students in an elementary school setting in the United States*. Unpublished doctoral dissertation, Boston University, Boston.

Cleghorn, A. & Genesee, F. (1984). Languages in contact: An ethnographic study of interaction in an immersion school. *TESOL Quarterly, 18*, 595–625.

Cohen, D. K. (1970). Immigrants and the schools. *Review of Educational Research, 40*, 13–27.

Conklin, N. F., & Lourie, M. A. (1983). *A host of tongues: Language communities in the United States*. New York: The Free Press.

Coppola, J. (1997). *Teachers learning about diversity: Effects on curricular and instructional decisions in literacy*. Unpublished doctoral dissertation, Boston University, Boston.

Corson, D. (1998). *Changing education for diversity*. London: Open University Press.

Corson, D. (2001). *Language diversity and education*. Mahwah, NJ: Lawrence Erlbaum Associates.

Cortes, C. E. (2000). *The children are watching: How the media teach about diversity*. New York: Teachers College Press.

Crawford, J. (1992). *Hold your tongue*. Reading, MA: Addison–Wesley.

Crawford, J. (2000b). *English–only vs. English–only: A tale of two initiatives*. Available: http://ourworld.compuserve.com/homepages/JWCRAWFORD/203–207.htm

Crawford, J. (2000a). *At war with diversity: U. S. language policy in an age of anxiety*. Clevedon, England: Multilingual Matters.

Crawford, J. (2001). *Census 2000: A guide for the perplexed* [Report]. Retrieved January 16, 2002, from http://ourworld.compuserve.com/homepages/JWCRAWFORD/census02.htm

Crystal, D. (1987). *The Cambridge encyclopedia of language*. Cambridge, England: Cambridge University Press.

Cummins, J. (1981). The role of primary language development in promoting educational success for language minority students. In B. E. Department (Ed.), *Schooling and language minority students: A theoretical framework* (pp. 3–49). Sacramento: California State Department of Education.

Cummins, J. (2000). *Language, Power, and Pedagogy: Bilingual Children in the Crossfire*. Buffalo, NY: Multilingual Matters.

Cummins, J., & Sayers, D. (1995). *Brave new schools: Challenging Cultural illiteracy*. New York: St. Martin's Press.

Delgado–Gaitan, C. (1990). *Literacy for empowerment: The role of parents in children's education*. London: Falmer Press.

Delpit, L. D. (1995). *Other people's children: cultural conflict in the classroom*. New York: New Press.

Dentler, R. A., & Hafner, A. L. (1997). *Hosting newcomers: Structuring educational opportunities for immigrant children*. New York: Teachers College.

Deschenes, S., Cuban, L., & Tyack, D. (2001). Mismatch: Historical perspectives on schools and students who don't fit them. *Teachers College Record, 103*(4), 525–547.

Dien, T. T. (1998). Language and literacy in Vietnamese American communities. In B. Pérez (Ed.), *Sociocultural contexts of language and literacy* (pp. 123–161). Mahwah, N J: Lawrence Erlbaum Associates.

Donovan, M. S., & Cross, C. T. E. (2002). *Minority students in special and gifted education.* Washington, DC: National Academy Press.

Edelsky, C. (1991). *With literacy and justice for all: Rethinking the social in language and education.* London: Falmer Press.

Faltis, C. J. (2001). Joinfostering: Teaching and learning in multilingual classrooms (3rd Edition ed.). Upper Saddle River, NJ: Merrill, Prentice Hall.

Fantini, A. (1985). *Language acquisition of a bilingual child: A sociolinguistic perspective.* San Diego: College Hill.

Fernandez, R. M., & Nielsen, F. (1986). Bilingualism and Hispanic scholastic achievement: Some baseline results. *Social Science Research, 15,* 43–70.

Fillmore, L. W. (1979). Individual differences in second language acquisition. In C. J. Fillmore, D. Kempler, & W. S.–Y. Wang (Eds.), *Individual differences in language ability and language behavior* (pp. 203–228). New York: Academic Press.

Fillmore, L. W. (1991). When learning a second language means losing the first. *Early Childhood Research Quarterly, 6,* 323–346.

Fishman, J. A. (1966). *Language loyalty in the US: The maintenance and perpetuation of non–English mother tongues by American ethnic and religious groups.* The Hague, Netherlands: Mouton.

Flaxman, E., Burnett, G., & Ascher, C. (1995). The unfulfilled mission of federal compensatory education programs. In E. Flaxman & A.H. Passow, (Eds.), *Changing populations /chaning Schools. Ninety–fourth yearbook of the National Society for the Study of Education, Part II* (102–123). Chicago: University of Chicago Press.

Fradd, S. H., & Boswell, T. D. (1996). Spanish as an economic resource in metropolitan Miami. *Bilingual Research Journal, 20,* 283–337.

Freeman, R. D. (1998). *Bilingual education and social change* (Vol. 14). Clevedon, England: Multilingual Matters.

Freire, P., & Macedo, D. (1987). *Literacy: Reading the word and the world.* South Hadley, MA: Bergin & Garvey Publishers.

Gass, S. M., & Selinker, L. (2001). *Second Language Acquisition.* Mahwah, NJ: Lawrence Erlbaum Associates.

Geneshi, C. (1981). Codeswitching in Chicano six–year–olds. In R. P. Duran (Ed.), *Latino language and communicative Behaviour* (pp. 133–152). Norwood, NJ: Ablex.

Gibson, M. A. (1993). The school performance of immigrant minorities: A comparative view. In E. Jacob & C. Jordan (Eds.), *Minority education: Anthropological perspectives* (pp. 113–128). Norwood, NJ: Ablex.

Grabe, W., & Kaplan, R. B. (1989). Writing in a second language: Contrastive rhetoric. In D. M.

Gedda, G. (2001). *U.S. informs Mexico of migration plan.* Retrieved November 29, 2001, from http://dailynews.yahoo.com/htx/ap/20011121/pl/us_mexico_2.html Graham, C. R., & Brown, C. (1996). The effects of acculturation on second language proficiency in a community with a two–way bilingual program. *The Bilingual Research Journal, 20,* 235–260.

Green, J. P. (1997). A meta–analysis of the Rossell and Baker review of bilingual education research. *Bilingual Research Journal, 21* (2 & 3), 103–122.

Grosjean, F. (1982). *Life with two languages: An introduction to bilingualism.* Cambridge, MA: Harvard University Press.

Guerrero, M. D. (1997). Spanish academic language proficiency: The case of bilingual education teachers in the United States. *Bilingual Research Journal, 21*(1), 3–109.

Gutiérrez, K. D., Baquedano–López, P., & Asato, J. (2000). "English for the children": The new literacy of the old world order, language policy and educational reform. *Bilingual Research Journal, 24*(1 & 2), 87–112.

Gutierrez, K. D., Larson, J., & Freuter, B. (1995). Cultural tensions in the scripted classroom: The value of the subjugated perspective. *Urban Education, 29* (4), 410–442.

Guxman, M. M. (1968). Some general regularities in the formation and development of national languages. In J. A. Fishman (Ed.), *Readings in the sociology of language* (pp. 766–779). The Hague, Netherlands: Mouton.

Guzman, B. (2001). *The Hispanic Population Census 2000 Brief.* Washington, DC: U.S. Census Bureau.

Haney, W. (2002). Revealing illusions of educational progress: Texas high–stakes tests and minority student performance. In Z. Beykont (Ed.), *The power of culture: Teaching across language differences* (pp. 25–42). Cambridge, MA: Harvard Education Publishing Group.

Heath, S. B. (1983). *Way with words: Language, life, and work in communities and classrooms.* Cambridge, England: Cambridge University Press.

Hirsch, E. D. J. (1987). *Cultural literacy: What every American needs to know.* Boston: Houghton Mifflin.

Hodgkinson, H. (2001). Educational demographics: What teachers should know. *Educational Leadership, 58*(4), 1–5.

Hornberger, N. H. (1992). Biliteracy contexts, continua, and contrasts: Policy and curriculum for Cambodian and Puerto Rican students in Philadelphia. *Education and Urban Society, 24*(2), 196–211.

Housen, A. (2002). Process and outcomes in the European School model of mulilingual education. *Bilingual Research Journal, 26*(1), 45–64.

Igoa, C. (1995). *The inner world of the immigrant child.* Mahwah, NJ: Lawrence Erlbaum Associates.

Institute for Women's Policy Research. (1997). *Briefing paper–The wage gap–women's and men's earnings.* Retrieved September 6, 2001, from Johnson & D. H. Roen (Eds.), *Richness in writing: Empowering ESL students* (pp. 263–283). New York: Longman.

Jones, A. (1988). Which girls are "learning to lose"? In S. Middleton (Ed.), *Women and education in Aotearoa* (pp. 143–152). Wellington, New Zealand: Allen & Unwin.

Karp, S. (2002). Let them eat tests. *Rethinking Schools, 16*(4), 3–4, 23.

Keller, G. D., & Van Hooft, K. S. (1982). A chronology of bilingualism and bilingual education in the United States. In J. A. Fishman & G. D. Keller (Eds.), *Bilinigual education for Hispanic students in the United States* (pp. 3–19). New York: Teachers College Press.

Kelley, M. P. F. (1995). Social and cultural capital in the urban ghetto: Implications for the economic sociology of immigration. In A. Portes (Ed.), *The econoic sociology of immigration: Essays on networks, ethnicity, and entrepreneurship* (pp. 213–247). New York: Russel Sage Foundation.

Kleinfeld, J. S. (1979). *Eskimo school on the Andreafsky: A study of effective bicultural education.* New York: Praeger.

Koski, W. S., & Levin, H. M. (2000). Twenty–five years after Rodriguez: What have we learned? *Teachers College Record, 102*(3), 480–513.

Kozol, J. (1992). *Savage inequalities: Children in America's schools*. New York: Harper Perennial.

Krashen, S. (2002). Don't trust Ed Trust. Substance, 27 (6), 3.

Ladson–Billings, G., & Tate IV, W. F. (1995). Toward a critical race theory of education. *Teachers College Record, 97*(1), 47–68.

LaFrance, M. (1991). School for scandal: Different educational experiences for females and males. *Gender and Education, 3*(1), 3–13.

Lau v. Nichols, *414* (U. S. 563, 94 S. Ct. 786 (1974).

Lee, J. (2002). Racial and ethnic achievement gap trends: Reversing the progress toward equity? *Educational Researcher, 31*(1), 3–12.

Lerner, M. (1957). *America as a civilization: Life and thought in the United States today.* New York: Simon & Schuster.

Lewis, E. G. (1977). Bilingualism and bilingual education: The ancient world to the Renaissance. In B. Spolsky & R. Cooper (Eds.), *Frontiers of bilingual education* (pp. 22–93). Rowley, MA: Newbury House.

Lyons, J. J. (1990). the past and future directions of federal bilingual education policy. In C. B. Cazden & C. E. Snow (Eds.), *English plus: Issues in bilingual education* (pp. 66–80). Newbury Park, CA: Sage.

Macedo, D. P. (1981). *Stereotyped attitudes towards various Portuguese accents*. Washington DC: National Clearinghouse for Bilingual Education.

Mackey, W. (1968). The description of bilingualism. In J. A. Fishman (Ed.), *Readings in the sociology of language* (pp. 554–584). The Hague, Netherlands: Mouton.

Mackey, W. F., & Beebe, V. N. (1977). *Bilingual schools for a bicultural community: Miami's adaptation to the Cuban refugees*. Rowley, MA: Newbury House.

Martin, M. O., Mullis, I. V. S., Gonzalez, E. J., Gregory, K. D., Smith, T. A., Chrostowski, S. J., Garden, R. A., & O'Connor, K. M. (2000). *TIMSS 1999 International Science Report: Findings from the IEA's repeat of the third international Mathematics and Science study at the eighth grade*. Boston: Lynch School of Education, Boston College.

McCarty, T. (2002). *A place to be Navajo: Rough Rock and the struggle for self–determination in indigenous schooling*. Mahwah, N. J: Lawrence Erlbaum Associates.

McCarty, T. L., & Watahomigie, L. J. (1998). Language and literacy in American Indian and Alaska native communities. In B. Perez (Ed.), *Sociocultural contexts of language and literacy* (pp. 69–98). Mahwah, N. J: Lawrence Erlbaum Associates.

McKay, S. L., & Wong, S. C. (Eds.). (1988). *Language Diversity: Problem or resource?* Cambridge, MA: Newbury House.

McQuillan, P. J., & Englert, K. S. (2001). The return to neighborhood schools, concentrated poverty, and educational opportunity: An agenda for reform. *Hastings Constitutional Law Quarterly, 28*(4), 739–770.

Moll, L. C. (1988). Some key issues in teaching Latino students. *Language Arts, 65*(5), 465–472.

Mora, J. K. (2001). *Proposition 227's second aniversary: Triumph or travesty?* Retrieved on February 19, 2003, from http://coe.sdsu.edu/people/jmora/prop227/227YearTwo.htm

Mullis, I. V. S., Martin, M. O., Gonzalez, E. J., Gregory, K. D., Garden, R. A., O'Connor, K. M., Chrostowski, S. J., & Smith, T. A. (2000). *TIMSS 1999: International Mathematics Report: Findings from the IEA's repeat of the third international Mathematics and Science study at the eighth grade*. Boston: Lynch School of Education Boston College..

National Center for Education Statistics. (1997). *America's teachers: Profile of a profession, 1993–1994.* Retrieved on February 19, 2003, from http://nces.ed.gov/pubs97/97460.html

National Center for Research on Teacher Learning. (1991). *Findings from the teacher education and learning to teach study: Final report.* East Lansing, MI: National Center for Research on Teacher Learning.

National Clearing hose for Bilingual Education. (2002a). *How many school–aged limited English proficient students are there in the U.S.?* [Chart]. Retrieved February 26, 2002, from http://www.ncbe.gwu.edu/askncbe/faqs/01leps.htm

National Clearing hose for Bilingual Education. (2002b, February 2002). *What are the most common language groups for LEP students?*[Chart]. Retrieved February 26, 2002, from http://www.ncbe.gwu.edu/askncbe/faqs/05toplangs.htm

Neuman, S. B., & Celano, D. (2001). Access to print in low–income and middle–income communities: An ecological study of four neighborhoods. *Reading Research Quarterly, 36*(1), 8–26.

Nevarez–La Torre, A. A. (1997). Influencing Latino Education: Church based community programs. *Education and Urban Society, 30*(1), 58–74.

Nieto, S. (2000). *Affirming diversity: The sociopolitical context of multuicultural education* (3. ed.). Reading, MA: Longman.

Oakes, J. (1985). *Keeping track: How schools structure inequality.* New Haven, CT: Yale University Press.

Ogbu, J. U. (1993). Frameworks—Variability in minority school performance: A problem in search of an explanation. In E. Jacob & C. Jordan(Eds.), *Minority education: Anthropological perspectives* (pp. 83–111). Norwood, N.J.: Ablex.

Ogbu, J. U., & Matute–Bianchi, M. E. (1986). Understanding sociocultural factors: Knowledge, indentity, and school adjustment. In Bilingual Education Office (Ed.), *Beyond language: Social and cultural factors in schooling language minority students* (pp. 73–142). Sacramento, California: State Department of Education.

Orenstein, P. (1994). *School girls.* New York: Anchor Books.

Payne, K. J., & Biddles, B. J. (1999). Poor school funding, child poverty, and mathematics achievement. *Educational Researcher, 28*(6), 4–13.

Payne, R. (1998). *Getting beyond race: The changing American culture.* Boulder, CO: Westview Press.

Perez, B. (Ed.). (1998). *Sociocultural context of languages and literacy.* Mahwah, NJ: Lawrence Erlbaum Associates.

Pierce, M. S., & Brisk, M. E. (2002). Sharing the bilingual journey: Situational autobiography in a family literacy context. *Bilingual Research Journal,26,* 575–597.

Portes, A. (1995). Children of immigrants: Segmented assimilation and its determinants. In A. Portes (Ed.), The economic sociology of immigration: Essays on networks, ethnicity, and entrepreneurship (pp. 248–280). New York: Russell Sage Foundation.

Portes, A., & Zhou, M. (1993). The new second generation: Segmented assimilation and its variants. In P. I. Ross (Ed.), *Interminority affairs in the United States: Pluralism at the crossroads.* (pp. 74–96). Newbury Park, CA: Sage.

Portes, A., & Rumbaut, R. G. (2001). *Legacies: The story of the immigrant second generation.* Berkeley: University of California Press.

Portes, A. with Rumbaut, R. G. (1996). *Immigrant America: A portrait.* Berkeley: University of California Press.

Portes, P. R. (1999). Social and psychological factors in the academic achievement of children of immigrants: A cultural history puzzle. *American Educational Research Journal, 36,* 489–507.

Portraits of success. (2002). *Rachel Carson Elementary, Transitional Bilingual Education.* (The Northeast and Islands Regional Educational Laboratory at Brown University). Retrieved June 13, 2002, from http://www.lab.brown.edu/public/NABE/portraits.taf?_function=detail&Data_entry_uid1=3

Ramirez, J. D. (1992). Executive summary. *Bilingual Research Journal, 16,* 1–62.

Richards, J. B. (1987). Success or failure?: Learning and the language minority student. In H. T. Trueba (Ed.), *Success or failure?: Learning and the language minority student* (pp. 109–130). Cambridge, MA: Newbury House.

Rickford, J. R. (1999). *African American vernacular English.* Oxford, England: Blackwell.

Rivera, C., Stansfield, C. W., Scialdone, L., & Sharkey, M. (2000). *An analysis of state policy for the inclusion and accommodation of English language learners in state assessment programs during 1998–1999.* Arlington, VA: George Washington University Center of Equity and Excellence in Education.

Romaine, S. (1995). *Bilingualism* (2nd ed.). New York: Basil Blackwell.

Saravia–Shore, M., & Arvizu, S. (1992). *Cross–cultural literacy: Ethnographies of communication in multiethnic classrooms.* New York: Garland.

Scheinfeld, D. R. (1993). *New beginnings: A guide to designing parenting programs for refugee and immigrant parents.* New York: International Catholic Child Bureau.

Schnalberg, L. (1995). Board relaxes bilingual education policy in California. *Education Week, 14*(41), 1.

Schonfeld, a. (1999). *Manifestations of gender distinction in the Japanese language.* Retrieved February 19, 2003, from http://www.coolest.com/jpfm.htm

Schumann, J. (1978). *The pidginization process: A model for second language acquisition.* Rowley, MA: Newbury House.

Shu, H., & Anderson, R. A. (1997). Role of radical awareness in the character and word acquisition of Chinese children. *Reading Research Quarterly, 32*(1), 78–89.

Silva, A. D. E. (1998). Emergent Spanish writing of a second grader in a whole language classroom. In B. Perez (Ed.), *Sociocultural contexts of language and literacy* (pp. 223–248). Mahwah, NJ: Lawrence Erlbaum Associates.

Siu, S.–F. (1992). *Toward an understanding of Chinese–American educational achievement* (Rep. No. 2). Baltimore, MD: Center on Families, Communities, Schools and Children's Learning.

Sizer, T. (1995, January 8). What's wrong with standard tests. *Education Week,* p. 58.

Sizer, T. R. (1992). *Horace's School: Redesigning the American high school.* Boston: Houghton Mifflin.

Spolsky, B. (1978). American Indian education. In B. Spolsky & R. L. Cooper (Eds.), *Case studies in bilingual education.* (pp. 332–361) Rowley, MA: Newbury House.

Suárez–Orozco, C., & Suárez–Orozco, M. M. (2001). *Children of immigration.* Cambridge, MA: Harvard University Press.

Suarez–Orozco, M. M. (1987). Towards a psychological understanding of Hispanic adaptation to American schooling. In H. T. Trueba (Ed.), *Success or failure?: Learning and the language minority student* (pp. 156–168). Cambridge, MA: Newbury Hosue.

Taylor, D. M. (1987). Social psychological barriers to effective childhood bilingualism. In P. Hornel, M. Palij, & D. Aaronson (Eds.), *Childhood bilingualism: Aspects of linguistic, cognitive and social development* (pp. 183–195). Hillsdale, NJ: Lawrence Erlbaum Associates.

Teitelbaum, H., & Hiller, R. J. (1977). Bilingual education: The legal mandate. *Harvard Educational Review, 47,* 138–170.

National Clearinghouse for Bilingual Education. (2001). *No child left behind Act of 2001. Title III: Language instruction for limited English proficient and immigrant students.* Washington, DC: U.S. Department fo Education.

Thomas, W. P., & Collier, V. P. (2002). *A national study of school effectiveness for language minority students' long–term academic achievement. Final Report. Executive Summary.* Santa Cruz, CA: Center for Research on Education, Diversity & Excellence.

Tollefson, J. W. (1991). *Planning Language, planning inequality.* New York: Longman.

Torres–Guzman, M. E. (1992). Stories of hope in the midst of despair: Culturally responsive education for Latino students in an alternative high school in New York City. In M. Saravia–Shore & S. Arvizu, (Eds.), *Cross–cultural literacy: Ethnographies of communication in multiethnic classrooms.* New York: Garland.

Trumbull, E., Rothstein–Fisch, C., Greenfield, P. M., & Quiroz, B. (2001). *Bridging cultures between home and school: A guide for teachers.* Mahwah, NJ: Lawrence Erlbaum Associates.

Tzeng, O. (1983). Cognitive processing of various orthographies. In M. Chu–Chang (Ed.), *Asian– and Pacific–American perspectives in bilingual education* (pp. 73–96). New York: Teachers College Press.

U. S. Census Bureau. (2000). *American fact finder,* [Tables and Charts]. Retrieved March 13, 2002, from http://factfinder.census.gov/servlet/BasicFactsServlet

U. S. Commission on Civil Rights. (1971). *The unfinished education: Outcomes for minorities in the five Southwestern states. Report II.* Washington, DC: US Government Printing Office.

U.S. Department of Education. (2000). *Twenty–Second annual report to Congress on the implimentation of the individuals with disabilities education act* (Rep. No. 22). Washington, DC:

Valdés, G. (1996). *Con respeto: Bridging the distances between culturally diverse families and schools: An ethnographic portrait.* New York: Teachers College Press.

Veltman, C. (1983). *Language shift in the United States.* New York: Mouton.

Verplaetse, L. S. (2000). How content teachers allocate turns to limited English proficient students. *Journal of Education, 182*(3), 19–35.

Von Maltitz, F. W. (1975). *Living and learning in two languages.* New York: McGraw–Hill.

Willig, A. C. (1985). A meta–analysis of selected studies on the effectiveness of bilingual education. *Review of Educational Research, 55*(3), 269–317.

Yoshida, M. (1978). The acquisition of English vocabulary by a Japanese–speaking child. In E. M. Hatch (Ed.), *Second language acquisition* (pp. 91–100). Rowley, MA: Newbury House.

Zeichner, K. (1993). *Educating teachers for cultural diversity.* Lansing National Center of Research on Teacher Learning, Michigan State University.

Zentella, A. C. (1997). *Growing up bilingual.* Oxford, England: Blackwell.

Zogby, J. (2001). *Submission to the United States Commission on Civil Rights (Report). Washington, DC: Arab American Institute Foundation.*

Author Index

Subject Index